Functional Programmi

Functional Programming in JavaScript

LUIS ATENCIO

MANNING

SHELTER ISLAND

Manning Publications Co.   Development editor: Marina Michaels
20 Baldwin Road   Technical development editor: Dean Iverson
PO Box 761   Review editor: Aleksandar Dragosavljevic
Shelter Island, NY 11964   Project editor: Tiffany Taylor
Copy editor: Tiffany Taylor
Proofreader: Katie Tennant
Technical proofreader: Daniel Lamb
Typesetter: Dennis Dalinnik
Cover designer: Leslie Haimes

Updated edition, 2017

ISBN: 9781617292828
Printed in the United States of America
2 3 4 5 6 7 8 9 10 – EBM – 21 20 19 18 17

To my wonderful wife, Ana.
Thank you for your unconditional support
and for being the source of passion and inspiration in my life.

brief contents

contents

preface

When I was in college and graduate school, my class schedule was focused on object-oriented design as the sole methodology for planning and architecting software systems. And, like many developers, I began my career writing object-oriented code and building entire systems based on this paradigm.

Throughout my development career, I've learned and followed programming languages closely, not only because I want to learn something cool, but also because I'm intrigued by the design decisions and philosophy that each language fosters. Just as a new language provides a different perspective on how to approach software problems, a new paradigm can achieve the same effect. Although the object-oriented approach continues to be the modus operandi of software design, learning about functional programming will open your eyes to new techniques that you can use on their own or in parallel with any other design paradigm that fits your application.

Functional programming has been around for years, but to me it was only a minor distraction. I had heard and read about the benefits of Haskell, Lisp, Scheme, and, more recently, Scala, Clojure, and F# in terms of expressiveness and being highly productive platforms; even Java, which has traditionally been known as a verbose language, has functional artifacts that make code more succinct. Eventually, the minor distraction became impossible to avoid. And guess what? JavaScript, that object-oriented language everyone uses, can be turned around 180 degrees and used functionally. It turns out that this is the most powerful and effective way to use JavaScript. It took me a long time to discover this, and in this book I want to make you aware of it so you don't have go on wondering why your JavaScript code is becoming so complex.

Throughout my journey as a developer, I've learned how to use functional programming principles to create code that is modular, expressive, robust, easy to reason about, and simple to test. Without a doubt, this has changed me as a software engineer, so I wanted to capture and jot down my experiences somehow—perhaps in a book. Naturally, I approached Manning, with the idea of writing a functional programming book using the Dart programming language. I was playing around with Dart at the time and thought that combining it with my functional background would be a fun, unexplored, uncharted territory. I wrote a proposal, and a week later I had an interview. During the interview, I learned that Manning was seeking a person to write a book about functional programming in JavaScript. Because JavaScript is a language I'm very much obsessed with, to say the least, I was thrilled to jump into this opportunity. By writing this book, I hope to help you develop the same skills and take your development in a new direction.

acknowledgments

Writing a book is not a trivial undertaking, and the tireless collaboration of many people with a variety of talents brought to life the manuscript you're holding (or reading onscreen).

The staff at Manning were incredible and instrumental in obtaining the level of quality we all hoped for, and I thank all of them from the bottom of my heart. Without them, this book would not have been possible. Special thanks to Marjan Bace and Mike Stephens for believing in the idea of this book and in me as an author; to Marina Michaels, for giving me a map and a flashlight to navigate this maze of book-writing challenges; to Susan Conant, for bringing me up to speed and teaching me my first lessons about what it means to write a technical book; to Bert Bates, for giving me my initial sparks of creativity and for his amazing insights on how to teach programming; and to everyone on the editorial and production teams, including Mary Piergies, Janet Vail, Kevin Sullivan, Tiffany Taylor, Katie Tennant, Dennis Dalinnik, and many others who worked behind the scenes.

I can't thank enough the amazing group of technical peer reviewers led by Aleksandar Dragosavljevic—Amy Teng, Andrew Meredith, Becky Huett, Daniel Lamb, David Barkol, Ed Griebel, Efran Cobisi, Ezra Simeloff, John Shea, Ken Fukuyama, Peter Edwards, Subhasis Ghosh, Tanner Slayton, Thorsten Szutzkus, Wilfredo Manrique, William E. Wheeler, and Yiling Lu—and the talented forum contributors. Their contributions included catching technical mistakes, errors in terminology, and typos, and making topic suggestions. Each pass through the review process and each piece of feedback implemented through the forum topics shaped and molded the manuscript.

On the technical side, special thanks to Dean Iverson, who served as the book's technical editor; Daniel Lamb, who served as the book's technical proofreader; and Brian Hanafee, for his thorough and in-depth evaluation of the entire book. They are the best technical editors I could have hoped for.

Last but not least, I thank my wife for always supporting me, and my family for pushing me to become better every day and not asking why I didn't call as often to check in while I was writing this book. Also, thanks go to my colleagues at work for purchasing early releases of the chapters. I am grateful to have the pleasure of working alongside such wonderful people.

about this book

Complexity is a huge beast to tame, and we'll never get rid of it entirely; it will always be an aspect of software development. I've spent countless hours and immeasurable brainpower trying to understand what a particular piece of code does. The secret is to control the complexity so it doesn't grow in proportion to the size of your code base—and functional programming can help. We're writing more JavaScript than ever before. We've gone from building small client-side event-handling routines, to heavy client-side architectures, to complete isomorphic (server + client) JavaScript applications. Functional programming isn't a tool—it's a way of thinking that can apply equally to any of these environments.

This book is designed to teach you how to apply functional programming techniques to your code using ECMAScript 6 JavaScript. The material is presented at a gradual, steady pace and covers both theoretical and practical aspects of functional programming. I provide additional information for advanced readers, to help you get deeper into some of the harder concepts.

Roadmap

This book has eight chapters and is divided into three parts that guide you from fundamental building blocks to more-advanced and practical applications of functional programming.

Part 1, "Think functionally," paints a high-level landscape of functional JavaScript. It also discusses core aspects of using JavaScript functionally and thinking like a functional programmer:

- Chapter 1 introduces some of the core functional concepts that are explained in later chapters and prepares you to make the functional leap. It introduces the main pillars of functional programming, including pure functions, side effects, and declarative programming.
- Chapter 2 establishes a level playing field for beginning and intermediate JavaScript developers and acts as a refresher for more-advanced readers. In addition, it's sprinkled with basic functional programming concepts to prepare you for the techniques discussed in part 2.

Part 2, "Get functional," focuses on core functional programming techniques, including function chains, currying, composition, monads, and more:

- Chapter 3 introduces function chains and explores writing programs as combinations of recursion and high-order functions like map, filter, and reduce. It teaches these concepts using the Lodash.js framework.
- Chapter 4 covers the popular techniques of currying and composition, which increase the modularity of your code. Using a functional framework such as Ramda.js, composition is the glue that orchestrates your entire JavaScript solution.
- Chapter 5 provides a deep dive into more-theoretical areas of functional programming, with a comprehensive and gradual discussion of functors and monads in the context of error handling.

Part 3, "Enhancing your functional skills," discusses the practical benefits of using functional programming to tackle real-world challenges:

- Chapter 6 reveals the inherent ease with which functional programs can be unit tested. In addition, it introduces a rigorous, automated testing mode called property-based testing.
- Chapter 7 takes a look at JavaScript's memory model, which is used to support the evaluation of functions. This chapter also discusses techniques that help optimize the execution time of functional JavaScript applications.
- Chapter 8 introduces some of the main challenges JavaScript developers face on a day-to-day basis when dealing with event-driven and asynchronous behavior. It discusses how functional programming can provide elegant solutions to reduce the complexity of existing imperative solutions with a related paradigm known as reactive programming, implemented using RxJS.

Who should read this book

Functional Programming in JavaScript is written for JavaScript developers with at least a basic understanding of object-oriented software and a general awareness of the challenges of modern web applications. Because JavaScript is such a ubiquitous language, if you want an introduction to functional programming and prefer a familiar syntax, you can take full advantage of this book instead of learning Haskell. (If you want to ease your way into Haskell, this book isn't the best resource, because each language has its own idiosyncrasies that are best understood by learning it directly.)

The book will help beginning and intermediate programmers heighten their JavaScript skills with higher-order functions, closures, function currying, composition, as well as new JavaScript ES6 features like lambda expressions, iterators, generators, and promises. Advanced developers will enjoy the comprehensive coverage of monads and reactive programming as well, which can help you implement innovative ways of tackling the arduous task of dealing with event-driven and asynchronous code, taking full advantage of the JavaScript platform.

How to use this book

If you're a beginner or intermediate JavaScript developer and functional programming is new to you, begin with chapter 1. If you're a strong JavaScript programmer, you can skim through chapter 2 and move quickly into chapter 3, which begins with function chains and overall functional design.

More-advanced users of functional JavaScript typically understand pure functions, currying, and composition, so you may skim chapter 4 and move into functors and monads in chapter 5.

Examples and source code

The code examples in this book use ECMAScript 6 JavaScript, which can run equally well on either the server (Node.js) or the client. Some examples show I/O and browser DOM APIs, but without regard for browser incompatibilities. I assume you have experience interacting at a basic level with HTML pages and the console. No specific browser-based JavaScript is used.

The book makes heavy use of functional JavaScript libraries like Lodash.js, Ramda.js, and others. You can find documentation and installation information in the appendix.

This book contains extensive code listings that showcase functional techniques and, where appropriate, compare imperative versus functional designs. You can find all the code samples at the publisher's website, https://www.manning.com/books/functional-programming-in-javascript, and on GitHub at https://github.com/luijar/functional-programming-js.

Typographical conventions

The following conventions are used throughout the book:

- *Italic* typeface is used to reference important terms.
- `Courier` typeface is used to denote code listings, as well as elements and attributes, methods names, classes, functions, and other programming artifacts.
- Code annotations accompany some of the source code listings, highlighting important concepts.

About the author

Luis Atencio (@luijar) is a staff software engineer for Citrix Systems in Ft. Lauderdale, Florida. He has a B.S. and an M.S. in Computer Science and now works full-time developing and architecting applications using JavaScript, Java, and PHP platforms. Luis is very involved in the community and has presented frequently at local meetups and conferences. He blogs about software engineering at luisatencio.net, writes articles for magazines and DZone, and is also the coauthor of *RxJS in Action* (forthcoming from Manning in 2017).

Author Online

Purchase of *Functional Programming in JavaScript* includes free access to a private web forum run by Manning Publications where you can make comments about the book, ask technical questions, and receive help from the author and from other users. To access the forum and subscribe to it, point your web browser to https://www.manning.com/books/functional-programming-in-javascript. This page provides information on how to get on the forum once you are registered, what kind of help is available, and the rules of conduct on the forum.

Manning's commitment to our readers is to provide a venue where a meaningful dialog between individual readers and between readers and the author can take place. It is not a commitment to any specific amount of participation on the part of the author, whose contribution to Author Online remains voluntary (and unpaid). We suggest you try asking the author some challenging questions lest his interest stray! The Author Online forum and the archives of previous discussions will be accessible from the publisher's website as long as the book is in print.

Part 1

Think functionally

I t's highly probable that most of your experience building professional applications has been with an object-oriented language. You may have heard or read about functional programming in other books, blogs, forums, and magazine articles, but you've probably never written any functional code. Don't worry; this is to be expected. I've done most of my development in an object-oriented environment as well. Writing functional code isn't difficult, but learning to think functionally and letting go of old habits is. The primary goal of part 1 of this book is to lay the foundation for and prepare your mind to embrace the functional techniques discussed in parts 2 and 3.

Chapter 1 discusses what functional programming is and the mindset you need to embrace it; it also introduces some of the most important techniques based on pure functions, immutability, side effects, and referential transparency. These form the backbone of all functional code and will help you transition into functional more easily. Also, these will be the guiding principles that set the stage for many of the design decisions we make in the following chapters.

Chapter 2 provides a first view of JavaScript as a functional language. Because it's so ubiquitous and mainstream, it's an ideal language with which to teach functional programming. If you aren't a strong JavaScript developer, this chapter will bring you up to speed with everything you need to know to understand functional JavaScript, such as higher-order functions, closures, and scoping rules.

Becoming functional

1

This chapter covers

- Thinking in functional terms
- Learning the what and why of functional programming
- Understanding the principles of immutability and pure functions
- Functional programming techniques and their impact on overall design

 OO makes code understandable by encapsulating moving parts.

FP makes code understandable by minimizing moving parts.

—Michael Feathers (Twitter)

If you're reading this book, chances are you're a JavaScript developer with a working knowledge of object-oriented or structured design, and you're curious about functional programming. Perhaps you've tried to learn it before and haven't been able to apply it successfully at work or on your personal projects. In either case, your main goal is to advance your development skills and improve the quality of your code. This book can help you accomplish that.

3

The rapid pace of web platforms, the evolution of browsers, and—most important—the demands of end users have all had a profound effect on the way we design web applications today. Users demand that web applications feel more like a native desktop or a mobile app with rich and responsive widgets. Naturally, these demands force JavaScript developers to think more broadly about the solution space and to adopt adequate programming paradigms and best practices that provide the best possible solutions.

As developers, we gravitate toward frameworks that help us create extensible and clean application architectures. Yet the complexity of our codebase still gets out of control, and we're challenged to reexamine the basic design principles of our code. Also, the web of today is radically different than it was years ago for JavaScript developers, because we can do many things now that weren't technically feasible before. We can choose to write large server-side applications with Node.js or push the bulk of the business logic onto the client, leaving a thin server behind. In either case, we need to interact with storage technology, spawn asynchronous processes, handle events, and much more.

Object-oriented design helps solve part of the problem; but because JavaScript is such a dynamic language with lots of shared state, it isn't long before we accumulate enough complexity to make our code unwieldy and hard to maintain. Object-oriented design certainly moves the needle in the right direction, but we need more. Perhaps you've heard the term *reactive programming* in recent years. This programming paradigm facilitates working with data flows and propagation of change. In JavaScript, this is extremely important when dealing with asynchronous or event-based code. Overall, what we need is a programming paradigm that encourages us to think carefully about our data and the functions that interact with it. When thinking about an application's design, ask yourself the following questions in terms of these design principles:

- *Extensibility*—Do I constantly refactor my code to support additional functionality?
- *Easy to modularize*—If I change one file, is another file affected?
- *Reusability*—Is there a lot of duplication?
- *Testability*—Do I struggle to unit test my functions?
- *Easy to reason about*—Is my code unstructured and hard to follow?

If you answer "Yes" or "I don't know" to any of these questions, then you've picked up the right book as a guide on the path to productivity. Functional programming (FP) is the programming paradigm you need. Although it's based on simple concepts, FP requires a shift in the way you think about problems. FP isn't a new tool or an API, but a different approach to problem solving that will become intuitive once you understand the basic principles.

In this chapter, I define what functional programming is and tell you how and why it's useful and important. I introduce the core principles of immutability and pure functions and talk about FP techniques and how those techniques affect your approach to designing programs. These techniques allow you to easily pick up reactive programming and use it to solve complex JavaScript tasks. But before we can get into all this, you need to learn why thinking functionally is important and how it can help you tackle the complexities of JavaScript programs.

1.1 Can functional programming help?

Learning functional programming has never been as important as it is today. The development community and major software companies are starting to realize the benefits of using FP techniques to power their business applications. Nowadays, most major programming languages (Scala, Java 8, F#, Python, JavaScript, and many more) provide either native or API-based functional support. Hence, FP skills are in high demand now and will continue to be in the years to come.

In the context of JavaScript, an FP mindset can be used to shape the incredibly expressive nature of the language and help you write code that is clean, modular, testable, and succinct so that you can be more productive at work. For many years, we've neglected the fact that JavaScript can be written more effectively in a functional style. This neglect is partly due to an overall misunderstanding of the JavaScript language, and also due to JavaScript's lack of native constructs to properly manage state; it's a dynamic platform that places the burden of managing this state on us (the ones responsible for introducing bugs into our applications). This may work well for small scripts, but it becomes harder to control as your code base grows. In a way, I think FP protects you from JavaScript itself. I discuss this further in chapter 2.

Writing functional JavaScript code addresses most of these concerns. Using a set of proven techniques and practices based on pure functions, you can write code that is easy to reason about in the face of increasing complexity. Writing JavaScript functionally is a two-for-one deal, because you not only improve the quality of your entire application, but also gain more proficiency in and a better understanding of the JavaScript language.

Because functional programming isn't a framework or a tool, but a way of writing code, thinking functionally is radically different from thinking in object-oriented terms. But how do you become functional? How do you begin to think functionally? Functional programming is intuitive once you've grasped its essence. Unlearning old habits is the hardest part and can be a huge paradigm shift for most people who come from an object-oriented background. Before you can learn to think functionally, first you must learn what FP is.

1.2 What is functional programming?

In simple terms, functional programming is a software development style that places a major emphasis on the use of functions. You might say, "Well, I already use functions on a day-to-day basis at work; what's the difference?" As I mentioned earlier, FP requires you to think a bit differently about how to approach the tasks you're facing. It's not a matter of just applying functions to come up with a result; the goal, rather, is to *abstract control flows and operations* on data with functions in order to *avoid side effects* and *reduce mutation of state* in your application. I know this sounds like a mouthful, but I'll visit each of these terms further and build on them throughout the book.

Normally, FP books start with computing Fibonacci numbers, but I'd rather start with a simple JavaScript program that displays text on an HTML page. What better text to print than the good ol' "Hello World":

```
document.querySelector('#msg').innerHTML = '<h1>Hello World</h1>';
```

> **NOTE** I mentioned earlier that because functional programming isn't a specific tool, but a way of writing code, you can apply it to write client-side (browser-based) as well as server-side applications (Node.js). Opening the browser and typing in some code is probably the easiest way to get JavaScript up and running, and that's all you'll need for this book.

This program is simple, but because everything is hardcoded, you can't use it to display messages dynamically. Say you wanted to change the formatting, the content, or perhaps the target element; you'd need to rewrite this entire expression. Maybe you decide to wrap this code with a function and make the change points parameters, so you can write it once and use it with any configuration:

```
function printMessage(elementId, format, message) {
    document.querySelector(`#${elementId}`).innerHTML =
        `<${format}>${message}</${format}>`;
}

printMessage('msg', 'h1','Hello World');
```

An improvement, indeed, but still not a completely reusable piece of code. Suppose you want to write to a file instead of an HTML page. You need to take the simple thought process of creating parameterized functions to a different level, where parameters aren't just scalar values but can also be functions themselves that provide additional functionality. Functional programming is a bit like using functions on steroids, because your sole objective is to evaluate and combine lots of functions with others to achieve greater behavior. I'll fast-forward a bit and show you a sneak peek at this same program using a functional approach.

> **Listing 1.1 Functional** `printMessage`

```
var printMessage = run(addToDom('msg'), h1, echo);

printMessage('Hello World');
```

Without a doubt, this looks radically different than the original. For starters, h1 isn't a scalar anymore; it's a function just like addToDom and echo. Visually, it feels as though you're creating a function from smaller functions.

There's a reason for this madness. Listing 1.1 captures the process of decomposing a program into smaller pieces that are more reusable, more reliable, and easier to understand, and then combining them to form an entire program that is easier to reason about as a whole. Every functional program follows this fundamental principle. For the time being, you'll use a magical function, run,[1] to invoke a series of functions sequentially, such as addToDom, h1, and echo. I'll explain run in detail later. Behind the scenes, it basically links each function in a chain-like manner by passing the return value of one as input to the next. In this case, the string "Hello World" returned from echo is passed into h1, and the result is finally passed into addToDom.

Why does the functional solution look this way? I like to think of it as basically parameterizing your code so that you can easily change it in a noninvasive manner—like adjusting an algorithm's initial conditions. With this foundation laid, you can now easily augment printMessage to repeat the message twice, use an h2 header, and write to the console instead of the DOM, all without having to rewrite any of the internal logic.

Listing 1.2 Extending `printMessage`

```
var printMessage = run(console.log, repeat(2), h2, echo);

printMessage('Get Functional');
```

This visually distinct approach isn't accidental. When comparing the functional to the nonfunctional solution, you may have noticed that there's a radical difference in style. Both print the same output, yet they look very different. This is due to FP's inherent declarative mode of development. In order to fully understand functional programming, first you must learn the fundamental concepts on which it's based:

- Declarative programming
- Pure functions
- Referential transparency
- Immutability

1.2.1 Functional programming is declarative

Functional programming falls under the umbrella of *declarative* programming paradigms: it's a paradigm that expresses a set of operations without revealing how they're implemented or how data flows through them. The more popular models used today, though, are *imperative* or *procedural*, and are supported in most structured and object-oriented languages like Java, C#, C++, and others. Imperative programming treats a computer program as merely a sequence of top-to-bottom statements that changes the state of the system in order to compute a result.

---

[1] For more details on this provisional run function, visit http://mng.bz/nmax.

Let's look at a simple imperative example. Suppose you need to square all the numbers in an array. An imperative program follows these steps:

```
var array = [0, 1, 2, 3, 4, 5, 6, 7, 8, 9];
for(let i = 0; i < array.length; i++) {
    array[i] = Math.pow(array[i], 2);
}
array; //-> [0, 1, 4, 9, 16, 25, 36, 49, 64, 81]
```

Imperative programming tells the computer, in great detail, *how* to perform a certain task (looping through and applying the square formula to each number, in this case). This is the most common way of writing this code and will most likely be your first approach to tackling this problem.

Declarative programming, on the other hand, separates program description from evaluation. It focuses on the use of *expressions* to describe what the logic of a program is without necessarily specifying its control flow or state changes. An example of declarative programming is found in SQL statements. SQL queries are composed of statements that describe what the outcome of a query should look like, abstracting the internal mechanism for data retrieval. In chapter 3, I show an example of using a SQL-like overlay over your functional code to give meaning to both your application and the data that runs through it.

Shifting to a functional approach to tackle this same task, you only need to be concerned with applying the right behavior at each element and cede control of looping to other parts of the system. You can let `Array.map()` do most of the heavy lifting:

```
[0, 1, 2, 3, 4, 5, 6, 7, 8, 9].map(
        function(num) {
            return Math.pow(num, 2);
        });
```

← **Map takes a function that computes the square of each number**

```
//-> [0, 1, 4, 9, 16, 25, 36, 49, 64, 81]
```

Compared with the previous example, you see that this code frees you from the responsibility of properly managing a loop counter and array index access; put simply, the more code you have, the more places there are for bugs to occur. Also, standard loops aren't reusable artifacts unless they're abstracted with functions. And that's precisely what we'll do. In chapter 3, I demonstrate how to remove manual loops completely from your code in favor of first-class, higher-order functions like map, reduce, and filter, which accept functions as parameters so that your code is more reusable, extensible, and declarative. This is what I did with the magical run function in listings 1.1 and 1.2.

Abstracting loops with functions lets you take advantage of *lambda expressions* or *arrow functions*, introduced in ES6 JavaScript. Lambda expressions provide a succinct alternative to anonymous functions that can be passed in as a function argument, in the spirit of writing less:

```
[0, 1, 2, 3, 4, 5, 6, 7, 8, 9].map(num => Math.pow(num, 2));

//-> [0, 1, 4, 9, 16, 25, 36, 49, 64, 81]
```

> ### Translating lambda notation to regular function notation
>
> Lambda expressions provide an enormous syntactical advantage over regular function notations because they reduce the structure of a function call down to the most important pieces. This ES6 lambda expression
>
> ```
> num => Math.pow(num, 2)
> ```
>
> is equivalent to the following function:
>
> ```
> function(num) {
>     return Math.pow(num, 2);
> }
> ```

Why remove loops from your code? A loop is an imperative control structure that's hard to reuse and difficult to plug in to other operations. In addition, it implies code that's constantly changing or mutating in response to new iterations. You'll learn that functional programs aim for *statelessness* and *immutability* as much as possible. Stateless code has zero chance of changing or breaking global state. To achieve this, you'll use functions that avoid side effects and changes of state, known as *pure functions.*

1.2.2 Pure functions and the problem with side effects

Functional programming is based on the premise that you build immutable programs based on the building blocks of pure functions. A pure function has the following qualities:

- It depends only on the input provided and not on any hidden or external state that may change during its evaluation or between calls.
- It doesn't inflict changes beyond their scope, such as modifying a global object or a parameter passed by reference.

Intuitively, any function that doesn't meet these requirements is "impure." Programming with immutability can feel strange at first. After all, the whole point of imperative design, which is what we're accustomed to, is to declare that variables are to mutate from one statement to the next (they're "variable," after all). This is a natural thing for us to do. Consider the following function:

```
var counter = 0;
function increment() {
    return ++counter;
}
```

This function is impure because it reads/modifies an external variable, `counter`, which isn't local to the function's scope. Generally, functions have side effects when reading from or writing to external resources, as shown in figure 1.1. Another example is the popular function `Date.now()`; its output certainly isn't predicable and consistent, because it always depends on a constantly changing factor: time.

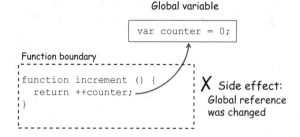

Global variable

```
var counter = 0;
```

Function boundary
```
function increment () {
    return ++counter;
}
```

X Side effect:
Global reference
was changed

Figure 1.1 Function `increment()` causes side effects by reading/modifying an external variable, `counter`. Its result is unpredictable because `counter` can change at any time between calls.

In this case, `counter` is accessed via an implicit global variable (in browser-based JavaScript, it's the `window` object). Another common side effect occurs when accessing instance data via the `this` keyword. The behavior of `this` in JavaScript is unlike it is in any other programming language because it determines the runtime context of a function. This often leads to code that's hard to reason about, which is why I avoid it when possible. I revisit this topic in the next chapter. Side effects can occur in many situations, including these:

- Changing a variable, property, or data structure globally
- Changing the original value of a function's argument
- Processing user input
- Throwing an exception, unless it's caught within the same function
- Printing to the screen or logging
- Querying the HTML documents, browser cookies, or databases

If you're unable to create and modify objects or print to the console, what practical value would you get from a program like this? Indeed, pure functions can be hard to use in a world full of dynamic behavior and mutation. But practical functional programming doesn't restrict *all* changes of state; it just provides a framework to help you manage and reduce them, while allowing you to separate the pure from the impure. Impure code produces *externally visible* side effects like those listed earlier, and in this book I examine ways to deal with this.

To talk more concretely about these issues, suppose you're a developer on a team implementing an application to manage a school's student data. Listing 1.3 shows a small imperative program that finds a student record by Social Security number and renders it in the browser (again, the use of the browser is immaterial; you could just as easily write to the console, a database, or a file). I refer to and expand this program throughout the book as a typical, real-world scenario that involves side effects by interacting with an external local object store (like an array of objects) and doing some level of IO.

Listing 1.3 Imperative `showStudent` function with side effects

```
function showStudent(ssn) {
    let student = db.get(ssn);
    if(student !== null) {
        document.querySelector(`#${elementId}`).innerHTML =
            `${student.ssn},
             ${student.firstname},
             ${student.lastname}`;
    }
    else {
        throw new Error('Student not found!');
    }
}
 showStudent('444-44-4444');
```

Accesses object storage to look up a student by SSN. Assume this is a synchronous operation for now; I deal with asynchronous code much later in the book.

Reaches outside the function to read the elementId

Throws an exception for an invalid student

Runs this program with SSN 444-44-4444 and appends the student details to the page

Let's analyze this code further. This function clearly exposes a few side effects that ripple beyond its scope:

- It interacts with an external variable (db) for data access because the function signature doesn't declare this parameter. At any point in time, this reference could become null or change from one call to the next, yielding completely different results and compromising the integrity of the program.
- The global variable elementId can change at any time, outside your control.
- HTML elements are directly modified. The HTML document (DOM) is itself a mutable, shared, global resource.
- It can potentially throw an exception if the student isn't found, which causes the entire program stack to unwind and end abruptly.

The function in listing 1.3 relies on external resources, which makes the code inflexible, hard to work with, and difficult to test. Pure functions, on the other hand, have clear contracts as part of their signatures that describe clearly all of the function's formal parameters (set of inputs), making them simpler to understand and use.

Let's put our functional hat on and use what you learned from the simple print-Message program against this real-life scenario. As you become more comfortable with functional programming in this book, you'll continue to improve this implementation with new techniques. At the moment, you can make two simple enhancements:

- Separate this long function into shorter functions, each with a single purpose.
- Reduce the number of side effects by explicitly defining all arguments needed for the functions to carry out their job.

Let's begin by separating the activities of fetching the student record from displaying it on the screen. Granted, the side effects from interacting with an external storage system and the DOM are unavoidable, but at least you can make them more manageable and single them out from the main logic. To do this, I'll introduce a popular FP technique called ⌈*currying.*⌉ With currying, you can partially set some of the arguments of a function in order to reduce them down to one. As shown in the next listing, you can apply curry to reduce find and append to unary functions that can easily combine via run.

Python
functools
Partial

unary
functions

Listing 1.4 Decomposing the showStudent program

```
const find = curry((db, id) => {
  let obj = db.find(id);
  if(obj === null) {
    throw new Error('Object not found!');
  }
  return obj;
});

const csv = student =>
  `${student.ssn}, ${student.firstname}, ${student.lastname}`;

const append = curry((selector, info) => {
    document.querySelector(selector).innerHTML = info;
});
```

The find function needs a reference to the object store and the ID of the student to look up.

Converts a student object into comma-separated values

To display a student's details on the page, you need the element ID and the student data.

You don't need to understand currying now, but it's important to see that being able to reduce the length of these functions lets you write showStudent as the combination of these smaller parts:

```
var showStudent = run(
  append('#student-info'),
  csv,
  find(db));

showStudent('444-44-4444');
```

Partially sets the HTML element ID to use in the function

Partially sets a data access object to point to the students table

Although this program has been only marginally improved, it's beginning to show many benefits:

- It's a lot more flexible, because it now has three reusable components.
- This fine-grained function reuse is a strategy for increasing your productivity, because you can dramatically reduce the footprint of code that must be actively managed.
- You enhance the code's readability by following a declarative style that provides a clear view of the high-level steps carried out by this program.
- More important, interaction with the HTML objects is moved into its own function, isolating the pure from the non-pure (impure) behavior. I explain currying and managing pure and impure parts in depth in chapter 4.

This program still has some loose ends that need to be tightened, but reducing side effects will make it less brittle to changing external conditions. If you look closer at the `find` function, you'll notice it has a `null`-check branching statement that can produce an exception. For many reasons, which we'll study later, it's beneficial to guarantee a consistent return value from a function, making its result consistent and predicable. This is a quality of pure functions called *referential transparency.*

1.2.3 Referential transparency and substitutability

Referential transparency is a more formal way of defining a pure function. *Purity* in this sense refers to the existence of a pure mapping between a function's arguments and its return value. Hence, if a function consistently yields the same result on the same input, it's said to be *referentially transparent.* For instance, the stateful `increment` function shown earlier isn't referentially transparent because its return value is heavily dependent on the external variable `counter`. Here it is again:

```
var counter = 0;

function increment() {
    return ++counter;
}
```

In order to make it referentially transparent, you need to remove its dependent state—the outer variable—and make it an explicit formal parameter of the function signature. You can convert it to ES6 lambda form:

```
var increment = counter => counter + 1;
```

Now this function is stable and always returns the same output when provided with the same input. Otherwise, the function's return value is being influenced by some external factor.

We seek this quality in functions because it not only makes code easier to test, but also allows us to *reason about entire programs* much more easily. Referential transparency or *equational correctness* is inherited from math, but functions in programming languages behave nothing like mathematical functions; so achieving referential transparency is strictly on us. Using the magical `run` function again, figure 1.2 shows how to use the imperative versus the functional version of `increment`.

Programs built this way are much easier to reason about because you can form a mental model of the state of the system and achieve the desired outcome through *rewriting* or *substitution.* Let's look at this more concretely and assume that any program can be defined as a set of functions that processes a given input and produces an output. Here it is in pseudo form:

```
Program = [Input] + [func1, func2, func3, ...] -> Output
```

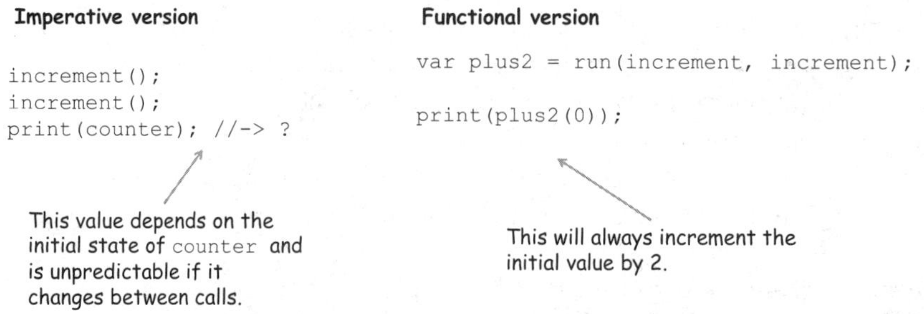

Imperative version

```
increment();
increment();
print(counter); //-> ?
```

This value depends on the
initial state of counter and
is unpredictable if it
changes between calls.

Functional version

```
var plus2 = run(increment, increment);

print(plus2(0));
```

This will always increment the
initial value by 2.

**Figure 1.2   Comparison of working with imperative and functional versions of
increment. The result of the imperative version is unpredictable and can be inconsistent
because the external counter variable may change at any time, compromising the result
of successive invocations of the function. The referentially transparent functional version
is always equationally correct and leaves no room for errors.**

If the functions [func1, func2, func3, ...] are pure, you can easily rewrite this program by inlining the values produced by them—[val1, val2, val3, ...]—without altering the result. Consider a simple example of computing a student's average grade:

```
var input = [80, 90, 100];
var average = (arr) => divide(sum(arr), size(arr));
average (input); //-> 90
```

Because the functions sum and size are referentially transparent, you can easily rewrite this expression for the given input as

```
var average = divide(270, 3); //-> 90
```

Because divide is always pure, it can be rewritten further using its mathematical notation; so for this input, the average is always $270/3 = 90$. Referential transparency makes it possible to reason about programs in this systematic, almost mathematical, way. The entire program can be implemented as follows:

```
var sum = (total, current) => total + current;
var total = arr => arr.reduce(sum);
var size = arr => arr.length;
var divide = (a, b) => a / b;
var average = arr => divide(total(arr), size(arr));
average(input); //-> 90
```

Another new function: reduce.
Just like map, reduce iterates
through an entire collection. By
providing a sum function, it can
be used to tally the result of
adding each number in the array.

In chapter 4, we'll look at
ways of combining an average
function into a composition.

Although I don't plan to apply equational reasoning to every program in the book, it's important to understand that this is implicit in any purely functional program, and that it wouldn't be possible if functions had side effects. In chapter 6, I come back to the importance of this principle in the context of unit testing functional code. Defining all function arguments up front avoids side effects in most cases, as with scalar values; but when objects are passed by reference, you must be cautious not to inadvertently mutate them.

1.2.4 Preserving immutable data

Immutable data is data that can't be changed after it's been created. In JavaScript, as with many other languages, all primitive types (`String`, `Number`, and so on) are inherently immutable. But other objects, like arrays, aren't immutable; even if they're passed as input to a function, you can still cause a side effect by changing the original content. Consider this simple array-sorting code:

```
var sortDesc = arr => {
    return arr.sort(
        (a, b) => b - a
    );
};
```

At a glance, this code seems perfectly fine and side effect–free. It does what you'd expect it to do—you provide an array, and it returns the same array sorted in descending order:

```
var arr = [1,2,3,4,5,6,7,8,9];
sortDesc(arr); //-> [9,8,7,6,5,4,3,2,1]
```

Unfortunately, the `Array.sort` function is stateful and causes the side effect of sorting the array in place—the original reference is changed. This is a serious flaw in the language and one that we'll overcome in future chapters.

Now that you've had a glimpse of the fundamental principles behind functional programming (declarative, pure, and immutable), I can express what it is more succinctly: *functional programming refers to the declarative evaluation of pure functions to create immutable programs by avoiding externally observable side effects.* Not such a mouthful after all. I've only scratched the surface in terms of the practical benefits of writing functional applications, but by now you're beginning to understand what it means to think with this mindset.

 Most of the issues JavaScript developers face nowadays are due to the heavy use of large functions that rely greatly on externally shared variables, do lots of branching, and have no clear structure. Unfortunately, this is the situation for many JavaScript applications today—even successful ones made up of many files that execute together, forming a shared mesh of mutable, global data that can be hard to track and debug.

Being forced to think in terms of pure operations and looking at functions as sealed *units of work* that never mutate data can definitely reduce the potential for bugs. Understanding these core principles is important in order to reap the benefits functional programming brings to your code, which will guide you on the path to overcoming complexity.

1.3 Benefits of functional programming

In order to benefit from functional programming, you must learn to think functionally and have the proper tools. In this section, I introduce some core techniques that are indispensable for your toolbox in order to develop your *functional awareness*—the instinct of looking at problems as a combination of simple functions that together provide a complete solution. The topics introduced in this section also serve as a brief introduction to some of the upcoming chapters in the book. If a concept is hard to grasp now, don't worry; it will become clearer as you progress through the rest of the chapters.

Now let's explore at a high level the benefits FP brings to your JavaScript applications. The following subsections explain how it can

- Encourage you to decompose tasks into simple functions
- Process data using fluent chains
- Decrease the complexity of event-driven code by enabling reactive paradigms

1.3.1 Encouraging the decomposition of complex tasks

At a high level, functional programming is effectively the interplay between decomposition (breaking programs into small pieces) and composition (joining the pieces back together). It's this duality that makes functional programs modular and so effective. As I mentioned previously, the unit of modularity, or *unit of work*, is the function itself. Thinking functionally typically begins with decomposition by learning to break a particular task into logical subtasks (functions), as shown in the decomposition of showStudent in figure 1.3.

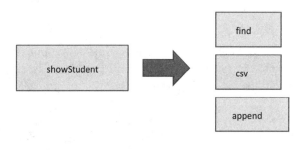

Figure 1.3 The process of decomposing breaks showStudent into smaller parts. These subtasks are independent and simpler to understand, so that when combined, they help solve the bigger picture.

If need be, these subtasks can be decomposed further until you arrive at simpler, pure functions, each of which is an independent unit of work. Remember that this was the thought process I followed when refactoring showStudent in listing 1.4. Modularization in FP is closely related to the *singularity* principle, which states that functions should have a single purpose; this was also evident in the code for average, shown earlier. Purity and referential transparency encourage you to think this way because in order to glue simple functions together, they must agree on the types of inputs and outputs. From referential transparency, you learn that a function's complexity is sometimes directly related to the number of arguments it receives (this is merely a practical observation and not a formal concept indicating that the lower the number of function parameters, the simpler the function tends to be).

All along, I've been using run to combine functions to make up whole programs. It's time to uncover this dark magic. In reality, run is an alias for one of the most important techniques: *composition*. The composition of two functions is another function that results from taking the output of one and plugging it into the next. Assume that you have two functions f and g. Formally, this can be expressed as follows:

```
f • g = f(g(x))
```

This formula reads "f composed of g," which creates a loose, type-safe relationship between g's return value and f's argument. The requirement for two functions to be compatible is that they must agree in the number of arguments as well as their types. We'll look at this closely in chapter 3. For now, let's diagram the composition of show-Student in figure 1.4, this time using the correct function, compose:

```
var showStudent = compose(append('#student-info'), csv, find(db));

showStudent('444-44-4444');
```

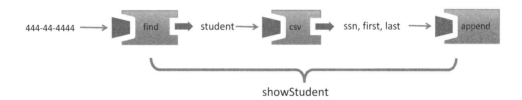

Figure 1.4 The flow of data when composing two functions. The return value from `find` must be compatible in type and arity with the arguments to `csv`, which in turn returns information that `append` can use. Note that in order to make the flow of data clear, I flipped the order of the function calls.

Understanding compose is crucial for learning how to implementing modularity and reusability in functional applications; I discuss this at length in chapter 4. Functional composition leads to code in which the meaning of the entire expression can be understood from the meaning of its individual pieces—a quality that becomes hard to achieve in other paradigms.

In addition, functional composition raises the level of abstraction so that you can clearly outline all the steps performed in this code without being exposed to any of its underlying details. Because compose accepts other functions as arguments, it's known as a *higher-order function*. But composition isn't the only way to create fluent, modular code; in this book, you'll also learn how to build sequences of operations by connecting operations in a chain-like manner.

1.3.2 *Processing data using fluent chains*

In addition to `map`, you can import a repertoire of many higher-order functions into any JavaScript project through some powerful and optimized functional libraries. In chapters 3 and 4, I give a tour of many of these higher-order functions implemented in popular JavaScript functional toolkits like Lodash.js and Ramda.js; they overlap in many aspects, but each brings unique features that can facilitate assembling function chains.

If you've written some JQuery code before, you're probably familiar with this idiom. A *chain* is a sequential invocation of functions that share a common object return value (such as the `$` or `jQuery` object). Like composition, this idiom allows you to write terse and concise code, and it's typically used a lot in functional as well as reactive programming JavaScript libraries (more on this later). To show this, let's tackle a different problem. Suppose you're tasked with writing a program that computes the average grade for students who have enrolled in more than one class. Given this array of enrollment data

```
let enrollment = [
  {enrolled: 2, grade: 100},
  {enrolled: 2, grade: 80},
  {enrolled: 1, grade: 89}
];
```

an imperative approach might look like this:

```
var totalGrades = 0;
var totalStudentsFound = 0;
for(let i = 0; i < enrollment.length; i++) {
    let student = enrollment [i];
    if(student !== null) {
       if(student.enrolled > 1) {
          totalGrades+= student.grade;
          totalStudentsFound++;
       }
    }
 }
 var average = totalGrades / totalStudentsFound; //-> 90
```

Just as before, decomposing this problem with a functional mindset, you can identify three major steps:

- Selecting the proper set of students (whose enrollment is greater than one)
- Extracting their grades
- Calculating their average grade

Now you can use Lodash to stitch together functions representing these steps, forming a functional chain, as shown in listing 1.5 (for a full explanation of what each of these functions does, you can visit the appendix for directions on where to find the proper documentation). A function chain is a *lazy evaluated* program, which means it defers its execution until needed. This benefits performance because you can avoid executing entire sequences of code that won't be used anywhere else, saving precious CPU cycles. This effectively simulates the *call-by-need* behavior built into other functional languages.

Listing 1.5 Programming with function chains

```
_.chain(enrollment)
  .filter(student => student.enrolled > 1)
  .pluck('grade')
  .average()
  .value(); //-> 90
```

Calling _.value() kicks off the execution of all operations in the chain.

Don't be too concerned at this point with everything that's happening in this code. For now, compare it to the imperative version, and notice how you can eliminate the need to declare and change variables, loops, and if-else statements. As you'll learn in chapter 7, many imperative control-flow mechanisms like loops and branches increase the level of complexity of your functions because they execute different paths depending on certain conditions, making them incredibly difficult to test.

To be fair, though, this example skips a lot of error-handling code found in typical real-world programs. Earlier, I mentioned that throwing exceptions was a cause of side effects. Exceptions don't exist in academic functional programming, but in real life you won't be able to escape them. There's a distinction between pure error handling and exception handling. The goal is to implement pure error handling as much as possible and allow exceptions to fire in truly exceptional conditions, just like the ones described earlier.

Fortunately, by applying some purely functional design patterns, you won't need to sacrifice this level of expressiveness to provide robust error-handling logic for your code. This is the main topic of discussion in chapter 5.

So far, you've seen how FP can help you create modular, testable, extensible applications. How well does it work when you need to interact with asynchronous or event-based data coming from user input, remote web requests, file systems, or persistent storage?

1.3.3 *Reacting to the complexity of asynchronous applications*

If you remember the last time you had to fetch remote data, handle user input, or interact with local storage, you probably recall writing entire sections of business logic into nested sequences of callback functions. This callback pattern breaks the linear flow of your code and becomes hard to read, because it's cluttered with nested forms of success- and error-handling logic. This is all about to change.

As I said earlier, learning functional programming, especially for JavaScript developers, is extremely important today. When building large applications, a lot of the focus has shifted from object-oriented frameworks like Backbone.js to frameworks that favor a reactive programming paradigm. Web frameworks like Angular.js are still widely used today; but new players in the field, such as RxJS, embrace the power of FP to tackle very challenging tasks.

Reactive programming is probably one of the most exciting and interesting applications of functional programming. You can use it to dramatically reduce the complexity in asynchronous and event-driven code that you, as JavaScript developers, deal with on a daily basis on the client as well as the server.

The main benefit of adopting a reactive paradigm is that it raises the level of abstraction of your code, allowing you to focus on specific business logic while forgetting about the arduous boilerplate code associated with setting up asynchronous and event-based programs. Also, this emerging paradigm takes full advantage of FP's ability to chain or compose functions together.

Events come in many flavors: mouse clicks, text field changes, focus changes, handling new HTTP requests, database queries, file writes, and so on. Suppose you need to read and validate a student's SSN. A typical imperative approach might look like the next listing.

> **Listing 1.6   Imperative program that reads and validates a student's SSN**

```
var valid = false;
var elem = document.querySelector('#student-ssn');
elem.onkeyup = function(event) {
   var val = elem.value;
   if(val !== null && val.length !== 0) {
      val = val.replace(/^\s*|\s*$|\-s/g, '');
      if(val.length --- 9) {
         console.log(`Valid SSN: ${val}!`);
         valid = true;
      }
   }
   else {
      console.log(`Invalid SSN: ${val}!`);
   }
};
```

Side effects in reaching out to data outside the function scope

Trims and cleans up input, mutating data in place

Nested branching logic

For such a simple task, this is beginning to look complex; and the code lacks the desired level of modularity with all business logic in a single place. Also, this function isn't reusable due to its dependency on external state. Because reactive programming is based on functional programming, it benefits from the use of pure functions to process data with the same familiar operations like map and reduce and the terseness of lambda expressions. So learning functional is half the battle when learning reactive!

This paradigm is enabled through a very important artifact called an *observable*. Observables let you subscribe to a stream of data that you can process by composing and chaining operations together elegantly. Let's see it in action and subscribe to a simple input field for a student's SSN.

Listing 1.7   Functional program that reads and validates a student's SSN

```
Rx.Observable.fromEvent(
     document.querySelector('#student-ssn'), 'keyup')
  .pluck('srcElement', 'value')
  .map(ssn => ssn.replace(/^\s*|\s*$|\-/g, ''))
  .filter(ssn => ssn !== null && ssn.length === 9)
  .subscribe(validSsn => {
    console.log(`Valid SSN ${validSsn}`);
  });
```

Can you see the similarity between listing 1.7 and programming with chains in listing 1.5? This shows that whether you're processing a collection of elements or user input, it's all abstracted out and treated in the exact same manner. I have much more to say about this in chapter 8.

One of the most important takeaways is that all the operations performed in listing 1.7 are completely immutable, and all the business logic is segregated into individual functions. You don't *have* to use functional with reactive, but thinking functionally *forces* you to do so—and when you do, you unlock a truly amazing architecture based on *functional reactive programming* (FRP).

Functional programming is a paradigm shift that can dramatically transform the way you tackle solutions to any programming challenges. So is FP a replacement for the more popular object-oriented design? Fortunately, applying functional programming to your code isn't an all-or-nothing approach, as noted in the Michael Feathers quote at the beginning of this chapter. In fact, lots of applications can benefit from using FP alongside an object-oriented architecture. Due to rigid control for immutability and shared state, FP is also known for making multithreaded programming more straightforward. Because JavaScript is a single-threaded platform, this isn't something we need to worry about or cover in this book. In the next chapter, I spend some time highlighting some of the key differences between functional and object-oriented design, which I believe will help you grok the functional way of thinking more easily.

In this chapter, I briefly touched on topics that will be covered in depth throughout the book as you sink deeper into a functional frame of mind. If you've been following all the concepts so far, that's great, but don't worry if you missed a few things—that just means you've picked up the right book. In traditional OOP, you're accustomed to programming in the imperative/procedural style; changing this will require you to make a drastic shift in your thought processes as you begin to tackle problems the "functional way."

1.4   Summary

- Code that uses pure functions has zero chance of changing or breaking global state, which helps make your code more testable and maintainable.
- Functional programming is done in a declarative style that's easy to reason about. This improves the overall readability of the application and makes your code leaner through a combination of functions and lambda expressions.
- Data processing in a collection of elements is done fluently via function chains that link operations such as `map` and `reduce`.
- Functional programming treats functions as building blocks by relying on first-class, higher-order functions to improve the modularity and reusability of your code.
- You can reduce the complexity of event-based programs by combining functional with reactive programming.

Higher-order JavaScript

This chapter covers

- Why JavaScript is a suitable functional language
- JavaScript as a language that enables multiparadigm development
- Immutability and policies for change
- Understanding higher-order and first-class functions
- Exploring the concepts of closures and scopes
- Practical use of closures

Natural language has no dominant paradigm, and neither does JavaScript. Developers can select from a grab bag of approaches— procedural, functional, and object-oriented—and blend them as appropriate.

—Angus Croll, *If Hemingway Wrote JavaScript*

As applications get bigger, so does their complexity. No matter how good you think you are, turmoil is unavoidable if you don't have the proper programming models

23

in place. In chapter 1, I explained the reasons functional programming is a compelling paradigm to adopt. But paradigms by themselves are just programming models that need the right host language to come to life.

In this chapter, I take you on a fast-pass tour of a hybrid language that mixes both object-oriented as well as functional programming: JavaScript. Of course, this is by no means an extensive study of the language; rather, I'll focus on what allows JavaScript to be used functionally as well as where it falls short. One example of this is the lack of support for immutability. In addition, this chapter covers higher-order functions and closures, which together form the backbone that allows you to write JavaScript in a functional style. Without further ado, let's dive in.

2.1   Why JavaScript?

I began by answering the question, "Why functional?" Another question that comes to mind is, "Why JavaScript?" The answer to this question is simple: omnipresence. JavaScript is a dynamically typed, object-oriented, general-purpose language with an immensely expressive syntax. It's one of the most ubiquitous languages ever created and can be seen in the development of mobile applications, websites, web servers, desktop and embedded applications, and even databases. Given its extraordinary adoption as the *language of the web*, it begs to reason that JavaScript is by far the most widely used FP language ever created.

Despite its C-like syntax, JavaScript draws lots of inspiration from functional languages like Lisp and Scheme. Their commonalities lie in their support for higher-order functions, closures, array literals, and other features that make JavaScript a superb platform for applying FP techniques. In fact, functions are the main *units of work* in JavaScript, which means they're used not only to drive the behavior of your applications, but also to define objects, create modules, and handle events.

JavaScript is actively evolving and improving. Backed by the ECMAScript (ES) standard, its next major release, ES6, adds many more features to the language: arrow functions, constants, iterators, promises, and other features that suit functional programming very well.

Despite the fact that it has lots of powerful functional features, it's important to know that JavaScript is as object-oriented as it is functional. Unfortunately, the latter is rarely seen; most developers use mutable operations, imperative control structures, and instance state changes on objects, which are all virtually eliminated when adopting a functional style. Nevertheless, I feel it's important to spend some time talking about JavaScript as an object-oriented language first so that you can better appreciate the key differences between the two paradigms. This will allow you to leap into functional programming more easily.

2.2   Functional vs. object-oriented programming

Both functional and object-oriented programming (OOP) can be used to develop midsize-to-large systems. Hybrid languages like Scala and F#, for instance, blend both paradigms into a single language. JavaScript has a similar capability, and mastering it involves learning to use a combination of both; deciding where to draw the line depends on personal preference and the demands of the problem you're tackling. Understanding where functional and object-oriented approaches intercept and differ can help you transition from one to the other, or think in terms of either one.

Consider a simple model for a learning-management system involving a `Student` object. From a class or type hierarchy point of view, it's natural to think of `Student` as a subtype of `Person`, which encompasses basic attributes like first name, last name, address, and so on.

Object-oriented JavaScript

When I define a relationship between one object and another by saying it's a *subtype* or *derived type*, I'm referring to the *prototypal* relationship that exists between the objects. It's important to clarify that although JavaScript is object-oriented, it doesn't have *classical* inheritance as you may have seen in other languages like Java.

In ES6, this mechanism for setting up prototype links between objects has been (erroneously, according to many) sugar-coated with keywords such as `class` and `extends`. This makes coding object inheritance more straightforward but hides the real work and power of JavaScript's prototype mechanism. I won't cover object-oriented JavaScript in this book (toward the end of this chapter, I provide a reference to a book that discusses this and other topics in depth).

Extra functionality can be added by deriving `Student` further with a more specific type, such as `CollegeStudent`. At their core, object-oriented programs favor the creation of new derived objects as the principal means to gain code reuse. In this case, `CollegeStudent` will reuse all the data and behavior from its parent types. But adding more functionality to existing objects can be tricky when it doesn't necessarily apply to all of its descendants. Although `firstname` and `lastname` apply to `Person` and all of its children, `workAddress` is arguably more relevant as part of an `Employee` object (derived from `Person`) than a `Student` object. The reason for painting this model is that the main difference between object-oriented and functional applications is how this data (the object's properties) and behavior (functions) are organized.

Object-oriented applications, which are mostly imperative, rely heavily on object-based encapsulation to protect the integrity of their mutable state, both direct and inherited, in order to expose or manipulate that state via instance methods. As a result, there's a tight coupling between an object's data and its fine-grained behavior, forming a cohesive package; this is the goal in object-oriented programs and why the central form of abstraction is the object.

Alternatively, functional programming removes the need to hide data from the callers and typically works with a smaller set of very simple data types. Because everything is immutable, you're free to work with objects directly, but this time through generalized functions that live outside of an object's scope. In other words, data is loosely coupled to behavior. As you can see in figure 2.1, instead of fine-grained instance methods, functional code relies on more coarse-grained operations that can crosscut or work across many data types. In this paradigm, *functions become the main form of abstraction.*

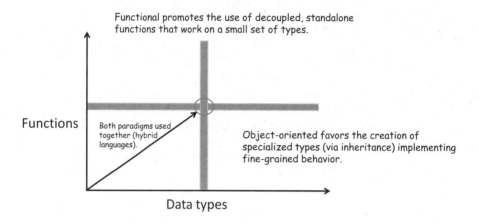

Figure 2.1   Object-oriented programming promotes logically connecting many data types with specialized behavior, whereas functional programming focuses on connecting operations on those data types via composition. There's a sweet spot where both paradigms can be used productively. Hybrid languages like Scala, F#, and JavaScript allow you to work with both.

Looking at figure 2.1, you see the two paradigms differ as you move up and to the right. In practice, some of the best object-oriented code I've seen uses both paradigms together—at their intersection. To do this, you need to treat objects as immutable entities or values and separate their functionality into functions that work on these objects. So a method on Person that looks like this

```
get fullname() {
    return [this._firstname, this._lastname].join(' ');
}
```
⟵ With methods, you're encouraged to use "this" to access the object's state.

can be split out as follows:

```
var fullname =
    person => [person.firstname, person.lastname].join(' ');
```
⟵ "this" is effectively replaced with the object passed in.

As you know, JavaScript is a dynamically typed language (which means you never have to write explicit types next to object references), so fullname() will work with any type derived from Person (or any object with properties firstname and lastname, for that matter), as shown in figure 2.2. Given its dynamic nature, JavaScript functions support the use of generalized polymorphic functions. In other words, functions that use references to base types (such as Person) work on objects of derived types (such as Student or CollegeStudent).

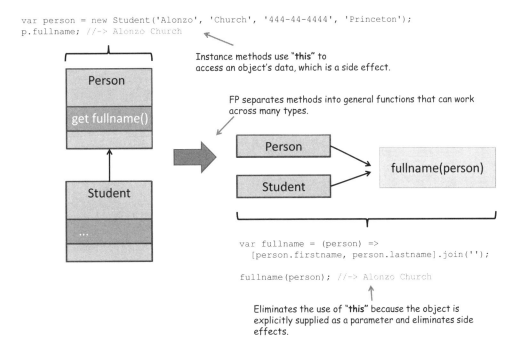

Figure 2.2 The focus of OOP is to create inheritance hierarchies (such as Student from Parent) with methods and data tightly bound together. Functional programming, on the other hand, favors general polymorphic functions that crosscut different data types and avoid the use of this.

As you can see in figure 2.2, separating fullname() into a standalone function encourages you to avoid using the this reference to access object data. Using this is problematic because it gives you access to instance-level data outside of the method scope, which causes side effects. Using FP, object data is not intimately coupled to specific parts of your code and is far more reusable and maintainable.

Instead of creating lots of derived types, you can extend the behavior of a function by passing other functions as arguments. To illustrate, let's define the simple data model in the following listing, which contains the class Student that derives from Person. I use this model in most of the examples throughout this book.

Listing 2.1   Defining the `Person` and `Student` classes

```
class Person {
   constructor(firstname, lastname, ssn) {
      this._firstname = firstname;
      this._lastname = lastname;
      this._ssn = ssn;
      this._address = null;
      this._birthYear = null;
   }

   get ssn() {
      return this._ssn;
   }

   get firstname() {
      return this._firstname;
   }

   get lastname() {
      return this._lastname;
   }

   get address() {
      return this._address;
   }

   get birthYear() {
      return this._birthYear;
   }

   set birthYear(year) {              ◄─
      this._birthYear = year;
   }

   set address(addr){                 ◄─
      this._address = addr;
   }

   toString() {
      return `Person(${this._firstname}, ${this._lastname})`;
   }
}

class Student extends Person {
   constructor(firstname, lastname, ssn, school) {
      super(firstname, lastname, ssn);
      this._school = school;
   }

   get school() {
      return this._school;
   }
}
```

> Using setter methods isn't meant to support object mutations, but is a way to easily create objects that have different properties without really long constructors. After objects are created and populated, their state never changes (we'll study ways to handle this later in this chapter).

Finding and running code examples

The code samples for this book can be found at www.manning.com/books/functional-programming-in-javascript and at https://github.com/luijar/functional-programming-js. Feel free to check out the project and begin practicing functional programming on your own. I recommend that you run any of the unit tests and play with the different programs. At the time of this writing, because not all JavaScript ES6 features have been implemented across all browsers, I use the Babel transpiler (formerly known as 6to5) to convert ES6 code into equivalent ES5 code.

Some features don't need transpilation and can be turned on with a browser setting like Chrome's Enable Experimental JavaScript. If you're running in experimental mode, it's important to enable *strict mode* by adding the statement `'use strict';` at the beginning of your JavaScript file.

Given a person, your task is to find all of their friends that live in the same country as this person. Also, given a student, your task is to find other students living in the same country and attending the same school. The object-oriented solution tightly couples operations, via this and super, to the object and parent object, respectively:

```
// Person class
peopleInSameCountry(friends) {
    var result = [];
    for (let idx in friends) {
        var friend = friends [idx];
        if (this.address.country === friend.address.country) {
            result.push(friend);
        }
    }
    return result;
};
// Student class
studentsInSameCountryAndSchool(friends) {
    var closeFriends = super.peopleInSameCountry(friends);    ←─┐ Uses super to
    var result = [];                                              request data from
    for (let idx in closeFriends) {                               the parent class
        var friend = closeFriends[idx];
        if (friend.school === this.school) {
            result.push(friend);
        }
    }
    return result;
};
```

On the other hand, because FP is based on purity and referential transparency, by isolating the behavior from the state you can add more operations by defining and combining new functions that work on those types. Doing this, you end up with simple objects in charge of storing data, and versatile functions that can work on those objects as arguments, which can be composed to achieve specialized functionality. You haven't learned about composition yet (it's covered in chapter 4), but it's important to highlight another fundamental difference between the paradigms. In essence, what inheritance does for OOP, composition does for FP in terms of applying new behavior to different data types.[1] To run this code, you'll use the following dataset:

```
var curry = new Student('Haskell', 'Curry',
    '111-11-1111', 'Penn State');
curry.address = new Address('US');

var turing = new Student('Alan', 'Turing',
    '222-22-2222', 'Princeton');
turing.address = new Address('England');

var church = new Student('Alonzo', 'Church',
   '333-33-3333', 'Princeton');
church.address = new Address('US');

var kleene = new Student('Stephen', 'Kleene',
    '444-44-4444', 'Princeton');
kleene.address = new Address('US');
```

The object-oriented approach uses the method in `Student` to find all other students who attend the same school:

```
church.studentsInSameCountryAndSchool([curry, turing, kleene]);
//-> [kleene]
```

The functional solution, on the other hand, breaks the problem into smaller functions:

```
function selector(country, school) {
    return function(student) {
        return student.address.country() === country &&
            student.school() === school;
    };
}

var findStudentsBy = function(friends, selector) {
    return friends.filter(selector);
};

findStudentsBy([curry, turing, church, kleene],
  selector('US', 'Princeton'));

//-> [church, kleene]
```

Creates a selector function that knows how to compare students' country and school

Navigates the object graphs. Later in this chapter, I'll show you a better approach to access object attributes.

Uses the filter operation on arrays and injects the special behavior via a selector function

---

[1] This reference applies more strongly to object-oriented practitioners than to the paradigm itself. Many authorities in the field, including the Gang of Four, prefer object composition over class inheritance, based on LSP.

By applying functional programming, you create an entirely new function, `find-StudentsBy`, that's much easier to work with. Keep in mind that this new function works with any objects that relate to `Person`, as well as any school and country combination.

This clearly demonstrates the differences between the two paradigms. Object-oriented design focuses on the nature of data and data relationships, whereas functional programming focuses on the operations performed—behavior. Table 2.1 summarizes other key differences that are worth noticing as I talk about them in this chapter and others to come.

Table 2.1 Comparing some important qualities of object-oriented and functional programming. These qualities are themes that are discussed throughout this book.

	Functional	**Object-oriented**
Unit of composition	Functions	Objects (classes)
Programming style	Declarative	Imperative
Data and behavior	Loosely coupled into pure, stand-alone functions	Tightly coupled in classes with methods
State management	Treats objects as immutable values	Favors mutation of objects via instance methods
Control flow	Functions and recursion	Loops and conditionals
Thread safety	Enables concurrent programming	Difficult to achieve
Encapsulation	Not needed because everything is immutable	Needed to protect data integrity

Despite their differences, building applications by blending these paradigms can be a powerful approach. On the one hand, you get a rich domain model with natural relationships among its constituent types; and on the other, you have a set of pure functions that can work on these types. Where you draw the line will depend on how comfortable you feel using either paradigm. Because JavaScript is as object-oriented as it is functional, using it functionally will require some special attention in terms of controlling state changes.

2.2.1 *Managing the state of JavaScript objects*

The *state* of a program can be defined as a snapshot of the data stored in all of its objects at any moment in time. Sadly, JavaScript is one of the worst languages when it comes to securing an object's state. A JavaScript object is highly dynamic, and you can modify, add, or delete its properties at any point in time. In listing 2.1, if you expect `_address` to be encapsulated (the use of the underscore is purely syntactic) within `Person`, you're wrong. You have complete access to this property outside of the class to do whatever you please or even to delete it.

With freedom comes great responsibility. Although this may give you the liberty to do many slick things like dynamic property creation, it can also lead to code that's extremely difficult to maintain in midsize-to-large programs.

I mentioned in chapter 1 that working with pure functions makes your code easier to maintain and reason about. Is there such a thing as a pure object? An immutable object that contains immutable functionality can be considered pure. The same level of reasoning that applies to functions translates just as well to simple objects. Managing state in JavaScript is crucial in our quest to use it as a functional language. There are some practices and patterns you can use to manage immutability, which we'll visit in the next sections, but complete encapsulation and protection of data will weigh heavily in your discipline to enforce it.

2.2.2   *Treating objects as values*

Strings and numbers are probably the easiest data types to work with in any programming language. Why do you think that is? Part of the reason is that, traditionally, these primitive types are inherently immutable, which gives us a certain peace of mind that other user-defined types don't. In functional programming, we call types that behave this way *values*. In chapter 1, you learned to think about immutability, and this requires effectively treating any object as a value; doing so allows you to work with functions that pass objects around and not worry about them being altered.

Despite all the syntactic sugar added around classes in ES6, JavaScript objects are nothing more than bags of attributes that can be added, removed, and changed at any time. What can you do to remedy this? Many programming languages support constructs that make an object's properties immutable. One example is Java's `final` keyword. Also, languages like F# have immutable variables by default, unless stated otherwise. At present, you don't have this luxury in JavaScript. Although JavaScript primitive types can't be changed, the state of the variable that refers to a primitive type can. Therefore, you need to be able to provide, or at least emulate, immutable references to data so that your user-defined objects behave as if they were immutable.

ES6 uses the `const` keyword to create constant references. This moves the needle in the right direction because constants can't be reassigned or re-declared. In practical functional programming, you can use `const` as a means to bring simple configuration data (URL strings, database names, and so on) into your functional program if need be. Although reading from an external variable is a side effect, the platform provides special semantics to constants so they won't change unexpectedly between function calls. Here's an example of declaring a constant value:

```
const gravity_ms = 9.806;

gravity_ms = 20;
```
JavaScript runtime won't allow this reassignment

But this doesn't solve the problems of mutability to the level that FP requires. You can prevent a variable from being reassigned, but how can you prevent an object's internal state from changing? This code would be perfectly acceptable:

```
const student = new Student('Alonzo', 'Church',
    '666-66-6666', 'Princeton');

student.lastname = 'Mourning';
```

Property has
been changed ←

What you need is a stricter policy for immutability; and encapsulation is a good strategy to protect against mutations. For simple object structures, a good alternative is to adopt the *Value Object* pattern. A value object is one whose equality doesn't depend on identity or reference, just on its value; once declared, its state may not change. In addition to numbers and strings, some examples of value objects are types like `tuple`, `pair`, `point`, `zipCode`, `coordinate`, `money`, `date`, and others. Here's an implementation for `zipCode`:

```
function zipCode(code, location) {
   let _code = code;
   let _location = location || '';

   return {
      code: function () {
         return _code;
      },
      location: function () {
         return _location;
      },
      fromString: function (str) {
         let parts = str.split('-');
         return zipCode(parts[0], parts[1]);
      },
      toString: function () {
         return _code + '-' + _location;
      }
   };
}

const princetonZip = zipCode('08544', '3345');
princetonZip.toString(); //-> '08544-3345'
```

In JavaScript, you can use functions and guard access to a ZIP code's internal state by returning an *object literal interface* that exposes a small set of methods to the caller and treats `_code` and `_location` as pseudo-private variables. These variables are only accessible in the object literal via *closures*, which you'll see later in this chapter.

The returned object effectively behaves like a primitive that has no mutating methods.[2] Hence, the `toString` method, although not a pure function, behaves like one and is a pure string representation of this object. Value objects are lightweight and

[2] The object's internal state may be protected, but its behavior is still subject to mutation because you can dynamically remove or replace any of its methods.

easy to work with in both functional and OOP. In conjunction with `const`, you can create objects with semantics similar to those of a string or number. Let's consider another example:

```
function coordinate(lat, long) {
   let _lat = lat;
   let _long = long;

   return {
      latitude: function () {
         return _lat;
      },
      longitude: function () {
         return _long;
      },
      translate: function (dx, dy) {
         return coordinate(_lat + dx, _long + dy);
      },
      toString: function () {
         return '(' + _lat + ',' + _long + ')';
      }
   };
}

const greenwich = coordinate(51.4778, 0.0015);
greenwich.toString(); //-> '(51.4778, 0.0015)'
```

Returns a new copy with the translated coordinates

Using methods to return new copies (as in `translate`) is another way to implement immutability. Applying a translation operation on this object yields a new `coordinate` object:

```
greenwich.translate(10, 10).toString(); //-> '(61.4778, 10.0015)'
```

Value Object is an object-oriented design pattern that was inspired by functional programming. This is another example of how the paradigms elegantly complement each other. This pattern is ideal, but it's not enough for modeling entire real-world problem domains. In practice, it's likely your code will need to handle hierarchical data (as you saw with `Person` and `Student` earlier) as well as interact with legacy objects. Luckily, JavaScript has a mechanism to emulate this using with `Object.freeze`.

2.2.3   *Deep-freezing moving parts*

JavaScript's new class syntax doesn't define keywords to mark fields as immutable, but it does support an internal mechanism for doing so by controlling some hidden object metaproperties like `writable`. By setting this property to `false`, JavaScript's `Object.freeze()` function can prevent an object's state from changing. Let's begin by freezing the `person` object from listing 2.1:

```
var person = Object.freeze(new Person('Haskell', 'Curry', '444-44-4444'));
person.firstname = 'Bob';
```

Not allowed

Executing the preceding code makes the attributes of person effectively read-only. Any attempt to change them (_firstname, in this case) will result in an error:

```
TypeError: Cannot assign to read only property '_firstname' of #<Person>
```

Object.freeze() can also immobilize inherited attributes. So freezing an instance of Student works exactly the same way and follows the object's prototype chain protecting every inherited Person attribute. But it can't be used to freeze nested object attributes, as shown in figure 2.3.

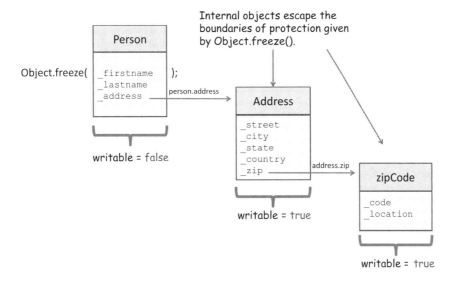

Figure 2.3 Although the Person type has been frozen, its internal object properties (like _address) haven't. So person.address.country is eligible to be changed at any time. Because only the top-level variables are frozen, this is a shallow freeze.

Here's the definition for the Address type:

```
class Address {
    constructor(country, state, city, zip, street) {
        this._country = country;
        this._state = state;
        this._city = city;
        this._zip = zip;
        this._street = street;
    }

    get street() {
        return this._street;
    }
}
```

```
    get city() {
        return this._city;
    }

    get state() {
        return this._state;
    }

    get zip() {
        return this._zip;
    }

    get country() {
        return this._country;
    }
}
```

Unfortunately, no errors will occur in the following code:

```
var person = new Person('Haskell', 'Curry', '444-44-4444');
person.address = new Address(
    'US', 'NJ', 'Princeton',
    zipCode('08544','1234'), 'Alexander St.');

    person = Object.freeze(person);

person.address._country = 'France'; //-> allowed!
person.address.country; //-> 'France'
```

`Object.freeze()` is a shallow operation. To get around this, you need to manually freeze an object's nested structure, as shown in the following listing.

Listing 2.2   Recursive function to deep-freeze an object

```
var isObject = (val) => val && typeof val === 'object';

function deepFreeze(obj) {
  if(isObject(obj)
     && !Object.isFrozen(obj)) {

      Object.keys(obj).
          forEach(name => deepFreeze(obj[name]));

      Object.freeze(obj);
  }
  return obj;
}
```

Skips any functions. Although, technically, functions may be mutated in JavaScript, you want to focus on data properties.

Maps over all properties and recursively calls Object.freeze() on non-frozen properties (I discuss the map function in chapter 3)

Ignores objects that have already been frozen; freezes ones that haven't

Calls itself recursively (I discuss recursion in chapter 3)

Freezes the root object

I've just shown some techniques you can use to enforce a level of immutability in your code, but it's unrealistic to expect that you can create entire applications without ever modifying any state. Thus, strict policies when creating new objects from originals (as with `coordinate.translate()`) are extremely beneficial in your quest to reduce the complexities and intricacies of JavaScript applications. Next, I discuss the best alternative to centrally managing object changes immutably using a functional approach called *lenses*.

2.2.4 *Navigating and modifying object graphs with lenses*

In OOP, you're accustomed to calling methods that change the internal contents of a stateful object. This has the disadvantage of never being able to guarantee the outcome of retrieving the state and may break the functionality of part of the system that expects the object to stay intact. You could opt to implement your own *copy-on-write* strategy and return new objects from each method call—a tedious and error-prone process, to say the least. A simple setter function in the Person class would look like this:

```
set lastname(lastname) {
    return new Person(this._firstname, lastname, this._ssn); ◁
};
```
> You'd have to manually copy the state of all other properties into a new instance (terrible!).

Now imagine having to do this for every single property of every type in your domain model. You need a solution for mutating stateful objects, in an immutable manner, that's unobtrusive and doesn't require hardcoding boilerplate code everywhere. *Lenses*, also known as *functional references*, are functional programming's solution to accessing and immutably manipulating attributes of stateful data types. Internally, lenses work similarly to a copy-on-write strategy by using an internal storage component that knows how to properly manage and copy state. You don't need to implement this yourself; rather, you can use a functional JavaScript library called Ramda.js (details about using this and other libraries can be found in the appendix). By default, Ramda exposes all of its functionality via the global object R. Using R.lensProp, you can create a lens that wraps over the lastname property of Person:

```
var person = new Person('Alonzo', 'Church', '444-44-4444');
var lastnameLens = R.lenseProp('lastName');
```

You can use R.view to read the contents of this property:

```
R.view(lastnameLens, person); //-> 'Church'
```

This is, for all practical purposes, similar to a get lastname() method. Nothing impressive so far. What about the setter? Here's where the magic comes in. Now, calling R.set creates and returns a brand-new copy of the object containing the new value and preserves the original instance state (copy-on-write semantics for free!):

```
var newPerson = R.set(lastnameLens, 'Mourning', person);
newPerson.lastname; //-> 'Mourning'
person.lastname; //-> 'Church'
```

Lenses are valuable because they give you an unobtrusive mechanism for manipulating objects, even if these are legacy objects or objects outside of your control. Lenses also support nested properties, like the address property of `Person`:

```
person.address = new Address(
    'US', 'NJ', 'Princeton', zipCode('08544','1234'),
    'Alexander St.');
```

Let's create a lens that navigates to the `address.zip` property:

```
var zipPath = ['address', 'zip'];
var zipLens = R.lens(R.path(zipPath), R.assocPath(zipPath));   ◁─┐ Defines getter
R.view(zipLens, person);   //-> zipCode('08544', '1234')           │ and setter
                                                                    │ behavior
```

Because lenses implement immutable setters, you can change the nested object and return a new object:

```
var newPerson = R.set(zipLens, zipCode('90210', '5678'), person);
var newZip = R.view(zipLens, newPerson);        //-> zipCode('90210', '5678')
var originalZip = R.view(zipLens, person);      //-> zipCode('08544', '1234')
newZip.toString() !== originalZip.toString(); //-> true
```

This is great because now you have getter and setter semantics in a functional way. In addition to providing a protective immutable wrapper, lenses also fit extremely well with FP's philosophy of isolating field-access logic away from the object, eliminating the reliance on `this`, and giving you powerful functions that know how to reach into and manipulate the contents of any object.

Now that you understand how to work with objects properly, I'll shift gears and address the topic of functions. Functions drive the moving pieces of your application and are the heart of functional programming.

2.3   Functions

In functional programming, functions are the basic units of work, which means everything centers around them. A *function* is any callable expression that can be evaluated by applying the () operator to it. Functions can return either a computed value or undefined (void function) back to the caller. Because FP works a lot like math, functions are meaningful only when they produce a *usable result* (not null or undefined); otherwise, the assumption is that they modify external data and cause side effects to occur. For the purpose of this book, we can distinguish between *expressions* (functions that produce a value) and *statements* (functions that don't). Imperative and procedural programming are mostly made up of ordered sequences of statements; but FP is entirely expressional, so void functions don't serve a purpose in this paradigm.

JavaScript functions have two important characteristics that are the bread and butter of its functional style: they're first-class and higher-order. We'll explore both of these ideas in detail next.

2.3.1 *Functions as first-class citizens*

In JavaScript, the term *first-class* comes from making functions actual objects in the language—also called first-class citizens. You're probably used to seeing functions declared like this:

```
function multiplier(a,b) {
    return a * b;
}
```

But JavaScript offers more options. Like objects, a function can be

- Assigned to variables as an anonymous function or lambda expression (I explain the use of lambdas is more detail in chapter 3):

```
var square = function (x) {          Anonymous
    return x * x;                    function
}

var square = x => x * x;          ← Lambda
                                     expression
```

- Assigned to object properties as methods:

```
var obj = {
    method: function (x) { return x * x; }
};
```

Whereas a function call uses the `()` operator, as in `square(2)`, the function object is printed as follows:

```
square;
// function (x) {
//     return x * x;
// }
```

Although not common practice, functions can also be instantiated via constructors, which is proof of their first-class nature in JavaScript. The constructor takes the set of formal parameters, the function body, and the new keyword, like so:

```
var multiplier = new Function('a', 'b', 'return a * b');

multiplier(2, 3); //-> 6
```

In JavaScript, every function is an instance of the `Function` type. A function's `length` property can be used to retrieve the number of formal parameters, and methods such as `apply()` and `call()` can be used to call functions with contexts (more about them in the next section).

The right side of an anonymous function expression is a function object with an empty `name` property. You can use anonymous functions to extend or specialize a function's behavior by passing them as arguments. Consider JavaScript's native

`Array.sort(comparator)` as an example; it takes a comparator function object. By default, `sort` converts values being sorted into strings and uses their Unicode values as natural sorting criteria. This is limiting and often not what you intend. Let's look at a couple of examples:

```
var fruit = ['Coconut', 'apples'];
fruit.sort();  //->['Coconut', 'apples']
```

In Unicode, capital letters come before lowercase letters.

```
var ages = [1, 10, 21, 2];
ages.sort(); //->[1, 10, 2, 21]
```

Numbers are converted into strings and compared with their Unicode points.

As a result, `sort()` is a function whose behavior is frequently driven by the criteria implemented in the `comparator` function, which by itself is almost useless. You can force proper numerical comparisons and sort a list of people by age using a custom function argument:

```
people.sort((p1, p2) => p1.getAge() - p2.getAge());
```

The `comparator` function takes two parameters, p1 and p2, with the following contract:

- If `comparator` return less than 0, p1 comes before p2.
- If `comparator` returns 0, leave p1 and p2 unchanged.
- If `comparator` returns greater than 0, p1 comes after p2.

In addition to being assignable, JavaScript functions like `sort()` accept other functions as arguments and belong to a category called *higher-order functions*.

2.3.2 *Higher-order functions*

Because functions behave like regular objects, you can intuitively expect that they can be passed in as function arguments and returned from other functions. These are called *higher-order functions*. You saw the comparator function for `Array.sort()`; let's quickly look at some other examples.

The following snippet shows that functions can be passed in to other functions. The `applyOperation` function takes two arguments and applies any `operator` function to both of them:

```
function applyOperation(a, b, opt) {
    return opt(a,b);
}

var multiplier = (a, b) => a * b;

applyOperation(2, 3, multiplier); // -> 6
```

The opt() function can be passed as an argument to other functions.

In the next example, the add function takes an argument and returns a function that, in turn, receives a second argument and adds them together:

```
function add(a) {
   return function (b) {            ◁─┐   A function is returned
      return a + b;                   │   from another function.
   }
}
add(3)(3); //-> 6
```

Because functions are first-class and higher-order, JavaScript functions can *behave as values*, which implies that a function is nothing more than a yet-to-be-executed value defined immutably based on the input provided to the function. This principle is embedded in everything that you do in functional programming, especially when you get into function chains, as you'll see in chapter 3. When building function chains, you'll always rely on function names to point to a piece of a program that will be executed as part of an entire expression.

You can combine higher-order functions to create meaningful expressions from smaller pieces and simplify many programs that would otherwise be tedious to write. As an example, say you need to print a list of people who live in the United States. Your first approach would probably look like this imperative code:

```
function printPeopleInTheUs(people) {
   for (let i = 0; i < people.length; i++) {
     var thisPerson = people[i];
     if(thisPerson.address.country === 'US') {       Invokes each object's
       console.log(thisPerson);              ◁─┘      toString method
     }
   }
}                                      ┌─ p1, p2, and p3 are
printPeopleInTheUs([p1, p2, p3]);  ◁─┘   instances of Person.
```

Now, suppose you need to support printing people living in other countries, as well. With higher-order functions, you can nicely abstract out the action performed on each person: in this case, printing to the console. You can freely supply any action function you want to a higher-order printPeople function:

```
function printPeople(people, action) {
   for (let i = 0; i < people.length; i++) {
      action (people[i]);
   }
}

var action = function (person) {
   if(person.address.country === 'US') {
      console.log(person);
   }
}

printPeople(people,action);
```

A noticeable pattern that occurs in languages like JavaScript is that function names can be passive nouns like `multiplier`, `comparator`, and `action`. Because they're first-class, functions can be assigned to variables and executed at a later time. Let's refactor `printPeople` to take full advantage of higher-order functions:

```
function printPeople(people, selector, printer) {
    people.forEach(function (person) {
        if(selector(person)) {
            printer(person);
        }
    });
}

var inUs = person => person.address.country === 'US';

printPeople(people, inUs, console.log);
```

> forEach is the functional-style, preferred way of looping; I discuss it later in this chapter.

> By using higher-order functions, the declarative pattern is beginning to emerge. This expression makes clear what this program does.

This is the mindset you must develop to fully embrace functional programming. This exercise shows that the code is a lot more flexible than what you started with, because you can quickly swap (or configure) the criteria for selection as well as change where you want to print. Chapters 3 and 4 focus on this topic and the use of special libraries to fluently chain operations together and build complex programs from simple parts.

Looking ahead

I want to briefly pause my discussion of core JavaScript material to elaborate further on the program in this section and combine some concepts I've briefly touched on. This is a bit advanced for now, but soon you'll learn how to build programs this way using FP techniques. You can create supporting functions using lenses that you can use to access an object's properties:

```
var countryPath = ['address', 'country'];
var countryL = R.lens(R.path(countryPath), R.assocPath(countryPath));
var inCountry = R.curry((country, person) =>
        R.equals(R.view(countryL, person), country));
```

This is much more functional than before:

```
people.filter(inCountry('US')).map(console.log);
```

As you can see, the country name becomes another parameter that can be changed to anything you want. This is something to look forward to in the following chapters.

In JavaScript, functions not only are invoked, they're also applied. Let's talk about this unique quality of JavaScript's function-invocation mechanism.

2.3.3 *Types of function invocation*

JavaScript's function-invocation mechanism is an interesting part of the language and different from other programming languages. JavaScript gives you complete freedom to dictate the runtime context in which a function is invoked: the value of `this` in the function body. JavaScript functions can be invoked in many different ways:

- *As a global function*—The reference to `this` is set either to the `global` object or to `undefined` (in strict mode):

```
function doWork() {
    this.myVar = 'Some value';    ◁─┐  Calling doWork() globally
}                                    │  causes the "this" reference
doWork();                         ◁─┘  to point to the global object.
```

- *As a method*—The reference to `this` is set to the owner of the method. This is an important part of JavaScript's object-oriented nature:

```
var obj = {
    prop: 'Some property',
        getProp: function () {return this.prop}  ◁─┐  Invoking an object's
};                                                  │  method points "this"
obj.getProp();                                   ◁─┘  to the owning object.
```

- *As a constructor by prepending the call with* `new`—This implicitly returns the reference to the newly created object:

```
function MyType(arg) {                     ┌  Calling a function with new
    this.prop = arg;               ◁───┤  sets the "this" reference to
}                                      │  point to the object that's
                                  ◁───┤  being constructed and
var someVal = new MyType('some argument');    implicitly returned.
```

As you can see from these examples, unlike in other programming languages, the `this` reference is set based on how the function is used (globally, as an object method, as a constructor, and so on) and not by its lexical context (its location in the code). This can lead to code that's hard to understand, because you need to pay close attention to the context in which a function is executing.

I included this section because it's important for you to know as a JavaScript developer; but as I've indicated several times, the use of `this` in functional code is rarely seen (in fact, it's avoided at all costs). It's heavily used by library and tool implementers for special cases that demand bending the language context to perform incredible feats. These often involve the function methods `apply` and `call`.

2.3.4   *Function methods*

JavaScript supports calling functions via the function methods (like meta-functions) `call` and `apply`, which belong to the function's prototype. Both methods are used extensively when scaffolding code is built so that API users can create new functions from existing ones. Let's take a quick look at writing a `negate` function, for example:

```
function negate(func) {
    return function() {
        return !func.apply(null, arguments);
    };
}

function isNull(val) {
    return val === null;
}

var isNotNull = negate(isNull);

isNotNull(null); //-> false
isNotNull({});    //-> true
```

Creates the higher-order function negate, which takes a function as input and returns a function that negates its outcome

Uses Function.apply() to execute this function against the original arguments

Defines the function isNull

Defines the function isNotNull as the negation of isNull

The `negate` function creates a new function that invokes its argument and then logically negates it. This example uses `apply`, but you could use `call` the same way; the difference is that the latter accepts an argument list, whereas the former takes an array of arguments. The first argument, `thisArg`, can be used to manipulate the function context as needed. Here are both signatures:

```
Function.prototype.apply(thisArg, [argsArray])

Function.prototype.call(thisArg, arg1,arg2,...)
```

If `thisArg` refers to an object, it's set to the object the method is called on. If `thisArg` is `null`, the function context is set to the global object, and the function behaves like a simple global function. But if the method is a function in strict mode, the actual value of `null` is passed in.

Manipulating the function context through `thisArg` opens the door to many different techniques. This is discouraged in functional programming, because it never relies on the context state (recall that all data is provided to functions as arguments), so I won't spend any more time on this feature.

Although the notion of a shared global or object context isn't all that useful in functional JavaScript, there's one specific context we care about: the function context. To understand it, you must understand closures and scopes.

2.4 Closures and scopes

Prior to JavaScript, closures only existed in FP languages used in certain specific applications. JavaScript is the first to adopt it into mainstream development and significantly change the way in which we write code. Let's revisit the `zipCode` type:

```
function zipCode(code, location) {
    let _code = code;
    let _location = location || '';

    return {
        code: function () {
            return _code;
        },
        location: function () {
            return _location;
        },
      ...
    };
}
```

If you examine this code closely, you'll realize that the `zipCode` function returns an object literal that seems to have full access to variables declared outside of its scope. In other words, after `zipCode` has finished executing, the resulting object can still see information declared in this enclosing function:

```
const princetonZip = zipCode('08544', '3345');
princetonZip.code(); //-> '08544'
```

This is a bit mind-bending, and it's all thanks to the closure that forms around object and function declarations in JavaScript. Being able to access data this way has many practical uses; in this section, we'll look at using closures to emulate private variables, fetch data from the server, and force block-scoped variables.

A *closure* is a data structure that binds a function to its environment at the moment it's declared. It's based on the textual location of the function declaration; therefore, a closure is also called a *static* or *lexical scope* surrounding the function definition. Because it gives functions access to its surrounding state, it makes code clear and readable. As you'll see shortly, closures are instrumental not only in functional programs when you're working with higher-order functions, but also for event-handling and callbacks, emulating private variables, and mitigating some of JavaScript's pitfalls.

The rules that govern the behavior of a function's closure are closely related to JavaScript's scoping rules. A scope groups a set of variable bindings and defines a section of code in which a variable is defined. In essence, a closure is a function's inheritance of scopes akin to how an object's method has access to its inherited instance variables—both have references to their parents. Closures are readily seen in the case of nested functions. Here's a quick example:

```
function makeAddFunction(amount) {
    function add(number) {
        return number + amount;
    }
    return add;
}
```
> The add function is lexically bound in **makeAddFunction** and has access to the amount variable.

```
function makeExponentialFunction(base) {
    function raise (exponent) {
        return Math.pow(base, exponent);
    }
    return raise;
}
var addTenTo = makeAddFunction(10);
addTenTo(10); //-> 20

var raiseThreeTo = makeExponentialFunction(3);
raiseThreeTo(2); //-> 9
```
> The function raise() is lexically bound in **makeExponentialFunction** and has access to base.

It's important to notice in this example that even though the amount and base variables in both functions are no longer in the active scope, they're still accessible from the returned function when invoked. Essentially, you can imagine the nested functions add and raise as functions that package not only their computation but also a snapshot of all variables surrounding them. More generally, as shown in figure 2.4, a function's closure includes the following:

- All function parameters (params and params2, in this case)
- All variables in the outer scope (including all global variables, of course), as well as those declared after the function additionalVars

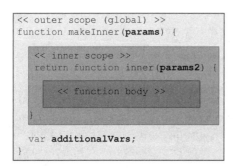

Figure 2.4   A closure contains variables that appear in the outer (global) scope, the parent function's inner scope, and the parent function's parameters and additional variables declared after the function declaration. The code defined in the function's body can access variables and objects defined in each of these scopes. All functions share the global scope.

Let's see this in action in the next listing.

Listing 2.3   Closures at work

```
var outerVar = 'Outer';
function makeInner(params) {
    var innerVar = 'Inner';
```
> Declares the global variable outerVar

> Declares the local variable to makeInner

```
                 function inner() {                              ◁────   Declaration of
                     console.log(                                        inner: innerVar
                         `I can see: ${outerVar}, ${innerVar}, and ${params}`);   and outerVar are
                 }                                                        part of inner's
                 return inner;                                            closure
             }
Invokes
makeInner
to return
function
inner
         ┗─▷  var inner = makeInner('Params');        Function inner is a valid
              inner();                          ◁──── function that outlives the
                                                       execution of its outer function
```

Running this code prints out the following:

```
'I can see: Outer, Inner, and Params'
```

At first glance, this may seem unintuitive and somewhat mystical. You'd expect that local variables—innerVar in this case—would cease to exist or be garbage-collected after makeInner returned, thereby printing undefined. Behind the scenes, it's again the magic of closures that makes this possible. The function returned from makeInner remembers all the variables in the scope at the time it was declared and also prevents them from being disposed of. The global scope is also part of this closure, giving access to outerVar as well; I'll revisit closures and what's inside a function context in chapter 7.

You may wonder how variables (like additionalVars) declared after a function is declared can also be included as part of its closure. To answer this, you need to understand that JavaScript has three forms of scoping: global scope, function scope, and a pseudo-block scope.

2.4.1 *Problems with the global scope*

Global scope is the simplest form of scoping, but also the worst. Any objects and variables declared in the outermost level of a script (not contained in any function) are part of the *global scope* and accessible from all JavaScript code. Recall that our goal in functional programming is to prevent any observable changes to ripple out from functions; but in the global scope, every line that executes causes visible changes to occur.

It's tempting to use global variables, but they're shared among all scripts loaded onto the page, which can easily lead to namespace collisions if your JavaScript code isn't packaged into modules. Polluting the global namespace can be problematic because you run the chance of overriding variables and functions declared in different files.

Global data has the detrimental effect of making programs hard to reason about because you're obligated to keep a mental note of the state of all variables at any point in time. This is one of the main reasons program complexity increases as your code becomes larger. It's also conducive to having side effects in your functions, because you inevitably create external dependencies when reading from or writing to it. It should be obvious at this point that when writing in an FP style, you'll avoid using global variables at all cost.

2.4.2   *JavaScript's function scope*

This is JavaScript's preferred scoping mechanism. Any variables declared in a function are local to that function and not visible anywhere else. Also, when a function returns, any local variables declared in are deleted with it. So in the function

```
function doWork() {
    let student = new Student(...);
    let address = new Address(...);
    // do more work
};
```

the variables `student` and `address` are bound in `doWork()` and are inaccessible by the outside world. As you can see in figure 2.5, resolving a variable by name is similar to the prototype name-resolution chain described earlier. It begins by checking the innermost scope and works its way outward. JavaScript's scoping mechanism works as follows:

1 It checks the variable's function scope.
2 If not in the local scope, it moves outward into the surrounding lexical scope, searching for the variable reference until it reaches the global scope.
3 If the variable can't be referenced, JavaScript returns `undefined`.

Consider this code sample:

```
var x = 'Some value';
function parentFunction() {
    function innerFunction() {
        console.log(x);
    }
    return innerFunction;
}
var inner = parentFunction();
inner();
```

When `inner` is called, the JavaScript runtime unwinds the lookup process for x in the sequence shown in figure 2.5.

Figure 2.5   JavaScript's *name-resolution order*, which first looks into the closest scope level surrounding a variable lookup and moves outward. It first checks the function's scope (local), then moves into its parent's scope (if there is one), and finally moves into the global scope. If the variable x isn't found, the function returns `undefined`.

If you have experience with any other programming language, you're probably used to function scope. But given JavaScript's C-like syntax, you may expect block scopes to work in similar ways.

2.4.3 *A pseudo-block scope*

Unfortunately, standard ES5 JavaScript doesn't support block-level scope, which is formed in brackets, {}, under control structures such as for, while, if, and switch statements. The exception is the error variable passed into a catch block. The with statement can do some level of block scope, but its use is discouraged and is removed in strict mode. In other C-like languages, a variable declared in an if statement (myVar, in this case) such as the following

```
if (someCondition) {
    var myVar = 10;
}
```

isn't accessible from outside the code block. This can be confusing for developers who are accustomed to that style and are new to JavaScript. Because JavaScript has function scope exclusively, any variables declared in a block are accessible at any point in the function. This can also be a nightmare for JavaScript developers, but there are ways to overcome it. Let's look at the problem at hand:

```
function doWork() {
    if (!myVar) {
      var myVar = 10;
    }
    console.log(myVar); //-> 10
}
doWork();
```

The variable myVar is declared in the if statement, but it's visible from outside the block. Strangely enough, running this code prints out the value 10. This can be baffling, especially for developers used to the more common block-level scope. An internal JavaScript mechanism hoists variable and function declarations to the top of the current scope—the function scope, in this case. This can make writing loops unsafe; pay attention to the following listing.

Listing 2.4 Ambiguous loop-counter problem

```
var arr = [1, 2, 3, 4];
function processArr() {

    function multipleBy10(val) {
        i = 10;
        return val * i;
    }

    for(var i = 0; i < arr.length; i++) {
      arr[i] = multipleBy10(arr[i]);
    }
```

```
      return arr;
}
processArr(); //-> [10, 2, 3, 4]
```

The loop counter i is moved to the top of the function and becomes part of the multipleBy10 function's closure. Forgetting to use the keyword var in i's declaration fails to create a locally scoped variable in multiplyBy and accidentally modifies the loop counter to 10. The loop-counter declaration is hoisted, set to undefined, and then later assigned the value 0 when the loop is run. In chapter 8, you'll see a recurrence of this ambiguity problem that occurs with computing nonblocking operations in loops.

Good IDEs and linters can help mitigate these issues, but even they aren't much help in the face of hundreds of lines of code. In the next chapter, we'll look at better solutions that are both more elegant and less error-prone than standard loops: techniques that take full advantage of higher-order functions and help mitigate these pitfalls. As you've seen throughout this chapter, ES6 JavaScript provides the let keyword to help resolve this loop-counter ambiguity by properly binding the loop counter to its enclosing block:

```
for(let i = 0; i < arr.length; i++) {          let resolves the hoisting
   // ...                                       problem and scopes i in
}                                               the right place. Outside
                                                the loop, i isn't defined.
i;  // i === undefined
```

This is a step in the right direction, and the reason why I prefer using let than var in scope-bounded variables, but manual loops have other shortcomings that we'll remedy in the next chapter. Now that you understand what makes up a function's closure and its interplay with scope mechanics, let's turn to some practical uses of closures.

2.4.4   *Practical applications of closures*

Closures have many practical applications that are important to apply when implementing large JavaScript programs. These aren't specific to functional programming, but they do take advantage of JavaScript's function mechanism:

- Emulating private variables
- Making asynchronous server-side calls
- Creating artificial block-scoped variables

EMULATING PRIVATE VARIABLES

Unlike JavaScript, many languages provide a built-in mechanism to define internal properties of an object by setting accessibility modifiers (like private). JavaScript doesn't have a native keyword for private variables and functions to be accessed only in the scope of an object. Encapsulation can play in favor of immutability because you can't change what you can't access.

Using closures, however, it's possible to emulate this behavior. One example is returning an object, much like `zipCode` and `coordinate` in the earlier example. These functions return object literals with methods that have access to any of the outer function's local variables, but don't expose these variables, therefore effectively making them private.

Closures can also provide a way to manage your global namespace to avoid globally shared data. Library and module authors take closures to the next level by hiding an entire module's private methods and data. This is referred to as the *Module pattern* because it uses a single *immediately invoked function expression* (IIFE) to encapsulate internal variables while allowing you to export the necessary set of functionality to the outside world and severely reduce the number of global references.

> **NOTE** As a general best practice, I recommend packaging all of your functional code inside well-encapsulated modules. You can transfer all the core principles of functional programming you've learned in this book to the level of modules.

Here's a short sample of a module skeleton:[3]

Names the function again so that any stack trace information resulting from an error clearly identifies the IIFE

Private variables aren't accessible from outside this function but are accessible to both methods.

```
var MyModule = (function MyModule(export)
    let _myPrivateVar = ...;

    export.method1 = function () {
      // do work
    };

    export.method2 = function () {
      // do work
    };

    return export;
}(MyModule || {}));
```

Methods to be exported globally under the object's scope, which creates a pseudo-namespace

Single object that privately encloses all hidden state and methods. You can invoke method1() using MyModule.method1().

The object `MyModule` is created globally and passed into a function expression, created with the `function` keyword, and immediately executed when the script is loaded. Due to JavaScript's function scope, `_myPrivateVar` and any other private variables are local to the wrapping function. The closure surrounding the two exported methods is what allows the object to safely access all of the module's internal properties. This is compelling because it keeps your global footprint low while exposing an object with

---

[3] For a more in-depth explanation of the different types of module patterns, see Ben Cherry's "JavaScript Module Pattern: In-Depth," *Adequately Good*, March 12, 2010, http://mng.bz/H9hk.

lots of encapsulated state and behavior. This module pattern has been adopted in all the functional libraries we'll use throughout this book.

MAKING ASYNCHRONOUS SERVER-SIDE CALLS

JavaScript's first-class, higher-order functions can be passed into other functions as callbacks. Callbacks are useful as hooks to handle events in an unobtrusive manner. Suppose you need to make a request to the server and want to be notified once the data has been received. The traditional idiom is to provide a callback function that will handle the response:

```
getJSON('/students',
    (students) => {
        getJSON('/students/grades',                          Processes both
            grades => processGrades(grades),        ◁         responses
            error => console.log(error.message));   ◁
    },                                                       Handles fetching
    (error) =>                                               grade errors
        console.log(error.message)          ◁
)                                                  Handles fetching
                                                   student errors
```

getJSON is a higher-order function that takes two callbacks as arguments: a success function and an error function. A common pattern that occurs with asynchronous code as well as event handling is that you can easily corner yourself into deeply nested function calls; this forms the unpleasant "callback pyramid of doom" when you need to make several subsequent remote calls to the server. As you've probably experienced, when code is deeply nested, it becomes hard to follow. In chapter 8, you'll learn best practices for how to basically flatten this code into more fluent and declarative expressions that chain together instead of nesting.

EMULATING BLOCKED-SCOPE VARIABLES

Using closures can provide an alternative solution to the ambiguous loop-counter variable example in listing 2.4. As I mentioned earlier, the underlying issue is JavaScript's lack of block-scope semantics, so the objective is to artificially create this block scope. What can you do about this? Using `let` mitigates many of the issues with the traditional looping mechanism, but a functional approach would be to take advantage of closures and JavaScript's function scope and consider using `forEach`. Now, instead of worrying about tying the loop counter and other variables in scope, you can effectively wrap the loop body inside the loop as if emulating a function-scope block under the loop statement. As you'll learn later, this helps you call asynchronous behavior while iterating over collections:

```
arr.forEach(function(elem, i) {
    ...
});
```

This chapter covered just the basics of JavaScript, to help you understand some of its limitations when it's used functionally and prepare you for the functional techniques covered in later chapters. If you seek a much deeper understanding of the language, there are entire books dedicated to this subject that teach the concepts of objects, inheritance, and closures much more thoroughly.

Want to become a JavaScript ninja?

The topics of objects, functions, scoping, and closures covered in this chapter are crucial to becoming a JavaScript expert. But I've only scratched the surface, to level the playing field so that we can focus strictly on functional programming for the remainder of the book. To obtain more information and take your JavaScript skills to a ninja level, I recommend that you read *Secrets of the JavaScript Ninja, Second Edition* by John Resig, Bear Bibeault, and Josip Maras (Manning, 2016, www.manning.com/books/secrets-of-the-javascript-ninja-second-edition).

Now that you have a solid JavaScript foundation, in the next chapter we'll look at data processing using some popular operations such as `map`, `reduce`, `filter`, and recursion.

2.5 *Summary*

- JavaScript is a versatile language with a powerful inclination toward OOP and functional programming.
- Implementing immutability into OOP allows it to mix nicely with functional programming.
- Higher-order and first-class JavaScript functions provide the backbone that allows JavaScript to be written functionally.
- Closures have many practical uses for information hiding, module development, and passing parameterized behavior into coarse-grained functions across multiple data types.

Part 2

Get functional

Part 1 answered the two most fundamental questions about this book: Why Functional? And why JavaScript? Now that you understand what functional programming brings to JavaScript development, I'll take it up a few notches. In part 2, I'll build on and discuss all the practical concepts and techniques you need in order to apply functional programming to solve real-world problems. In this part, you'll learn what it means to "get functional."

Chapter 3 takes a first look at some comprehensive functional programs by using declarative abstractions such as map, reduce, and filter, with the goal of creating code that's easy to reason about. It also covers the use of recursion as a means of iterating through different forms of data in a functional style.

Chapter 4 takes the concepts from chapter 3 and applies them to constructing function pipelines to streamline development and write in a point-free style. You'll learn that the key to building functional code is breaking up complex tasks into small, independent components that can be glued back together to form whole solutions via the principle of compositionality. The result is a modular and reusable code base.

Finally, in chapter 5 you'll learn fundamental design patterns that combat the increasing complexity of your applications and error handling. Functional composition is made more reliable and robust with abstract data types like functors and monads, which provide a layer of abstraction that makes your code fault-tolerant and resilient to exceptional conditions.

Applying the techniques discovered in part 2 will completely transform the way you code JavaScript. Also, this sets the stage for part 3, which deals with applying functional programming techniques to solve more-complex JavaScript problems involving asynchronous data and events.

Few data structures, *many operations*

> Computational processes are abstract beings that inhabit computers. As they evolve, processes manipulate other abstract things called data.
>
> —Harold Abelson and Gerald Jay Sussman (*Structure and Interpretation of Computer Programs*, MIT Press, 1979)

Part 1 of this book accomplished two important goals: on one hand, those chapters got your feet wet by teaching you how to think functionally and introducing the tools you'll need to use functional programming. Second, you took a condensed tour of many core JavaScript features, particularly higher-order functions, that will be used frequently throughout this chapter and the rest of the book. Now that you know how to make functions pure, it's time to learn how to connect them.

In this chapter, I'll introduce you to a few useful and practical operations like map, reduce, and filter that allow you to traverse and transform data structures in a sequential manner. These operations are so important that virtually all functional programs use them in one way or another. They also facilitate removing manual loops from your code, because most loops are just specific cases handled by these functions.

You'll also learn to use a functional JavaScript library called Lodash.js. It lets you process and understand not only the structure of your application, but also the structure of your data. In addition, I'll discuss the important role recursion plays in functional programming and the advantages of being able to think recursively. Building on these concepts, you'll learn to write concise, extensible, and declarative programs that clearly separate control flow from the main logic of your code.

3.1   *Understanding your application's control flow*

The path a program takes to arrive at a solution is known as its *control flow.* An imperative program describes its flow or path in great detail by exposing all the necessary steps needed to fulfill its task. These steps usually involve lots of loops and branches, as well as variables that change with each statement. At a high level, you can depict a simple imperative program like this:

```
var loop = optC();
while(loop) {
   var condition = optA();
   if(condition) {
     optB1();
   }
   else {
     optB2();
   }
   loop = optC();
}
optD();
```

Figure 3.1 shows a simple flowchart of this program.

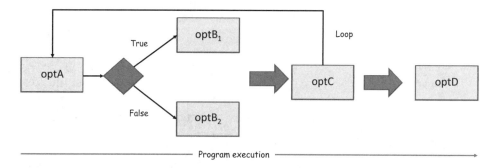

Figure 3.1   An imperative program made up of a series of operations (or statements) controlled by branches and loops

On the other hand, declarative programs, specifically functional ones, raise the level of abstraction by using a minimally structured flow made up of independent black-box operations that connect in a simple topology. These connected operations are nothing more than higher-order functions that move state from one operation to the next, as shown in figure 3.2. Working functionally with data structures such as arrays lends itself to this style of development and treats data and control flow as simple connections between high-level components.

Figure 3.2 Functional control among connected black-box operations. Information flows independently from one operation to the next (the operations are individual, pure functions). Branches and iterations are effectively reduced or even eliminated in favor of high-level abstractions.

This produces code more or less like the following:

```
optA().optB().optC().optD();
```

Connecting via dots suggests the presence of a shared object that contains these methods.

Chaining operations in this manner leads to concise, fluent, expressive programs that let you separate a program's control flow from its computational logic. Thus, you can reason about your code and your data more effectively.

3.2 *Method chaining*

Method chaining is an OOP pattern that allows multiple methods to be called in a single statement. When these methods all belong to the same object, method chaining is referred to as *method cascading*. Although this pattern is seen mostly in object-oriented applications, under certain conditions, such as working with immutable objects, it works just as well with functional programming. Because mutation of objects is prohibited in functional code, you may wonder how this is possible. Let's look at a string-manipulation example:

```
'Functional Programming'.substring(0, 10).toLowerCase() + ' is fun';
```

In this example, both `substring` and `toLowerCase` are string methods that operate on the owning string object (via `this`) and return new strings. The plus (+) operator is overloaded in JavaScript strings as syntactic sugar for concatenation—also producing a new string. The result of applying these transformations is a string that bears no reference to the original, which remains untouched; this is to be expected, because strings are, by design, immutable. From an object-oriented perspective, this is taken for granted; but from the functional programming side, this is ideal—you don't require lenses to work with strings.

If you refactor the previous code into a more functional style, it looks like this:

```
concat(toLowerCase(substring('Functional Programming', 1, 10))),' is fun');
```

This code follows the functional doctrine that all parameters should be explicitly defined in the function declaration; it has no side effects and doesn't mutate the original object. Arguably, writing this function inside out isn't as fluent as the method-chaining approach. It's also much harder to read, because you need to start peeling off the wrapped functions to understand what's truly happening.

Chaining methods belonging to a single object instance has its place in functional programming, as long as you respect the policy for change. Wouldn't it be nice to translate this pattern to work with arrays as well? The behavior we see in strings has also been extended to work with JavaScript arrays, but most people aren't familiar with it and resort to quick-and-dirty `for` loops.

3.3   *Function chaining*

Object-oriented programs use inheritance as the main mechanism for code reuse. Recall from the previous chapter that `Student` inherits from `Person`, and that all state and methods are inherited by the child type. You may have seen this pattern predominantly in purer object-oriented languages, especially in their data structure implementations. Java, for instance, has an explosion of concrete `List` classes for each need: `ArrayList`, `LinkedList`, `DoublyLinkedList`, `CopyOnWriteArrayList`, and others implement the basic `List` interface and derive from common parent classes, adding their own specific functionality.

Functional programming takes a different approach. Instead of creating new data structure classes to meet specific needs, it uses common ones like arrays and applies a number of coarse-grained, higher-order operations that are agnostic to the underlying representation of the data. These operations are designed to do the following:

- Accept function arguments in order to inject specialized behavior that solves your particular task
- Replace the traditional, manual looping mechanisms that contain mutations of temporary variables and side effects, thereby creating less code to maintain and fewer places where errors can occur

Let's survey these in detail. The examples in this chapter are based on a collection of `Person` objects. For brevity, I've declared only four objects, but the same concepts apply to larger collections:

```
const p1 = new Person('Haskell', 'Curry', '111-11-1111');
p1.address = new Address('US');
p1.birthYear = 1900;
```

```
const p2 = new Person('Barkley', 'Rosser', '222-22-2222');
p2.address = new Address('Greece');
p2.birthYear = 1907;

const p3 = new Person('John', 'von Neumann', '333-33-3333');
p3.address = new Address('Hungary');
p3.birthYear = 1903;

const p4 = new Person('Alonzo', 'Church', '444-44-4444');
p4.address = new Address('US');
p4.birthYear = 1903;
```

3.3.1 *Understanding lambda expressions*

Born from functional programming, *lambda expressions* (known as *fat-arrow functions* in the JavaScript world) encode one-line anonymous functions into a shorter syntax, compared to a traditional function declaration. You can have lambda functions with multiple lines, but one-liners are the most commonly used, as you saw in chapter 2. Whether you use lambdas or regular function syntax will depend on the readability of your code; under the hood, they're all the same. Here's a simple example of a function used to extract a person's name:

```
const name = p => p.fullname;
console.log(name(p1)); //-> 'Haskell Curry'
```

The compact notation (p) => p.fullname is syntactic sugar for a function that takes a parameter p and implicitly returns p.fullname. Figure 3.3 shows the structure of this new syntactic addition.

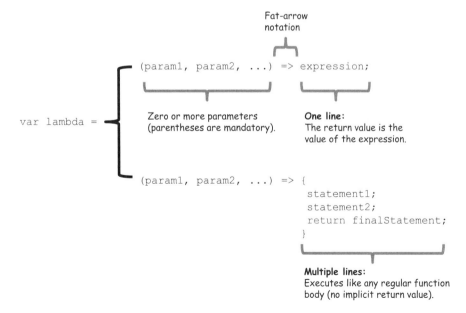

Figure 3.3 Dissecting the structure of arrow functions. The right side of a lambda function is either a single expression or an enclosed set of multiple statements.

Lambda expressions uphold the functional definition of a function because they encourage you to always return a value. In fact, for one-line expressions, the return value results from the value of the function body. Another point worth noting here is the relationship between first-class functions and lambdas. In this case, `name` points not to a concrete value, but (lazily) to a description of how to obtain it; in other words, `name` points to an arrow function that knows how to compute this data. This is why, in functional programming, you can use functions as values. I'll discuss this concept further in this chapter and lazy functions in chapter 7.

Furthermore, functional programming promotes the use of three central higher-order functions—`map`, `reduce`, and `filter`—that are designed to work well with lambda expressions. A lot of functional JavaScript code is based on processing lists of data; hence, the name of the original functional language, LISP (list processing), from which JavaScript is derived. JavaScript 5.1 provides native versions of these operations known as the functional *array extras*; but in order to create complete solutions that may involve other similar types of operations, I'll use the implementations provided in a functional library called Lodash.js. Its toolkit provides important artifacts that empower you to write functional programs, and it contains a rich repertoire of utility functions that handle many common programming tasks (see the appendix for details on how to install this library). Once it's installed, you can access its functionality via the global _ (underscore or low-dash) object. Let's get started with _.map.

The underscore in Lodash

Lodash uses the underscore convention because it began as a fork of the famous and widely used Undesrscore.js project (http://underscorejs.org/). Lodash still tracks Underscore's API closely, to the point that it can serve as a drop-in replacement. But behind the scenes, it's a complete rewrite in favor of more elegant ways to build function chains, as well as some performance enhancements that you'll learn about in chapter 7.

3.3.2 Transforming data with _.map

Suppose you need to transform all the elements in a large collection of data. For instance, given a list of student objects, you want to extract each person's full name. How many times have you had to write this sequence of statements?

```
var result = [];
var persons = [p1, p2, p3, p4];
for(let i = 0; i < persons.length; i++) {
    var p = persons[i];
    if(p !== null && p !== undefined) {
        result.push(p.fullname);
    }
}
```

The imperative approach assumes fullname is a method in Student.

map (also known as `collect`) is a higher-order function that applies an iterator function to each element in an array, in order, and returns a new array of equal length. Here's the same program, this time using a functional style with _.map:

```
_.map(persons,
    s => (s !== null && s !== undefined) ? s.fullname : ''
);
```

I got rid of all var declarations using higher-order functions.

A formal definition of this operation is as follows:

```
map(f, [e0, e1, e2...]) -> [r0, r1, r2...];  where, f(dn) = rn
```

map is extremely useful for parsing through entire collections of elements without having to write a single loop or deal with odd scoping problems. Also, it's immutable, because the result is an entirely new array. map works by taking a function f and a collection of n elements as input; it returns a new array of size n with elements computed from applying f to each element in a left-to-right manner. This is depicted in figure 3.4.

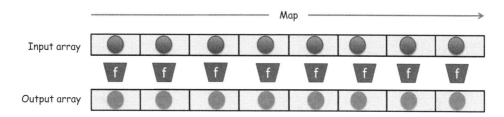

Figure 3.4 The map operation applies an iterator function f to each element in an array and returns an array of equal length.

This example of _.map iterates over an array of student objects and extracts their names. You use a lambda expression as the iterator function (which is common). This doesn't change the original array but, rather, returns a new one that contains the following:

```
['Haskell Curry', 'Barkley Rosser', 'John von Neumann', 'Alonzo Church']
```

Because it's always beneficial to understand one level below the abstraction layer, let's look at how _.map could be implemented.

Listing 3.1   Map implementation

```
function map(arr, fn) {
  const len = arr.length,
        result = new Array(len);
  for (let idx = 0; idx < len; ++idx) {
    result[idx] = fn(arr[idx], idx, arr);
  }
  return result;
}
```

Takes a function and an array, applies the function to each element, and returns a new array of the same size as the original

Result: An array of the same length as the input

Applies the function fn to each element in the array and puts the result back into an array

As you can see, internally, _.map is based on standard loops. This function handles iteration on your behalf, so you're only responsible for administering the proper functionality in the iterator function instead of having to worry about mundane concerns like incrementing loop variables and bounds checks. This is an example of how functional libraries bring your code to the same level as purer functional languages.

map is exclusively a left-to-right operation; for a right-to-left sweep, you must first reverse the array. For consistency, Lodash's _.reverse() matches JavaScript's Array .reverse(), which means it mutates the original array in place; it's important for you to be aware of when functions have side effects:

```
_(persons).reverse().map(
    p => (p !== null && p !== undefined) ? p.fullname : ''
);
```

Notice the use of a slightly different syntax in this example. Lodash provides a nice, noninvasive way to integrate your code with it. All that's needed for it to be able to manage your objects is for you to wrap them in the notation _(...). Afterward, you have complete control of its powerful functional arsenal to apply any transformations you need.

Mapping over containers
The concept of mapping over data structures (in this case, an array) to transform the constituent values has far-reaching implications. Just as you can map any function over an array, in chapter 5 you'll learn that you can also map a function over any object.

Now that you can apply a transformation function over your data, it's useful to be able to make conclusions or extract certain results based on the new structure. This is the work of the reduce function.

3.3.3 *Gathering results with _.reduce*

You know how to transform your data, but how do you gather meaningful results from it? Suppose you want to compute the country with the largest count from a collection of Person objects. You can use the reduce function to accomplish this.

reduce is a higher-order function that compresses an array of elements down to a single value. This value is computed from the accumulated result of invoking a function with an accumulator value against each element. This is easier to visualize by looking at the diagram in figure 3.5.

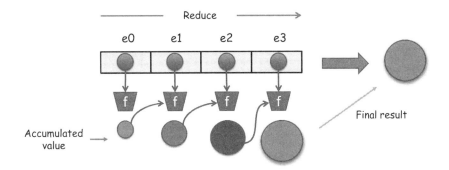

Figure 3.5 Reducing an array into a single value. Each iteration returns an accumulated value based on the previous result; this accumulated value is kept until you reach the end of the array. The final outcome of reduce is always a single value.

This diagram can be expressed more formally with the following notation:

```
reduce(f,[e0, e1, e2, e3],accum) -> f(f(f(f(acc, e0), e1, e2, e3)))) -> R
```

Now, let's look at a simplified implementation of the internals of reduce.

Listing 3.2 Implementing reduce

```
function reduce(arr, fn, accumulator) {
    let idx = -1,
        len = arr.length;

    if (!accumulator && len > 0) {
        accumulator = arr[++idx];
    }

    while (++idx < len) {
        accumulator = fn(accumulator,
        arr[idx], idx, arr);
    }
    return accumulator;
}
```

If no accumulator value is provided, the first element of the array is used to initialize it.

Invokes fn on each element, passing the accumulated value and the current element value

Returns the single accumulated value

reduce accepts the following parameters:

- fn—The iterator function is executed on every value in the array and contains as parameters the accumulated value, the current value, the index, and the array.
- accumulator—The initial value, which is then used to store the accumulated result that's passed in to every subsequent function call.

Let's write a simple program that gathers some statistics about a set of Person objects. Suppose you want find the number of people who live in a particular country; see the following listing.

Listing 3.3   Computing country counts

```
_(persons).reduce((stat, person) => {          Extracts a
    const country = person.address.country;    person's country
    stat[country] = _.isUndefined(stat[country]) ? 1 :    Creates a country entry
        stat[country] + 1;                                that's initialized to 1
    return stat;                                          and incremented with
}, {});                                                   every person living in
                                                          that country
         Starts the reduce       Returns the
         process with an empty    accumulated
         object (initializes the  object
         accumulator)
```

Running this code converts the input array into a single object containing a representation of the population by country:

```
{
    'US'     : 2,
    'Greece' : 1,
    'Hungary': 1
}
```

To simplify this task further, you can implement the ubiquitous map-reduce combination. Linking these functions, you can enhance the behavior of map and reduce by providing specialized behaviors as parameters. At a high level, this program's flow has the structure

```
_(persons).map(func1).reduce(func2);
```

where func1 and func2 implement the particular behavior you want. Separating the functions from the main flow, you get the code in the next listing.

Listing 3.4   Combining map and reduce to compute statistics

```
const getCountry = person => person.address.country;

const gatherStats = function (stat, criteria) {
    stat[criteria] = _.isUndefined(stat[criteria]) ? 1 :
```

```
        stat[criteria] + 1;
    return stat;
};
```

```
_(persons).map(getCountry).reduce(gatherStats, {});
```

Listing 3.4 uses `map` to preprocess the array of objects and extract all countries; then it uses `reduce` to collect the final result. This produces the same output as listing 3.3, but in a much cleaner and extensible way. Instead of direct property access, consider providing a lens (using Ramda) that focuses on the person's `address.city` property:

```
const cityPath = ['address','city'];
const cityLens = R.lens(R.path(cityPath), R.assocPath(cityPath));
```

And just as easily, you can compute counts based on the cities people reside in:

```
_(persons).map(R.view(cityLens)).reduce(gatherStats, {});
```

Alternatively, you can use `_.groupBy` to accomplish a similar outcome in an even more succinct way:

```
_.groupBy(persons, R.view(cityLens));
```

Unlike `map`, because `reduce` relies on an accumulated result, it can behave differently when applied left-to-right or right-to-left if not provided with a commutative operation. To illustrate this, consider a simple program that sums up the numbers in an array:

```
_([0,1,3,4,5]).reduce(_.add);   //-> 13
```

The same result can be obtained by reducing in reverse with `_.reduceRight`. This works as expected because addition is a commutative operation, but it can produce significantly different results for operations that aren't, like division. Using the same notation as before, `_.reduceRight` can be viewed as follows:

```
reduceRight(f, [e0, e1, e2],accum) -> f(e0, f(e1, f(e2, f(e3,accum)))) -> R
```

For instance, these two programs using `_.divide` will compute completely different values:

```
([1,3,4,5]).reduce(_.divide) !== ([1,3,4,5]).reduceRight(_.divide);
```

Furthermore, `reduce` is an apply-to-all operation, which means there's no way for it to be short-circuited so it doesn't run through the entire array. Suppose you need to validate a list of input values. You could think of validating an array of parameters as reducing it to a single Boolean value, indicating whether all parameters are valid.

Using `reduce`, however, would be a bit inefficient because you'd have to visit all values in the list. Once you've found an invalid input, there's no point continuing to check all of them. Let's look at a more efficient validation function that uses `_.some` and other functions you'll come to know and love: `_.isUndefined` and `_.isNull`. When applied against each element in the list, `_.some` returns as soon as it finds a passing (`true`) value:

```
const isNotValid = val => _.isUndefined(val) || _.isNull(val);
```
⟵ Value isn't valid when undefined or null

```
const notAllValid = args => _(args).some(isNotValid);
```
⟵ Function some returns as soon as it yields true. This is useful when checking that there's at least one valid value

```
notAllValid(['string', 0, null, undefined]);   //-> true
notAllValid(['string', 0, {}]);                 //-> false
```

You can also obtain the logical inverse of `notAllValid` (called `allValid`) using `_.every`, which checks whether the given predicate returns `true` for all elements:

```
const isValid = val => !_.isUndefined(val) && !_.isNull(val);
const allValid = args => _(args).every(isValid);

allValid(['string', 0, null]); //-> false
allValid(['string', 0, {}]);   //-> true
```

As you saw earlier, both `map` and `reduce` attempt to traverse the entire array. Often, you aren't interested in processing all elements in your data structure and would like to skip any `null` or `undefined` objects. It would be nice if you had a mechanism to remove or filter out certain elements from the list before the computation takes place. Let's visit `_.filter` next.

3.3.4   Removing unwanted elements with _.filter

When processing large collections of data, it's often necessary to remove elements that don't form part of your computations. For instance, say you want to count only people living in European countries, or people born in a certain year. Instead of cluttering your code with `if-else` statements, you can use `_.filter`.

`filter` (also known as `select`) is a higher-order function that iterates through an array of elements and returns a new array that's a subset of the original with values for which a predicate function p returns a result of `true`. In formal notation, this looks like the following (also see figure 3.6):

```
filter(p, [d0, d1, d2, d3...dn]) -> [d0,d1,...dn] (subset of original input)
```

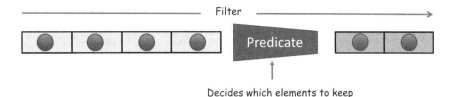

Decides which elements to keep

Figure 3.6 The `filter` operation takes an array as input and applies a selection criteria p that potentially yields a much smaller subset of the original array. The criteria p is also known as a *function predicate*.

A possible implementation of `filter` is shown in the following listing.

Listing 3.5 `filter` implementation

```
function filter(arr, predicate) {
    let idx = -1,
        len = arr.length,
        result = [];

    while (++idx < len) {
        let value = arr[idx];
        if (predicate(value, idx, this)) {
            result.push(value);
        }
    }
    return result;
}
```

Resulting array contains a subset of array values

Calls the predicate function. If the result is true, the value is kept; otherwise it's skipped.

In addition to the array, `filter` accepts a `predicate` function used to test each member of the array for inclusiveness. If the predicate yields `true`, the element is kept in the result; otherwise, the element is skipped. This is why `filter` is commonly used to remove invalid data from an array:

```
_(persons).filter(isValid).map(fullname);
```

But it can do much more than that. Suppose you need to extract only people born in 1903 from a collection of `Person` objects. Applying `_.filter` is much easier and cleaner than using conditional statements:

```
const bornIn1903 = person => person.birthYear === 1903;

_(persons).filter(bornIn1903).map(fullname).join(' and ');

//-> 'John von Neumann and Alonzo Church'
```

Array comprehension

map and `filter` are higher-order functions that return new arrays from existing ones. They exist in many functional programming languages like Haskell, Clojure, and others. An alternative to combining map and `filter` is to use a concept called *array comprehension*, also known as *list comprehension*. It's a functional feature that encapsulates the functionality of map and `filter` into a concise syntax using the `for...of` and `if` keywords, respectively:

```
[for (x of iterable) if (condition) x]
```

At the time of this writing, there's a proposal in ECMAScript 7 to include array comprehensions. They'll let you create concise expressions to assemble new arrays (which is why the entire expression is wrapped in []). For example, you can refactor the previous code in the following manner:

```
[for (p of people) if (p.birthYear === 1903) p.fullname]
   .join(' and ');
```

Applying all of these techniques based on these extensible and powerful functions allows you not only to write cleaner code but also to improve your understanding of the data. Using the declarative style, you can focus on what the output of the application will be instead of how to get there, facilitating deeper reasoning in your application.

3.4   *Reasoning about your code*

Recall that, in JavaScript, thousands of lines of code that share a global namespace can be loaded into a single page at once. Lately there's lots of interest in creating modules to compartmentalize business logic, but thousands of projects in production still don't do this.

What does it mean to "reason about your code"? I've used this term loosely in previous chapters to refer to the ability to look into any part of a program and easily build a mental model of what's happening. This model includes dynamic parts like the state of all variables and the outcomes of functions, as well as static parts such as the level of readability and expressiveness of your design. Both are important. You'll learn in this book that immutability and pure functions make building this model much easier.

Earlier, I highlighted the value of being able to link high-level operations together to build programs. An imperative program flow is radically different from a functional program flow. A functional flow gives you a clear picture as to the purpose of the program without revealing any of its internal details, so that you can reason more deeply about the code as well as how data flows into and out of the different stages to produce results.

3.4.1 *Declarative and lazy function chains*

Recall from chapter 1 that functional programs are made up of simple functions that in themselves don't accomplish much but, when put together, can solve complex tasks. In this section, you'll learn a way to build entire an program by linking a set of functions.

Functional programming's declarative model treats programs as the evaluation of independent, pure functions, which support you in building the necessary abstractions to gain fluency and expressiveness in your code. Doing so, you can form an ontology or vocabulary that clearly expresses the intent of your application. Building pure functions on top of the building blocks of map, reduce, and filter leads to writing in a style that makes code easy to reason about and understand at a glance.

The powerful effect of raising this level of abstraction is that you begin to think of operations as agnostic to the underlying data structures used. Theoretically speaking, whether you're working with arrays, linked lists, binary trees, or otherwise, it shouldn't change the semantic meaning of your program. For this reason, functional programming focuses on operations more than on the structure of the data.

For example, suppose you're tasked to read a list of names, normalize them, remove any duplicates, and sort the final result. First, let's write an imperative version of this program; later you'll refactor it into a functional style.

You can express the list of names as an array with unevenly formatted input strings:

```
var names = ['alonzo church', 'Haskell curry', 'stephen_kleene',
             'John Von Neumann', 'stephen_kleene'];
```

The imperative program is shown next.

Listing 3.6 Performing sequential operations on arrays (imperative approach)

```
var result = [];
for (let i = 0; i < names.length; i++) {        Loops through all
  var n = names[i];                              names in the array
  if (n !== undefined && n !== null) {
    var ns = n.replace(/_/, ' ').split(' ');     Checks to make sure
    for(let j = 0; j < ns.length; j++) {         all words are valid
      var p = ns[j];
      p = p.charAt(0).toUpperCase() + p.slice(1);  The array contains
      ns[j] = p;                                   inconsistently formatted
    }                                              data; this step normalizes
    if (result.indexOf(ns.join(' ')) < 0) {        (fixes) each element.
      result.push(ns.join(' '));
    }
  }                                                Eliminates duplicates by
}                                                  checking whether the name
result.sort();        Sorts the array             exists in the result
```

This code produces the desired output:

```
['Alonzo Church', 'Haskell Curry', 'John Von Neumann', 'Stephen Kleene']
```

The downside of imperative code is that it's targeted at solving a particular problem efficiently. The code in listing 3.6 can only be used to perform this particular task. Therefore, it runs at a far lower level of abstraction than functional code. The lower the level of abstraction, the lower the probability of reuse, and the greater the complexity and likelihood of errors.

On the other hand, the functional implementation merely connects black-box components together and cedes the responsibility to these well-established and tested APIs, as shown in the following listing. Notice how the cascade arrangement of function calls makes this code easier to read.

Listing 3.7   Performing sequential operations on arrays (functional approach)

```
_.chain(names)         ← Initializes a function chain
    .filter(isValid)     (discussed shortly)        Removes
    .map(s => s.replace(/_/, ' '))                  invalid values
    .uniq()                                         Normalizes
    .map(_.startCase)    ←        Throws away        values
    .sort()                  Sets  duplicates
    .value();                case
```

```
//-> ['Alonzo Church', 'Haskell Curry', 'John Von Neumann', 'Stephen Kleene']
```

The _.filter and _.map functions take care of all the heavy lifting of iterating through valid indexes in the names array. Your only job is to supply the specialized behavior in the remaining steps. You use the _.uniq function to throw away duplicate entries and _.startCase to capitalize each word; finally, you sort all the results.

I'd much rather write and read programs that look like listing 3.7, wouldn't you? Not just because of the sheer reduction in the amount of code, but also due to its simple and clear structure.

Let's continue exploring Lodash. This example revisits listing 3.4, which computes counts of all countries from an array of Person objects. For the purpose of this example, augment the gatherStats function slightly:

```
const gatherStats = function (stat, country) {
    if(!isValid(stat[country])) {
        stat[country] = {'name': country, 'count': 0};
    }
    stat[country].count++;
    return stat;
};
```

It now returns an object with the following structure:

```
{
    'US'     : {'name': 'US', count: 2},
    'Greece' : {'name': 'Greece', count: 1},
    'Hungary': {'name': 'Hungary', count: 1}
}
```

Using this structure guarantees unique entries for each country. Just for fun, let's inject a few more data points into the Person array you began the chapter with:

```
const p5 = new Person('David', 'Hilbert', '555-55-5555');
p5.address = new Address('Germany');
p5.birthYear = 1903;

const p6 = new Person('Alan', 'Turing', '666-66-6666');
p6.address = new Address('England');
p6.birthYear - 1912;

const p7 = new Person('Stephen', 'Kleene', '777-77-7777');
p7.address = new Address('US');
p7.birthYear = 1909;
```

The next task is to build a program that returns the country with the largest number of people in this dataset. Let's do this again by linking a function with the help of _.chain() and a few other artifacts.

Listing 3.8 Demonstrating lazy function chains with Lodash

```
_.chain(persons)                            ← Creates a lazy function chain
    .filter(isValid)                          to process the provided array
    .map(_.property('address.country'))     ← Uses _.property to extract the
    .reduce(gatherStats, {})                  person object's address.country
    .values()                                 property. This is Lodash's
    .sortBy('count')                          equivalent but less feature-rich
    .reverse()                                version of Ramda's R.view().
    .first()
    .value()
    .name;   //-> 'US'                       ← Executes all functions
                                               in the chain
```

The _.chain function can be used to augment the state of an input object by connecting operations that transform the input into the desired output. It's powerful because, unlike wrapping arrays with the shorthand _(...) object, it explicitly makes any function in the sequence chainable. Despite this being a complex program, you can avoid creating any variables, and all looping is effectively eliminated.

Another benefit of using _.chain is that you can create complex programs that behave lazily, so nothing executes until that last value() function is called. This can have a tremendous impact in your application because you can potentially skip running

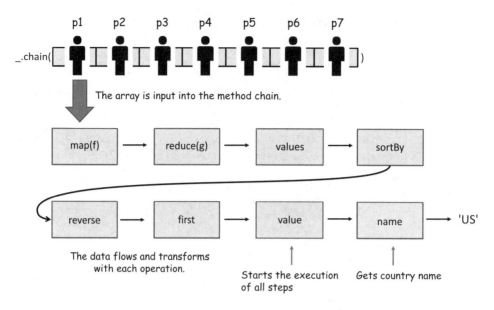

Figure 3.7 **Control of a program built using Lodash function chains. The array of person objects is processed through a series of operations. Along the way, the data flows and is finally transformed into a single value.**

entire functions when their results aren't needed (lazy evaluation will be discussed in chapter 7). This program's control flow is depicted in figure 3.7.

You're beginning to see why functional programs are superior. The imperative version of this task, I'll leave to your imagination. The reason listing 3.8 works so smoothly relates to the fundamental principles underlying FP—pure and side effect–free functions. Each function in the chain immutably operates on new arrays built from functions that precede it. By starting with a call to _.chain(), Lodash capitalizes on this pattern to provide a Swiss Army knife of utilities to satisfy most needs. This helps you transition into a style of programming called *point-free*; it's unique to functional programming, and I'll introduce it in the next chapter.

Being able to lazily define program pipelines has many more benefits than just readability. Because lazy programs are defined before they're evaluated, they can be optimized using techniques such as data-structure reuse and method fusion. These optimizations don't reduce the time it takes to execute functions per se; rather, they help to eliminate unnecessary invocations. I'll discuss this in more detail in chapter 7 when we study the performance of functional programs.

In listing 3.8, data is flowing from one node to the next in the network. Using higher-order functions declaratively makes it obvious how data transforms in each node, revealing more insights about your data.

3.4.2 SQL-like data: functions as data

Throughout this chapter, you've been exposed to an assortment of functions such as map, reduce, filter, groupBy, sortBy, uniq, and so on. The vocabulary formed around these functions can be used to clearly extrapolate information pertaining to your data. If you think outside the box for a second, you'll notice that these functions resemble SQL, which isn't accidental.

Developers are accustomed to using SQL and its features to understand and extrapolate meaning from data. For example, you can represent the collection's person objects as shown in table 3.1.

Table 3.1 Representing the data in the person list as a table

id	firstname	lastname	country	birthYear
0	Haskell	Curry	US	1900
1	Barkley	Rosser	Greece	1907
2	John	Von Neumann	Hungary	1903
3	Alonzo	Church	US	1903
4	David	Hilbert	Germany	1862
5	Alan	Turing	England	1912
6	Stephen	Kleene	US	1909

As it turns out, thinking in terms of a query language when building programs is similar to the operations applied to arrays in functional programming, which make use of a common vocabulary or algebra, if you will, to encourage a deeper reasoning about the nature of your data and how it's structured. The following SQL query

```
SELECT p.firstname FROM Person p
WHERE p.birthYear > 1903 and p.country IS NOT 'US'
GROUP BY p.firstname
```

makes it crystal clear what you should expect your data to look like after running this code. Before you implement the JavaScript version of this program, let's implement a few function aliases to help me make this point. Lodash supports a feature called *mixins* that can be used to extend the core library with additional functions and have them chained the same way:

```
_.mixin({'select':  _.map,
         'from':    _.chain,
         'where':   _.filter,
         'sortBy':  _.sortByOrder});
```

After applying this mixin object, you can write the following program.

Listing 3.9   Writing SQL-like JavaScript

```
_.from(persons)
  .where(p => p.birthYear > 1900 && p.address.country !== 'US')
  .sortBy(['firstname'])
  .select(p => p.firstname)
  .value();
```

Listing 3.9 creates aliases that map native SQL keywords to corresponding functions, so you may experience a closer realization of functional code to a query language.

> **JavaScript mixins**
>
> A mixin is an object that defines an abstract subset of functions relating to a particular type (in this case, a SQL command). This object isn't concretely used in code, other than to extend the behavior of another object (it's somewhat similar to a *trait* in other programming languages). The target object borrows all of functionality from the mixin.
>
> In the object-oriented world, it's also another way to reuse code without having to use inheritance or to simulate multiple inheritance in languages that don't support it (JavaScript being one of them). I won't cover mixins in this book, but they can be powerful when used correctly. If you want to learn more about mixins, I suggest reading https://javascriptweblog.wordpress.com/2011/05/31/a-fresh-look-at-javascript-mixins/.

You should be convinced by now that functional programming can behave as a powerful abstraction over imperative code. What better way of processing and parsing your data than to use query language semantics? Like SQL, this JavaScript code models the data in the form of functions, also known as *functions as data*. Because it's declarative, it describes *what* the data output is and not *how* it came to be. So far, I haven't needed any conventional looping statements in this chapter—and I don't intend to use them for the rest of the book. Instead, high-level abstractions replace looping.

Another technique commonly used to replace loops is recursion, which you can use to abstract iteration when tackling problems that are "self-similar" in nature. For these types of problems, sequential function chains are inefficient and inadequate. Recursion, on the other hand, implements its own ways of processing data by yielding the heavy lifting of standard looping to the language runtime.

3.5   *Learning to think recursively*

Sometimes a problem is difficult and complex to tackle head on. When this occurs, you should immediately look for ways to decompose it. If the problem can be broken down into smaller versions of itself, you may be able to solve the smaller version and build it up to solve the entire problem. Recursion is essential for array traversal in pure functional programming languages like Haskell, Scheme, and Erlang because they don't have looping constructs.

In JavaScript, recursion has many applications, such as parsing XML or HTML documents, graphs, and so on. In this section, I'll explain what recursion is and then work through an exercise that will teach you how to think recursively. Then we'll take a quick look at a few data structures you can parse through using recursion.

3.5.1   *What is recursion?*

Recursion is a technique designed to solve problems by decomposing them into smaller, self-similar problems that, when combined, arrive at the original solution. A recursive function has two main parts:

- Base cases (also known as the *terminating condition*)
- Recursive cases

The base cases are a set of inputs for which a recursive function computes a concrete result, without having to recur. The recursive case deals with a set of inputs (necessarily smaller than the original) for which the function calls itself. If the input isn't smaller, the recursion runs indefinitely until the program crashes. As the function recurs, the nature of the inputs unconditionally become smaller, finally reaching the instance for which the base case is triggered and the process terminates with a value.

Recall from chapter 2 that we used recursion to deep-freeze an entire nested object structure. The base case triggered when the object encountered was a primitive or had already been frozen; otherwise, the recursive step continued traversing the object structure as it found more unfrozen objects. Recursion was appropriate for this because at each level, the task to solve was exactly the same. Thinking recursively, though, can be a challenge, so let's begin there.

3.5.2   *Learning to think recursively*

Recursion isn't a simple concept to grasp. As with functional programming, the hardest part is unlearning conventional ways. The focus of this book is not to make you a master of recursion, and it's not a technique you'll use often; but it's important, and I'd like to exercise your brain and help you learn to analyze recursive problems better.

Recursive thinking takes itself or a modified version of itself into consideration. A recursive object is self-defining; for instance, think of the composition of branches in a tree. A branch has leaves as well as other branches, which in turn have more leaves and more branches. This process continues indefinitely and is halted only by a limiting external factor—the size of the tree, in this case.

With that in mind, let's do a warm-up exercise by tackling a simple problem: adding all the numbers in an array. We'll go from an imperative implementation to the most functional. The imperative side of your brain naturally visualizes a solution involving iterating through the array and keeping an accumulated value:

```
var acc = 0;
for(let i = 0; i < nums.length; i++) {
    acc += nums[i];
}
```

Your brain pushes you to consider the need for an accumulator, which is absolutely necessary when you're keeping a running total. But do you need to use a manual loop? At this point you're well aware that you have more weapons at your disposal in your functional arsenal (_.reduce):

```
_(nums).reduce((acc, current) => acc + current, 0);
```

Pushing manual iteration into the framework abstracts your application code from it. But you can do even better by ceding iteration entirely to the platform. The function _.reduce shows that you don't have to be concerned about looping or even the size of the list. You can compute the result by subsequently adding the first element to the rest and, thus, achieve recursive thinking. This thought process can be extended to picture summation as performing a sequence of operations in the following manner, which is known as *lateral thinking*:

```
sum[1,2,3,4,5,6,7,8,9] = 1 + sum[2,3,4,5,6,7,8,9]
                       = 1 + 2 + sum[3,4,5,6,7,8,9]
                       = 1 + 2 + 3 + sum[4,5,6,7,8,9]
```

Recursion and iteration are two sides of the same coin. In the absence of mutation, recursion offers a more expressive, powerful, and excellent alternative to iteration. In fact, pure functional languages don't even have standard looping constructs like do, for, and while, since all looping is done recursively. Recursion also leads to code that's easier to understand because it's premised on repeating the same actions multiple times on smaller input. The recursive solution in the following listing uses the Lodash _.first and _.rest functions to access the first element of the array or all but the first, respectively.

Listing 3.10   Performing recursive addition

```
function sum(arr) {
    if(_.isEmpty(arr)) {          ⟵───┤  Base case (terminating
        return 0;                      │  condition)
    }
    return _.first(arr) + sum(_.rest(arr));    ⟵───┐  Iterative case: calls itself
}                                                  │  on a smaller input using
sum([]); //-> 0                                    ┘  _.first and _.rest
sum([1,2,3,4,5,6,7,8,9]); //->45
```

Adding the empty array triggers the base case, naturally returning zero. Otherwise, for non-empty arrays, you proceed to recursively extract and sum the first elements together with the rest of the array. Behind the scenes, recursive calls are stacked on top of each other. As soon as the algorithm reaches the terminating condition, all the return statements are executed as the runtime unwinds the stack to let the addition take place. This is the mechanism by which recursion cedes looping to the language runtime. Here's a step-by-step view of the sum algorithm you just implemented:

```
1 + sum[2,3,4,5,6,7,8,9]
1 + 2 + sum[3,4,5,6,7,8,9]
1 + 2 + 3 + sum[4,5,6,7,8,9]
1 + 2 + 3 + 4 + sum[5,6,7,8,9]
1 + 2 + 3 + 4 + 5 + sum[6,7,8,9]
1 + 2 + 3 + 4 + 5 + 6 + sum[7,8,9]
1 + 2 + 3 + 4 + 5 + 6 + 7 + sum[8,9]
1 + 2 + 3 + 4 + 5 + 6 + 7 + 8 + sum[9]
1 + 2 + 3 + 4 + 5 + 6 + 7 + 8 + 9 + sum[]
1 + 2 + 3 + 4 + 5 + 6 + 7 + 8 + 9 + 0     -> halts, stack unwinds
1 + 2 + 3 + 4 + 5 + 6 + 7 + 8 + 9
1 + 2 + 3 + 4 + 5 + 6 + 7 + 17
1 + 2 + 3 + 4 + 5 + 6 + 24
1 + 2 + 3 + 4 + 5 + 30
1 + 2 + 3 + 4 + 35
1 + 2 + 3 + 39
1 + 2 + 42
1 + 44
45
```

At this point, it's natural to think about the performance of recursion versus manual iteration. After all, compilers have become extremely smart at optimizing loops. ES6 JavaScript brings an optimization feature called *tail-call optimization* that can bring the performance of these two features closer together. Consider this slightly different implementation of sum:

```
function sum(arr, acc = 0) {
    if(_.isEmpty(arr)) {
        return 0;
    }
    return sum(_.rest(arr), acc + _.first(arr));
}
```

Recursive call in tail position

This version places the recursive call as the last step in the function body, or in *tail position*. We'll explore the benefits of doing this further in chapter 7 when we look at functional optimizations.

3.5.3 *Recursively defined data structures*

You're probably wondering about the names passed in to the person objects we've been using as sample data. Back in the 1900s, the mathematics community behind functional programming (lambda calculus, category theory, and so on) was vibrant.

Much of the work published was based on joint ideas and theorems by leading univer-
sities under the tutelage of professors like Alonzo Church. In fact, many mathematicians like Barkley Rosser, Alan Turing, and Stephen Kleene, among others, were
doctoral students of Church's. They went on to have doctoral students of their own.
Figure 3.8 graphs this apprenticeship relationship (or a sliver of it).

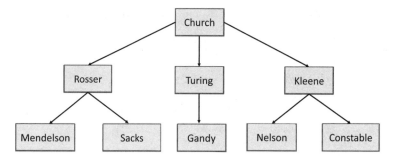

**Figure 3.8   Influential mathematicians who contributed to the development of
functional programming. The connected lines from parent to child nodes in the
tree structure represent a "student of" relationship.**

Structures like this are common in software because they can be used to model XML
documents, file systems, taxonomies, categories, menu widgets, faceted navigation,
social graphs, and more. So learning how to process them is vital. Figure 3.8 shows a set
of nodes with connections that denote advisor-student affiliations. Up to now, you've
used functional techniques to parse flat data structures, like arrays. But these operations
won't work on tree-like data. Because JavaScript doesn't have a built-in tree object, you
create a simple data structure based on nodes. A *node* is an object that contains a value, a
reference to its parent, and an array of children. In figure 3.8, Rosser has Church as its
parent node and Mendelson and Sacks as children. If a node has no parent, as is the
case with Church, it's considered the root. Here's the definition of the Node type.

Listing 3.11   Node object

```
class Node {
    constructor(val) {
      this._val = val;
      this._parent = null;
      this._children = [];
    }

    isRoot() {
       return isValid(this._parent);          ◁──  This function was
    }                                               created before.

    get children() {
      return this._children;
    }
```

```
    hasChildren() {
       return this._children.length > 0;
    }

    get value() {
      return this._val;
    }

    set value(val) {
      this._val = val;
    }

    append(child) {
       child._parent = this;
          this._children.push(child);
       return this;
    }

     toString() {
       return `Node (val: ${this._val}, children:
          ${this._children.length})`;
     }
}
```

Sets this
node's parent

Adds this child
node to the list
of children

Returns this same
node (convenient for
method cascading)

You can create new nodes like this:

```
const church = new Node(new Person('Alonzo', 'Church', '111-11-1111'));//
```

Repeat this for every
node in the tree.

Trees are recursively defined data structures that contain a root node:

Uses a static method to avoid confusion with
the more popular Array.prototype.map. A
static method can also be used effectively
as a standalone function.

```
class Tree {
   constructor(root) {
      this._root = root;
   }

   static map(node, fn, tree = null) {
      node.value = fn(node.value);
      if(tree === null) {
         tree = new Tree(node);
      }

      if(node.hasChildren()) {
        _.map(node.children, function (child) {
           Tree.map(child, fn, tree);
        });
      }
      return tree;
   }
```

Invokes the iterator function
and updates the value of the
node element in the tree

Similar to Array.prototype.map;
the result is a new structure.

If the node has no children, no
need to continue (base case).

Invokes the provided
function against
each child node

Recursive call
on each child
node

```
    get root() {
        return this._root;
    }
}
```

The node's main logic lies in the append method. Appending a child to a node sets the child's parent reference to it and adds the input node to the list of children. You populate the tree by linking nodes to other child nodes in the following manner, starting with the root, church:

```
church.append(rosser).append(turing).append(kleene);
kleene.append(nelson).append(constable);
rosser.append(mendelson).append(sacks);
turing.append(gandy);
```

Each node is in charge of wrapping a person object. The recursive algorithm performs a preorder traversal of the entire tree, beginning at the root and descending to all of its children. Due to its self-similar nature, traversing the tree from the root node is exactly like traversing it from any node: a recursive definition. For this, you use Tree.map, a higher-order function with semantics similar to Array.prototype.map, which accepts a function that's evaluated against each node value. As you can see, regardless of the data structure used to model this data (a tree, in this case), the semantics of this function should remain the same. Essentially, any data type can be mapped over by preserving its structure. I'll consider this notion of mapping structure preserving functions to types more formally in chapter 5.

A preorder traversal of this tree has the following steps, starting with root:

1 Display the data part of the root element
2 Traverse the left subtree by recursively calling the preorder function
3 Traverse the right subtree the same way

Figure 3.9 illustrates the path the algorithm takes.

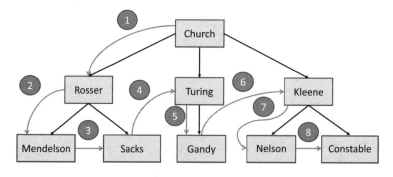

Figure 3.9   Recursive preorder traversal, starting with the root and descending all the way to the left before going to the right

The function `Tree.map` has two required inputs: the root node (which is basically the start of the tree) and the iterator function that transforms each node's value:

```
Tree.map(church, p => p.fullname);
```

This traverses the tree in preorder and applies the given function to each node, producing the following:

```
'Alonzo Church', 'Barkley Rosser', 'Elliot Mendelson', 'Gerald Sacks', 'Alan
Turing', 'Robin Gandy', 'Stephen Kleene', 'Nels Nelson', 'Robert Constable'
```

This idea of encapsulating data to control how it's accessed is key to functional programming when working with immutability and side effect–free data types. I'll expand on this idea further in chapter 5. Parsing data structures is one of the most fundamental aspects of software and the bread and butter of functional programming. This chapter took a deeper dive into the functional style of development using JavaScript's functional capabilities encoded in an extensible functional library called Lodash. This style favors a streamlined and flow-based model where high-level operations can be chained together as a sequence of steps, which contain the business logic needed to arrive at your result.

It's undeniable that writing flow-based code also benefits reusability and modularization, but I've only scratched the surface. I'll take this idea of flow-based programming to the next level in chapter 4, where I'll focus on constructing real function pipelines.

3.6 Summary

- You can write extensible code with the higher-order functions `map`, `reduce`, and `filter`.
- Lodash is a vehicle for data processing, creating programs via control chains where data flows and transformations are clearly demarcated.
- Functional programming's declarative style creates code that's easier to reason about.
- Mapping high-level abstractions to a SQL vocabulary reveals a deeper understanding of your data.
- Recursion solves self-similar problems and is required to parse through recursively defined data structures.

Toward modular, reusable code

4

This chapter covers

- Comparing function chains and pipelines
- Introducing the Ramda.js functional library
- Exploring the concepts of currying, partial application, and function binding
- Creating modular programs with functional composition
- Enhancing your program's flow with function combinators

A complex system that works is invariably found to have evolved from a simple system that worked.

—John Gall, *The Systems Bible* (General Systemantics Press, 2012)

Modularity is one of the most important qualities of large software projects; it represents the degree to which programs can be separated into smaller, independent parts. Modular programs posses the distinct quality that their meaning can be derived from the meaning of their constituent parts. These parts (or subprograms) become reusable components that can be incorporated as a whole or in pieces into other systems. This makes your code more maintainable and readable while making you more productive. As a simple use case, think of how Unix shell programs are written:

```
tr 'A-Z' 'a-z' <words.in | uniq | sort
```

Even if you have no experience with Unix programming, you can clearly see that this code involves a sequence of steps that transforms words from uppercase to lowercase, removes duplicates, and sorts the remainder. The pipe operator (| in this case) connects these commands. It's remarkable that by having clear contracts describing the inputs and outputs, small programs can be glued together to solve complex tasks. If you imagine having to write this program in traditional imperative JavaScript, a few loops, string comparisons, and perhaps a few conditional statements and global variables keeping track of everything come to mind. This probably isn't very modular, per se. In programming, we like to solve problems by breaking them into smaller pieces and reconstructing those pieces to form a solution.

In chapter 3, we used high-level functions to solve similar types of issues using tightly coupled method chains that cascade over a single wrapper object. In this chapter, we'll extend this idea further to create loosely coupled pipelines via functional composition, which will allow you to build whole programs from independent components with more flexibility. These components can be as small as functions or as big as entire modules that separately don't provide much value but together give meaning to the whole.

Creating modular code isn't an easy task. We'll look at important functional techniques like partial evaluation and composition, with the aid of a functional framework called Ramda.js, to bring code to the right level of abstraction in order to express solutions in a point-free manner via declarative function pipelines.

4.1 Method chains vs. function pipelines

Chapter 3 left off with method chains used to connect a series of functions together, revealing a style of functional programming much different from any other development style. But there's another approach for connecting functions, called *pipelining*.

When studying functions, it's useful to describe them in terms of their inputs and outputs. The notation used in Haskell, for example, is popular in the functional community, and you'll see it used in many places (see figure 4.1).

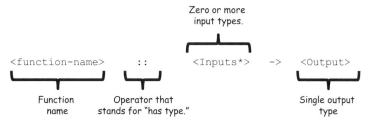

Figure 4.1 Haskell notation for defining a function. This notation describes the function name, followed by an operator that sets the types of the function's inputs and outputs.

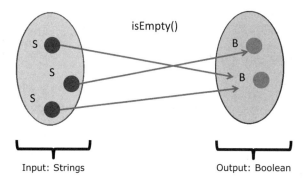

Input: Strings   **Output: Boolean**

Figure 4.2 The function `isEmpty` is a referentially transparent map between the set of all string values and the set of all Boolean values.

Remember that, in functional programming, a function is a mathematical mapping between inputs and output types, as shown in figure 4.2. For instance, a simple function like `isEmpty` that takes a string and returns a Boolean can be expressed in this notation as

```
isEmpty :: String -> Boolean
```

This function is a referentially transparent mapping between the set of all input values of type `String` and the set of all `Boolean` values. Here's the JavaScript lambda form together with its function signature:

```
// isEmpty :: String -> Boolean
const isEmpty = s => !s || !s.trim();
```

Viewing functions as mappings of types is necessary to understand how they can be chained and pipelined:

- Chaining methods together (tightly coupled, limited expressiveness)
- Arranging function pipelines (loosely coupled, flexible)

4.1.1   Chaining methods together

Recall from chapter 3 that the `map` and `filter` functions take an array as input and return a new one. These functions can be chained together tightly via the implicit Lodash wrapper object, which manages the creation of new data structures behind the scenes. Here's an example from chapter 3:

```
_.chain(names)
   .filter(isValid)
   .map(s => s.replace(/_/, ' '))
   .uniq()
   .map(_.startCase)
   .sort()
   .value();
```

After each "dot," you can only invoke other methods from the Lodash managed chain.

This is clearly a syntactical improvement over imperative code and drastically improves its readability. Unfortunately, it's contrived and tightly coupled to the owning object that confines the number of methods you can apply in the chain, which limits expressiveness of the code. In this case, you're obliged to use only the set of operations provided by Lodash, and you wouldn't be able to easily connect functions from different libraries (or your own) into one program.

> **NOTE** There are ways to extend an object with additional functionality using mixins, but you're still responsible for managing the mixin object yourself. I don't cover mixins in this book, but you can read about them in "A fresh look at JavaScript Mixins" (Angus Croll, *JavaScript, JavaScript* …, May 30, 2011, http://mng.bz/15Zj).

At a high level, you can visualize a simple sequence of array methods as shown in figure 4.3. It would be best to break the chain (so to speak) and have a lot more freedom to arrange a sequence of independent functions; you can achieve this with function pipelines.

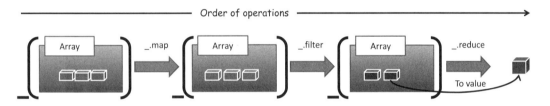

Figure 4.3 A chain of arrays is made up of methods invoked sequentially via the owning object. Internally, each method returns a new array containing the result of each function call.

4.1.2 Arranging functions in a pipeline

Functional programming removes the limitations present in method chaining and provides the flexibility to combine any set of functions, no matter where they come from. A *pipeline* is a directional sequence of functions loosely arranged so that the output of one is input into the next. Figure 4.4 illustrates this abstractly by connecting functions that work with different types of objects.

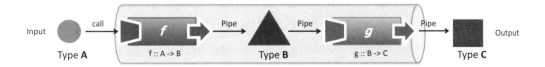

Figure 4.4 A Function pipeline that starts with a function f and input of type A and generates an object of type B, subsequently passed into g, which outputs an object of type C as the final result. Functions f and g can belong to any library or can be your own functions.

In this chapter, you'll learn techniques that can arrange function calls into high-level, succinct function pipelines, just like figure 4.4. If this diagram looks familiar, it's because this pattern is equivalent to the *pipes and filters* object-oriented design pattern seen in many enterprise applications, which was inspired by functional programming (the filters in this case became the individual functions).

Comparing figures 4.3 and 4.4 reveals a key difference between the approaches: chaining makes tight connections via an object's methods, whereas a pipeline links inputs and outputs of any functions—arriving at loosely coupled components. But for this linkage to be possible, the connecting functions must be compatible in terms of arity and type, which we'll examine next.

4.2 Requirements for compatible functions

Object-oriented programs use pipelines sporadically, in specific scenarios (authentication/authorization is usually one of them); on the other hand, functional programming relies on pipelines as the sole method of building programs. Depending on the task at hand, there's usually quite a gap between a problem definition and a proposed solution; therefore, computations must be carried out in well-defined stages. These stages are represented by functions that execute with the condition that their inputs and outputs be compatible in two ways:

- *Type*—The type returned by one function must match the argument type of a receiving function.
- *Arity*—A receiving function must declare at least one parameter in order to handle the value returned from a preceding function call.

4.2.1 Type-compatible functions

When designing function pipelines, it's important that there exists a level of compatibility between what functions return and what they accept. In terms of type, this isn't as big a concern in JavaScript as it is with statically typed languages, because JavaScript is loosely typed. Hence, if an object behaves like a certain type in practice, it's that type. This is also known as *duck typing*: "If it walks like a duck and talks like a duck, it's a duck."

> **NOTE** Statically typed languages have the advantage of using type systems to alert you about potential problems without having to run your code. Type systems are an important topic in functional programming but aren't covered in this book.

JavaScript's dynamic dispatch mechanism attempts to find properties and methods in your objects regardless of type information. Although this is extremely flexible, you often need to know what types of values a function is expecting; having this clearly defined (perhaps documented in code using the Haskell notation) makes your programs easier to understand.

Formally speaking, two functions f and g are type-compatible if the output of f has a type equivalent to the set of inputs of g. For example, here's a simple program to process a student's Social Security number:

```
trim     :: String  -> String
normalize :: String  -> String
```

Trims leading and trailing whitespace

Removes any dashes from the input string

At this point, you should be able to follow the correspondence between the input of normalize and the output of trim so that you can invoke them in a simple, manual, pipeline sequence, as shown in the following listing.

Listing 4.1 Building a manual function pipeline with `trim` and `normalize`

```
// trim :: String -> String
const trim = (str) => str.replace(/^\s*|\s*$/g, '');

// normalize :: String -> String
const normalize = (str) => str.replace(/\-/g, '');

normalize(trim(' 444-44-4444 ')); //-> '444444444'
```

Manually calls both functions in a simple sequential pipeline (you'll see how to automate this technique later). Calls the function purposely with leading and trailing whitespace.

Types are certainly important but, in JavaScript, not as critical as being compatible with the number of arguments a function accepts.

4.2.2 *Functions and arity: the case for tuples*

Arity can be defined as the number of arguments a function accepts; it's also referred to as the function's *length.* We usually take arity for granted in other programming paradigms, but in functional programming, as a corollary to referential transparency, the number of arguments a function declares is often directly proportional to its complexity. For instance, a function that works on a single string is likely much simpler than one taking three or four arguments:

```
// isValid :: String -> Boolean
function isValid(str) {
    ...
}
```

Easy to use

```
// makeAsyncHttp:: String, String, Array -> Boolean
function makeAsyncHttp (method, url, data) {
    ...
}
```

Harder to use, because all arguments must be computed first

Pure functions that expect a single argument are the simplest to use because the implication is that they serve a single purpose—a singular responsibility. Our goal is to work with functions with as few arguments as possible, because they're more flexible and versatile than those that depend on multiple arguments. Unfortunately, unary functions aren't easy to come by. In real life, isValid can be embellished with an error message that clearly describes what happened:

```
isValid :: String -> (Boolean, String)

isValid(' 444-444-44444'); //-> (false, 'Input is too long!')
```

> Returns a structure that holds the status of the validation and possibly an error message

But how can you return two different values? Functional languages have support for a structure called a *tuple*. It's a finite, ordered list of elements, usually grouping two or three values at a time, and written (a, b, c). Based on this concept, you can use a tuple as a return value from isValid that groups a status with a possible error message, to be returned as a single entity and subsequently passed to another function if need be. Let's explore tuples in more detail.

Tuples are immutable structures that pack together items of different types so that they can be passed into other functions. There are other ways of returning ad hoc data, such as object literals or arrays:

```
return {                            or   return [false, 'Input is too long!'];
    status : false,
    message: 'Input is too long!'
};
```

But when it comes to transferring data between functions, tuples offer more advantages:

- *Immutable*—Once created, you can't change a tuple's internal contents.
- *Avoid creating ad hoc types*—Tuples can relate values that may have no relationship at all to each other. So defining and instantiating new types solely for grouping data together makes your model unnecessarily convoluted.
- *Avoid creating heterogeneous arrays*—Working with arrays containing different types of elements is hard because it leads to writing code filled with lots of defensive type checks. Traditionally, arrays are meant to store objects of the same type.

Moreover, tuples behave much like the value objects shown in chapter 2. One concrete use case is in the concept of a Status, a simple data type containing a status flag and a message: (false, 'Some error occurred!'). Unlike other functional languages, such as Scala, JavaScript has no native support for a Tuple data type. For instance, given the following Scala tuple definition

```
var t = (30, 60, 90)
```

you can access each individual part like this:

```
var sumAnglesTriangle = t._1 + t._2 + t._3 = 180
```

But JavaScript provides all the tools out of the box required for you to implement your own version of `Tuple`, as shown next.

Listing 4.2   Typed `Tuple` data type

Reads the provided argument types the tuple will contain

Declares an internal type _T in charge of making sure the types match the corresponding values

Extracts the values to be stored in the tuple

Checks for non-null values. Functional data types shouldn't permit null values to permeate.

Checks that the tuple has the correct arity with respect to the number of types defined

Makes the tuple instance immutable

Extracts all values from the tuple as an array. You can use this with ES6 assignment destructuring to map tuple values into variables.

```
const Tuple = function( /* types */ ) {
  const typeInfo = Array.prototype.slice.call(arguments, 0);
  const _T - function( /* values */ ) {
    const values = Array.prototype.slice.call(arguments, 0);
    if(values.some(
        val => val === null || val === undefined)) {
      throw new ReferenceError('Tuples may not
        have any null values');
    }
    if(values.length !== typeInfo.length) {
      throw new TypeError('Tuple arity does
        not match its prototype');
    }
    values.map((val, index) => {
      this['_' + (index + 1)] = checkType(typeInfo[index])(val);
    }, this);
    Object.freeze(this);
  };
  _T.prototype.values = () => {
    return Object.keys(this)
      .map(k => this[k], this);
  };
  return _T;
};
```

Checks that each value passed in matches the correct type in the tuple definition using the checkType function (shown later). Every tuple element will translate to a property of the tuple referred to by ._n, where n is the index of the element (starting at 1).

The `Tuple` object in listing 4.2 is an immutable, fixed-length structure used to hold a heterogeneous set of *n* typed values that can be used for inter-function communication. For instance, you can use it to build quick value objects, such as `Status`:

```
const Status = Tuple(Boolean, String);
```

Let's finish the student SSN validation example to take advantage of tuples.

Listing 4.3   Using tuples for the `isValid` function

```
// trim :: String  -> String
const trim = (str) => str.replace(/^\s*|\s*$/g, '');

// normalize :: String  -> String
const normalize = (str) => str.replace(/\-/g, '');

// isValid :: String -> Status
const isValid = function (str) {
    if(str.length === 0){
        return new Status(false,
            'Invald input. Expected non-empty value!');
    }
    else {
        return new Status(true, 'Success!');
    }
}

isValid(normalize(strim('444-44-4444'))); //-> (true, 'Success!')
```

> **Declares a Status type that holds values for status (Boolean) and message (String)**

The occurrence of 2-tuples is so frequent in software that it's worth making them first-class objects. When combined with JavaScript ES6 support for *destructured assignment,* you can map tuple values to variables in a clean manner. Using tuples, the following code creates an object called `StringPair`.

Listing 4.4   `StringPair` type

```
const StringPair = Tuple(String, String);
const name = new StringPair('Barkley', 'Rosser');

[first, last] = name.values();
first; //-> 'Barkley'
last;  //-> 'Rosser'

const fullname = new StringPair('J', 'Barkley', 'Rosser');
```

> **Throws an arity mismatch error**

Tuples are one way to reduce a function's arity, but there's a better alternative for cases in which tuples aren't sufficient. Let's spice things up a bit by introducing *function currying,* which not only abstracts arity but also encourages modularity and reusability.

4.3   *Curried function evaluation*

Passing a function's return value as input to a unary function is straightforward, but what if the target function expects more parameters? In order to understand currying in JavaScript, first you must understand the difference between a *curried* and a regular (non-curried) evaluation. In JavaScript, a regular or non-curried function call is permitted to execute with missing arguments. In other words, if you define a function `f(a,b,c)` and call it with just `a`, the evaluation proceeds, and the JavaScript runtime sets b and c to undefined, as shown in figure 4.5. This is unfortunate and most likely the reason why currying isn't a built-in feature of the language. As you can imagine, not declaring any arguments and relying on the arguments object within functions only exacerbates this issue.

Evaluating: Runs as:

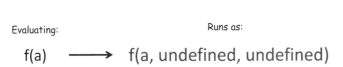

Figure 4.5 Calling a non-curried function with missing arguments causes the function to eagerly evaluate missing parameters and fill them with undefined.

On the other hand, a curried function is one where all arguments have been explicitly defined so that, when called with a subset of the arguments, it returns a new function that waits for the rest of the parameters to be supplied before running. Figure 4.6 represents this visually.

Evaluating: Returns:

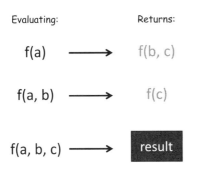

Figure 4.6 Evaluating a curried function f. The function produces a concrete result only when all arguments have been provided; otherwise, it returns another function that waits for these parameters to be passed in.

Currying is a technique that converts a multivariable function into a stepwise sequence of unary functions by suspending or "procrastinating" its execution until all arguments have been provided, which could happen later. Here's the formal definition of a curry of three parameters:

```
curry(f) :: ((a,b,c) -> d) -> a -> b -> c -> d
```

This formal notation suggests that curry is a mapping from functions to functions that deconstructs the input (a,b,c) into separate single-argument invocations. In pure functional programming languages, like Haskell, currying is a built-in feature and automatically part of all function definitions. Because JavaScript doesn't automatically curry functions, you need to write some supporting code to enable this. Before we go into auto-currying, let's start with a simple scenario of manually currying two arguments.

Listing 4.5   Manual currying with two arguments

```
function curry2(fn) {
    return function(firstArg) {
        return function(secondArg) {
            return fn(firstArg, secondArg);
        };
    };
}
```

First invocation of curry2 captures the first argument

Second invocation captures the second argument

Returns the result of applying this function with both arguments

As you can see, currying is another case of a lexical scope (a closure) where the returned functions are nothing more than trivial nested function wrappers to capture the arguments for later use. Here's a simple example:

```
const name = curry2(function (last, first) {
    return new StringPair('Barkley', 'Rosser');
});

[first, last] = name('Curry')('Haskell').values();
first;//-> 'Curry'
last; //-> 'Haskell'

name('Curry'); //-> Function
```

When supplied both arguments, evaluates the function completely

When supplied only one argument, returns another function rather than evaluating with undefined

Let's take another look at curry2, implementing the checkType function used in the Tuple type shown in listing 4.2. This example use functions from another functional library called Ramda.js.

Another functional library?

Like Lodash, Ramda.js provides lots of useful functions to connect functional programs and also enables a pure functional style of coding. The reason for using it is that its parameters are conveniently arranged to facilitate currying, partial application, and composition, which I'll cover later in this chapter. For more details about setting up Ramda, see the appendix.

Once it's installed, you can use the global variable R to access all of its functionality, such as R.is:

```
// checkType :: Type -> Object -> Object
const checkType = R.curry((typeDef, obj) => {
    if(!R.is(typeDef, obj)) {
        let type = typeof obj;
        throw new TypeError(`Type mismatch. Expected
```

Uses R.is() to check type information

```
        [${typeDef}] but found [${type}]`);
   }
   return obj;
});

checkType(String)('Curry'); //->'Curry'
checkType(Number)(3); //-> 3
checkType(Number)(3.5); //-> 3.5

let now = new Date();
checkType(Date)(now);   //-> now
checkType(Object)({}); //-> {}
checkType(String)(42); //-> TypeError
```

For simple tasks, curry2 is adequate; but as you start building more-complex function-ality, you'll need to handle any number of arguments automatically. Normally, I'd show you the function internals, but curry is a particularly long and convoluted func-tion to explain, so I'll spare you the headache and move into a more useful discussion (you can find curry and its flavors—curryRight, curryN, and so on—implemented in both Lodash and Ramda).

You can use R.curry to simulate the automatic currying mechanism in pure func-tional languages that works on any number of arguments. You can imagine automatic currying as artificially creating nested function scopes corresponding to the number of arguments declared. This example curries fullname:

```
// fullname :: (String, String) -> String
const fullname = function (first, last) {
    ...
}
```

The multiple arguments are transformed into unary functions of this form:

```
// fullname :: String -> String -> String
const fullname =
    function (first) {
        return function (last)  {
            ...
    }
}
```

Now let's jump into some of the practical applications of currying. In particular, it can be used to implement popular design patterns:

- Emulating function interfaces
- Implementing reusable, modular function templates

4.3.1   *Emulating function factories*

In the object-oriented world, interfaces are abstract types used to define a contract that classes must implement. If you create an interface with the function findStudent(ssn), concrete implementers of this interface must implement this function. Consider the following "short" Java example to illustrate this concept:

```java
public interface StudentStore {
    Student findStudent(String ssn);
}

public class DbStudentStore implements StudentStore {
    public Student findStudent(String ssn) {
        // ...
        ResultSet rs = jdbcStmt.executeQuery(sql);
        while(rs.next()){
            String ssn  = rs.getString("ssn");
            String name = rs.getString("firstname") +
                rs.getString("lastanme");
            return new Student(ssn, name);
        }
    }
}

public class CacheStudentStore implements StudentStore {
    public Student findStudent(String ssn) {
        // ...
        return cache.get(ssn);
    }
}
```

Sorry for the long-winded code snippet (Java is that verbose!). This code shows two implementations of the same interface: one that reads students from a database and the other that reads from a cache. But from the point of the view of the calling code, it cares only about calling the method and not where the object came from. This is the beauty of object-oriented design via the *factory method pattern*. Using a function factory, you can obtain the proper implementation:

```javascript
StudentStore store = getStudentStore();
store.findStudent("444-44-4444");
```

You have no reason to miss out in the functional programming world, and currying is the solution. Translating the Java code into JavaScript, you can create a function that looks up student objects in a data store as well as an array (these are the two implementers):

```javascript
// fetchStudentFromDb :: DB -> (String -> Student)
const fetchStudentFromDb = R.curry(function (db, ssn) {      ⟵  Looks up in
    return find(db, ssn);                                        an object DB
});

// fetchStudentFromArray :: Array -> (String -> Student)
const fetchStudentFromArray = R.curry(function (arr, ssn) {   ⟵  Looks up in
    return arr[ssn];                                              an array
});
```

Because the functions are curried, you can separate the function definition from evaluation with a generic factory method findStudent, whose implementation details could have originated from either implementation:

```
const findStudent = useDb ? fetchStudentFromDb(db)
                          : fetchStudentFromArray(arr);

findStudent('444-44-4444');
```

Now, findStudent can be passed to other modules without the caller knowing the concrete implementation (this will be important in chapter 6 for unit testing to mock interaction with the object store). In matters of reuse, currying also allows you to create a family of function templates.

4.3.2 *Implementing reusable function templates*

Suppose you need to configure different logging functions to handle different states in your application, such as errors, warnings, debug, and so on. Function templates define a family of related functions based on the number of arguments that are curried at the moment of creation. This example will use the popular library Log4js, a logging framework for JavaScript that is far superior to the typical console.log. You can find installation information in the appendix. Here's the basic setup:

```
const logger = new Log4js.getLogger('StudentEvents');
logger.info('Student added successfully!');
```

But with Log4js, you can do much more. Suppose you need instead to display messages on the screen in a pop-up. You can configure an appender to do so:

```
logger.addAppender(new Log4js.JSAlertAppender());
```

You can also change the layout by configuring the layout provider so that it outputs messages in JSON format instead of plain text:

```
appender.setLayout(new Log4js.JSONLayout());
```

There are many settings you can configure, and copying and pasting this code into each file causes lots of duplication. Instead, let's use currying to define a reusable function template (a logger module, if you will), which will give you the utmost flexibility and reuse.

Listing 4.6 Creating a logger function template

```
const logger = function(appender, layout, name, level, message) {
    const appenders = {
        'alert': new Log4js.JSAlertAppender(),          ◁——  Defines a set of
        'console': new Log4js.BrowserConsoleAppender()        canned appenders
    };
```

```
        const layouts = {
            'basic': new Log4js.BasicLayout(),          ◁──┐  Defines a set of
            'json': new Log4js.JSONLayout(),               │  canned layout
            'xml' : new Log4js.XMLLayout()                 │  providers
        };
        const appender = appenders[appender];
        appender.setLayout(layouts[layout]);
        const logger = new Log4js.getLogger(name);     ──┐  Issues a logging statement
        logger.addAppender(appender);                     │  with all configuration
        logger.log(level, message, null);              ◁──┘  parameters applied
};
```

Now, by currying `logger`, you can centrally manage and reuse appropriate loggers for each occasion:

```
const log = R.curry(logger)('alert', 'json', 'FJS');        ◁──┐  Evaluates all
                                                               │  but the last two
log('ERROR', 'Error condition detected!!');                    │  arguments

// -> this will popup an alert dialog with the requested message
```

If you're implementing multiple error-handling statements into one function or file, you also have the flexibility of partially setting all but the last parameter:

```
const logError = R.curry(logger)('console', 'basic', 'FJS', 'ERROR');
logError('Error code 404 detected!!');
logError('Error code 402 detected!!');
```

Behind the scenes, subsequent calls to curry are called on this function, finally yielding a unary function. The fact that you're able to create new functions from existing ones and pass any number of parameters to them leads to easily building functions in steps as arguments are defined.

In addition to gaining lots of reusability in your code, as I mentioned, the principal motivation behind currying is to convert multiargument functions into unary functions. Alternatives to currying are *partial function application* and *parameter binding*, which are moderately supported by the JavaScript language, to produce functions of smaller arity that also work well when plugged into function pipelines.

4.4   *Partial application and parameter binding*

Partial application is an operation that initializes a subset of a nonvariadic function's parameters to fixed values, creating a function of smaller arity. In simpler terms, if you have a function with five parameters, and you supply three of the arguments, you end up with a function that expects the last two.

Like currying, partial application can be used to directly reduce the length of a function, but in a slightly different manner. Because a curried function is, essentially, a partially applied function, there tends to be confusion about the techniques. Their main difference lies in the internal mechanism and control over parameter passing. I'll attempt to clarify:

- Currying generates nested unary functions at each partial invocation. Internally, the final result is generated from the step-wise composition of these unary functions. Also, variations of curry allow you to partially evaluate a number of arguments; therefore, it gives you complete control over when and how evaluation takes place.

- Partial application binds (assigns) a function's arguments to predefined values and generates a new function of fewer arguments. The resulting function contains the fixed parameters in its closure and is *completely evaluated* on the subsequent call.

Now that this is clear, let's move on to examine a possible implementation of partial.

Listing 4.7 Implementation of partial

Creates a new function with all parameters partially applied →

Uses Function.apply() to invoke this function with the proper context and all bound arguments →

```
function partial() {
    let fn = this, boundArgs = Array.prototype.slice.call(arguments);
    let placeholder = <<partialPlaceholderObj>>;          ←
    let bound = function() {
        let position = 0, length = boundArgs.length;
        let args = Array(length);
        for (let i = 0; i < length; i++) {
            args[i] = boundArgs[i] === placeholder        ←
                ? arguments[position++] : boundArgs[i];
        }

        while (position < arguments.length) {
            args.push(arguments[position++]);
        }
        return fn.apply(this, args);
    };
    return bound;
});
```

Implementations of partial in libraries such as Lodash use the underscore object as the placeholder. Other ad hoc implementations use undefined to suggest this parameter should be skipped.

The placeholder object partialPlaceholderObj skips defining a function's parameter for a later call, so you can pick which parameters are bound and which are supplied as part of the call (examples shortly).

For this discussion of partial application and function binding, we'll go back to using Lodash, because it has slightly better support for function binding than Ramda. On the surface, however, using _.partial has a similar feel to using R.curry, and both support placeholder arguments with their respective placeholder objects. With the same logger function shown earlier, you can partially apply certain parameters to create more-specific behavior:

```
const consoleLog = _.partial(logger, 'console', 'json', 'FJS Partial');
```

Let's use this function to reemphasize the difference between curry and partial. After applying these three arguments, the resulting consoleLog function expects the other two arguments when called (not in steps, but all at once). So, unlike currying, calling `consoleLog` with just one argument won't return a new function and will instead evaluate with the last one set to `undefined`. But you can continue applying partial arguments to `consoleLog` by using `_.partial` again:

```
const consoleInfoLog = _.partial(consoleLog, 'INFO');
consoleInfoLog('INFO logger configured with partial');
```

Currying is an automated way of using partial applications—this is its main difference from `partial`. Another variation is *function binding*, which is also available natively in JavaScript as `Function.prototype.bind()`.[1] It works a bit differently than `partial` does:

```
const log =_.bind(logger, undefined, 'console', 'json', 'FJS Binding');
log('WARN', 'FP is too awesome!');
```

What is this `undefined` second argument to `_.bind`? Bind lets you create bound functions, which can execute within the context of an owning object (passing `undefined` tells the runtime to bind this function to the global context). Let's see some practical uses of `_.partial` and `_.bind` that do the following:

- Extend the core language
- Bind delayed functions

4.4.1   *Extending the core language*

Partial application can be used to extend core data types like `String` and `Number` with useful utilities than enhance the expressiveness of the language. Just be mindful that extending the language this way may make your code less portable to platform upgrades if new, conflicting methods are added to the language. Consider the following examples:

> Using a placeholder, you can partially apply substring starting at index zero and create a function that expects an offset value.

```
// Take the first N characters
String.prototype.first = _.partial(String.prototype.substring, 0, _);

'Functional Programming'.first(3); // -> 'Fun'

// Convert any name into a Last, First format
String.prototype.asName =
    _.partial(String.prototype.replace, /(\w+)\s(\w+)/, '$2, $1');

'Alonzo Church'.asName(); //->  'Church, Alonzo'
```

> Partially applies certain parameters to create specific behavior

---

[1] See "Function.prototype.bind()," *Mozilla Developer Network*, http://mng.bz/MY75.

```
// Converts a string into an array
String.prototype.explode =
    _.partial(String.prototype.match, /[\w]/gi);

'ABC'.explode(); //->  ['A', 'B', 'C']

// Parses a simple URL
String.prototype.parseUrl = _.partial(String.prototype.match,
/(http[s]?|ftp):\/\/([^:\/\s]+)\.([^:\/\s]{2,5})/);

[ 'http://example.com', 'http', 'example', 'com' ]
```

Partially applies match with specific regex expressions to transform a string into an array containing specific data

Before implementing your own function, make sure to feature-check it first so you can stay on top of new language updates:

```
if(!String.prototype.explode) {
    String.prototype.explode = _.partial(String.prototype.match, /[\w]/gi);
}
```

There are cases where partial application doesn't work, such as when you're working with delayed functions like `setTimeout`. For this, you need to use function binding.

4.4.2 Binding into delayed functions

Using function binding to set the context object is important when you're working with methods that expect a certain owning object to be present. For instance, functions such as `setTimeout` and `setInterval` in the browser expect the `this` reference to be set to global context, the `window` object; otherwise, they don't work. Passing `undefined` tells the runtime to do just this. For instance, `setTimeout` can be used to create a simple scheduler object to run delayed tasks. Here's an example of using both `_.bind` and `_.partial`:

```
const Scheduler = (function () {
    const delayedFn = _.bind(setTimeout, undefined, _, _);

    return {
      delay5:  _.partial(delayedFn, _, 5000),
      delay10: _.partial(delayedFn, _, 10000),
      delay:   _.partial(delayedFn, _, _)
    };
})();

Scheduler.delay5(function () {
   consoleLog('Executing After 5 seconds!')
});
```

Using `Scheduler`, you can invoke any piece of code wrapped in a function body with a certain delay (this timer isn't guaranteed by the runtime engine, but that's a separate issue). Because both `bind` and `partial` are functions returning other functions, you can easily nest them. As you can see in the previous code, you build each delay operation from the composition of a bound function and a partially applied function. Function binding isn't as useful as partial application in functional programming, and it's also a bit trickier to use, because it involves once again setting the function context. I cover it here in case you run into it when exploring this topic on your own.

Both partial application and currying are useful. Currying is the most widely used technique to create function wrappers that abstract a function's behavior, either to preset its arguments or to partially evaluate them. This is beneficial because pure functions with fewer arguments are easier to work with than functions with many arguments. Either approach facilitates supplying the proper arguments so that functions don't have to blatantly access objects outside of their scope, while reducing them to unary functions. Isolating the logic of obtaining this necessary data makes functions more reusable; and, more important, it simplifies their composition.

4.5   *Composing function pipelines*

In chapter 1, we talked about the importance of being able to split a problem into smaller, simpler subproblems (or tasks) in order to put them back together to arrive at a solution—like pieces in a puzzle. The intention of functional programs is to gain the required structure that leads to composition, the backbone of functional programming. By now you understand the concepts of purity and side effect–free functions that make this such a powerful technique. Recall that a side effect–free function is one that doesn't depend on any external data; everything the function needs must be provided as arguments. In order to properly use composition, your functions must be side effect–free.

Furthermore, if a program is built from pure functions, the resulting program is itself pure, allowing it to be composed further as a part of even more-complex solutions without antagonizing other parts of the system. This topic is extremely important to understand, because it will be the central theme of the book going forward. So before we dive into functional composition, let's take a moment to understand it with a concrete example that composes widgets in an HTML page.

4.5.1   *Understanding composition with HTML widgets*

The idea of composition is intuitive and certainly not unique to functional programming. Consider how HTML widgets are laid out on a page. Complex widgets are built from the combination of simple ones, which in turn can form part of even bigger widgets. For instance, combining three input text boxes with an empty container produces a simple student form, as shown in figure 4.7.

The student form is a now a component (itself a widget) that can be composed with others into a more complex component to create an entire student console form (see figure 4.8). You get the idea; the student console widget could be plugged in to a bigger dashboard if need be. In this case, we say the console is *composed of* (or made up of) the address and bio forms. Objects with simple behavior (which don't have external dependencies) compose fairly well and can be used to build complex structures from simple ones, like interlocking building blocks.

Figure 4.7   Combining three simple input text widgets with a container widget to create a bio form component

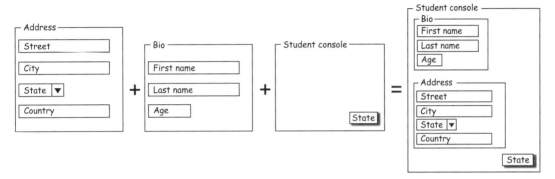

Figure 4.8   Student console widget built from smaller widgets including an address form, a bio form, a button, and a container

To demonstrate, let's create a recursive tuple definition called Node:

```
const Node = Tuple(Object, Tuple);
```

This can be used to hold an object and a reference to another node (tuple). It turns out this is the functional definition of a list of elements, made up recursively of a head and a tail. Using a curried function called element

```
const element = R.curry((val, tuple) => new Node(val, tuple));
```

you can create a null-terminated list of any type. Figure 4.9 shows a simple list of numbers.

```
var grades = element(1, element(2, element(3, element(4, null))));
```

Head   Tail

Figure 4.9   Highlighting the head and tail sections forming a list of numbers. The head and tail are readily available as functions for array processing in functional languages.

This is more or less how lists are constructed in languages like ML and Haskell. On the other hand, complex objects with high degrees of coupling to other external objects don't have clear rules for composition and can be extremely hard to work with. Functional composition can have a similar fate when side effects and mutations are present. Now, let's dive into the composition of functions.

4.5.2   *Functional composition: separating description from evaluation*

In essence, *functional composition* is a process used to group together complex behavior that has been broken into simpler tasks. I defined it briefly in chapter 1, and now I'll explain it in detail. Let's go over a quick example that uses Ramda's R.compose to combine two pure functions:

```
const str = `We can only see a short distance
             ahead but we can see plenty there
             that needs to be done`;

const explode = (str) => str.split(/\s+/);              Splits a sentence into
                                                        an array of words

const count = (arr) => arr.length;                      Counts the
                                                        words
const countWords = R.compose(count, explode);

countWords(str); //-> 19
```

Arguably, this code is easy to read, and its meaning easily derived by glancing at the function's constituent parts. The interesting quality of this program is that evaluation never takes place until countWords is run; in other words, the functions passed by name (explode and count) are dormant within the composition. The result of composition is another function that waits to be called with its respective argument: the argument to countWords. This is the beauty of function composition: *separating a function's description from its evaluation.*

I'll explain what happens behind the scenes. The call to countWords(str) runs explode with the given sentence and passes its output (array of strings) into count, which computes the length of the array. Composition connects outputs with inputs, creating true function pipelines. Let's examine a more formal definition. Consider two functions f and g with their respective input and output types:

```
g :: A -> B           g is a function
f :: B -> C           from type A to B.

                      f is a function
                      from type B to C.
```

Figure 4.10 draws a set of arrows connecting all groups. This abstract example shows a function (arrow) f that takes an argument of type B and returns a C. Another function (arrow) g takes an A and returns a B. The composition of g :: A -> B and f :: B -> C,

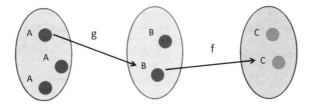

Figure 4.10 Showing the set of input and output types for functions f and g. Function g maps A values to B values, and function f maps B values to C values. Composition happens because f and g are compatible.

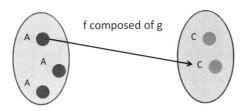

Figure 4.11 The composition of two functions is a new function directly mapping the inputs of the first function to the output of the second. The composition is also a referentially transparent mapping between inputs and outputs.

pronounced ("f composed of g"), results in another function (arrow) from A -> C, as shown in figure 4.11. This can be expressed more formally as

```
f • g = f(g) = compose :: ((B -> C), (A -> B)) -> (A -> C)
```

Recall that with referential transparency, functions are nothing more than arrows connecting one object of a group to another.

This leads to another important software development principle, which is the backbone of modular systems. Because composition loosely binds type-compatible functions at their boundaries (inputs and outputs), it fairly satisfies the principle of *programming to interfaces.* In the previous example, you have a function explode :: String -> [String] composed with the function count :: [String] -> Number; in other words, each function only knows or cares about the next function's interface and isn't worried about its implementation. Although it isn't part of the JavaScript language, compose can be naturally expressed as a higher-order function.

Listing 4.8 Implementation of compose

```
function compose(/* fns */) {
    let args = arguments;
    let start = args.length - 1;
    return function() {
        let i = start;
        let result = args[start].apply(this, arguments);
        while (i--)
            result = args[i].call(this, result);
        return result;
    };
}
```

The output of compose is another function that's called on actual arguments.

Dynamically applies the function on the arguments passed in

Iteratively invokes the subsequent functions based on the previous return value

Luckily, Ramda provides an implementation of `R.compose` that you can use so you don't have to implement this yourself. Let's write a validation program that checks for a valid SSN (you'll reuse a lot of these helper functions throughout the book):

```
const trim = (str) => str.replace(/^\s*|\s*$/g, '');        ◁──┐  Removes any spaces
                                                               │  before and after the input

const normalize = (str) => str.replace(/\-/g, '');         ◁──┐  Removes all dashes
                                                               │
                                                                  Checks the
const validLength = (param, str) => str.length === param;  ◁──┘  length of a string

                                                                  Configures the function
const checkLengthSsn = _.partial(validLength, 9);          ◁──   with parameter 9 to check
                                                                  the length of an SSN (9)
```

From these functions, you can create others:

```
                                                              ┌  Composes normalize
                                                              │  and trim results in the
const cleanInput = R.compose(normalize, trim);             ◁──┘  cleanInput function
const isValidSsn = R.compose(checkLengthSsn, cleanInput);  ◁─┐
                                                             │   Composes cleanInput
cleanInput(' 444-44-4444 ');   //-> '444444444'              │   further with
isValidSsn(' 444-44-4444 ');   //-> true                     │   checkLengthSsn to
                                                             └   yield a new function
```

Taking this fundamental concept further, as you can see in figure 4.12, entire programs can be built with the combination of simple functions.

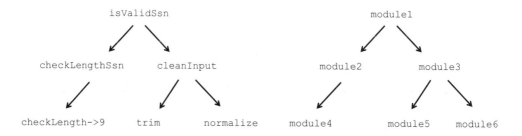

Figure 4.12 Complex functions can be built by composing simple functions. Just as functions combine, entire programs made from different modules (containing more functions) that can also combine in this fashion.

This concept isn't limited to functions; entire programs can be built from the combination of other side effect–free, pure programs or modules. (Based on the earlier definition of a function, used throughout this book, I'll use the terms *function*, *program*, and *module* loosely to refer to any executable unit with inputs and output.)

Composition is a *conjunctive operation*, which means it joins elements using a logical AND operator. For instance, the function `isValidSsn` is made from `checkLengthSsn` *and* `cleanInput`. In this manner, programs are derivations of the sum of all their parts. In chapter 5, we'll tackle problems that require disjunctive behavior to express conditions where functions can return one of two results, A OR B.

Alternatively, you can augment JavaScript's `Function` prototype to add `compose`. Here's the exact same behavior in a style similar to function chaining from chapter 3:

```
Function.prototype.compose = R.compose;

const cleanInput = checkLengthSsn.compose(normalize).compose(trim);
```

Functions are again chained with dots.

If you like this better, feel free to use it. In the next chapter, you'll learn that this mechanism of chaining methods is prevalent in functional algebraic data types called *monads*. Personally, I recommend sticking to the more functional form, because it's much more succinct and flexible and works better in conjunction with functional libraries.

4.5.3 *Composition with functional libraries*

One of the benefits of working with a functional library such as Ramda is that all functions have been properly configured with currying in mind, making them versatile when composed into function pipelines. Let's look at another example. Here's a list of students with their respective grades in a class:

```
const students = ['Rosser', 'Turing', 'Kleene', 'Church'];
const grades   = [80, 100, 90, 99];
```

Suppose you need to find the student with the highest grade in the class. You learned in chapter 3 that working with collections of data is one of the cornerstones of functional programming. The code in listing 4.9 is made up of the composition of several curried functions, each in charge of transforming this data in a particular way:

- `R.zip`—Creates a new array by pairing the contents of adjacent arrays. In this case, pairing these two arrays yields `[['Rosser', 80], ['Turing', 100], ...]`.
- `R.prop`—Specifies the value to be used in sorting. In this case, passing a 1 points to the second element of a subarray (grade).
- `R.sortBy`—Performs a natural ascending sort of the array by the given property.
- `R.reverse`—Reverses the entire array to get the highest number at the first element.
- `R.pluck`—Builds an array by extracting an element at a specified index. Passing a 0 points to the student name element.
- `R.head`—Takes the first element.

Listing 4.9   Computing the smartest student

```
const smartestStudent = R.compose(
    R.head,
    R.pluck(0),
    R.reverse,
    R.sortBy(R.prop(1)),
    R.zip);

smartestStudent(students, grades); //-> 'Turing'
```

Creates the function smartestStudent, defined as the composition of a series of Ramda functions

Passing both arrays to the function begins by calling R.zip(). At each step the data is immutably transformed from one expression to the next until the final result is obtained, extracted using R.head().

Using composition can be challenging, especially when you're just getting acquainted with the framework or you're just beginning to understand the problem domain. When I use composition in my own work, I often find myself thinking about where I should begin. Again, the hardest part is the exercise of breaking a task into smaller pieces; once this is finalized, composition is compelling for recombining functions.

In addition, something you'll soon realize and begin to love about functional composition is how you're naturally drawn to expressing the entire solution succinctly in one or two lines. Because you're forced to create functions that map to the different stages in your algorithm, you begin to build an ontology with which you can stitch together expressions that describe parts of your solution, allowing team members to more quickly understand your code. The following listing is similar to an exercise from chapter 3.

Listing 4.10   Using descriptive function aliases

```
const first = R.head;
const getName = R.pluck(0);
const reverse = R.reverse;
const sortByGrade = R.sortBy(R.prop(1));
const combine = R.zip;

R.compose(first, getName, reverse, sortByGrade, combine);
```

Although this instance of the program is easier to read, there's no added reusability because these functions are specific to the particular task at hand. Rather, I recommend getting acquainted with the functional vocabulary of head, pluck, zip, and others, so that, through practice, you gain comprehensive knowledge of your functional framework of choice. It will make the transition to other frameworks or other functional languages easier, because they all use many of the same naming conventions. This will quickly pay dividends in your productivity.

Listings 4.9 and 4.10 uses pure functions to express an entire solution, but you know this isn't always possible. As an application developer, you'll face many situations where you need to do things like read from local storage and make remote HTTP requests, among other tasks, which unavoidably create side effects. For this, you must be able to isolate and separate the impure from the pure code; as you'll see in chapter 6, this will make testing extremely simple.

4.5.4 Coping with pure and impure code

Impure code causes externally observable side effects after it's run and has external dependencies to access data beyond the scope of its constituent functions. It only takes one function to be impure for your entire program to follow suit.

With that said, you don't have to make your functions 100% pure to reap the benefits of functional programming. Although this is the perfect scenario, you must also learn to tolerate pure and impure behavior by creating a clear separation between the two and isolating the impurity as much as possible—ideally, in single functions. Then composition can be used to glue the pure and impure pieces back together. Recall from chapter 1 that you began implementing the requirements for the `showStudent` function, which looked like this:

```
const showStudent = compose(append, csv, findStudent);
```

One way or another, most of these functions emit side effects through the arguments they receive:

- `findStudent` uses a reference to a local object store or some external array.
- `append` directly writes and modifies HTML elements.

Let's continue improving this program by using `curry` to partially evaluate the invariable parameters of each function. You'll also add code to sanitize the input parameter and refactor the HTML operations with more fine-grained functions. Finally, you'll make the `find` operation more functional by dislodging it from the object store.

Listing 4.11 showStudent program using currying and composition

```
// findObject :: DB -> String -> Object
const findObject = R.curry((db, id) => {
   const obj = find(db, id);
   if(obj === null) {
     throw new Error(`Object with ID [${id}] not found`);
   }
   return obj;
});

// findStudent :: String -> Student
const findStudent = findObject(DB('students'));

const csv = ({ssn, firstname, lastname}) =>
    `${ssn}, ${firstname}, ${lastname}`;

// append :: String -> String -> String
const append = R.curry((elementId, info) => {
   document.querySelector(elementId).innerHTML = info;
   return info;
});
```

Refactored find() method that takes the storage object as a parameter to allow for easier composition

Partially evaluates fetchRecord by pointing to the students object store, creating a new function called findStudent

```
// showStudent :: String -> Integer
const showStudent = R.compose(
    append('#student-info'),
    csv,
    findStudent,
    normalize,
    trim);
```

◁ **Uses composition to put the entire program together in a single executable**

```
showStudent('44444-4444');   //-> 444-44-4444, Alonzo, Church
```

The code in listing 4.11 defines four functions that make up `showStudent` (I added their type signatures so that you can more easily follow the correspondence between each successive invocation). This program executes all the functions beginning with `trim` and works backward until it calls `append`, linking the output of one function and passing it to the next. But wait a second; remember the Unix program with which I started the chapter? This program executes each function in a left-to-right manner using the Unix built-in pipe | operator. Piping functions evaluates programs in the opposite order of composition (see figure 4.13).

```
tr 'A-Z' 'a-z' <words.in | uniq | sort
```
①   ②   ③

Figure 4.13   A simple Unix shell program, piping together a sequence of functions or programs

If the thought of composing functions in this naturally reversed flow feels odd to you, or you visualize your programs as a left-associative sequence, you can use Ramda's mirror function to `compose`, called `pipe`, which achieves the same results:

```
R.pipe(
    trim,
    normalize,
    findStudent,
    csv,
    append('#student-info'));
```

As evidence of how important this is, F# provides built-in support for this using its pipe-forward operator |>. In JavaScript, we don't have this luxury, but we can safely rely on functional libraries to do the job effectively. Note from both `R.pipe` and `R.compose` that you're creating new functions without having to explicitly declare any of their formal arguments, as you'd normally have to. Functional composition encourages this writing style, which goes by the name of *point-free coding*.

4.5.5   *Introducing point-free programming*

If you look closer at the function in listing 4.10, you can see that it doesn't show the parameters of any of its constituent functions, as would a traditional function declaration. Here it is again:

```
R.compose(first, getName, reverse, sortByGrade, combine);
```

Using `compose` (or `pipe`) means never having to declare arguments (known as the *points* of a function), making your code declarative and more succinct or *point-free.*

Point-free programming brings functional JavaScript code closer to that of Haskell and the Unix philosophy. It can be used to increase the level of abstraction by forcing you to think of composing high-level components instead of worrying about the low-level details of function evaluation. Currying plays an important role because it gives you the flexibility to partially define all but the last argument of an inlined function reference. This style of coding is also known as *tacit programming*, much like the Unix program from the start of the chapter, which is written next in a point-free way.

```
const runProgram = R.pipe(
    R.map(R.toLower),
    R.uniq,
    R.sortBy(R.identity));
```

Uses the identity function, which returns the argument it was called with. It has subtle but practical applications (explained in the next section).

```
runProgram(['Functional', 'Programming', 'Curry',
    'Memoization', 'Partial', 'Curry', 'Programming']);

//-> [curry, functional, memoization, partial, programming]
```

The program in listing 4.12 is made up of point-free function expressions that are defined only by name (some with an argument partially defined), without declaring what types of arguments they take or how they're connected within the bigger expression. As composition morphs into this coding style, it's important to keep in mind that overdoing it can create obscure or obfuscated programs. Not everything has to be point-free. In some cases, breaking out your function composition into two or three at a time can go a long way.

Point-free code can raise questions related to error handling and debugging. In other words, because throwing exceptions causes side effects to occur, should you resort to returning `null` from within composed functions? Checking for `null` within functions is acceptable but adds a lot of duplicated, boilerplate code and assumes you return sensible default values for the program to proceed. Also, how would you attempt to debug all of these commands, which appear on a single line? These are valid concerns and will be addressed in the next chapter, where I'll present more point-free programs that include automatic support for error handling.

Another obvious concern is how to handle situations where you need to use conditional logic or have some way of running multiple functions in sequence. In the next section, I'll discuss helpful utilities to manage your application's control flow.

4.6   *Managing control flow with functional combinators*

In chapter 3, I gave a comparison of a program's control flow in both imperative and functional paradigms and highlighted the significant differences between them. Imperative code uses procedural control mechanisms like `if-else` and `for` to drive a program's flow, but functional programming doesn't. As we leave the imperative world behind, we need to find alternatives to fill in that gap; for this, we can use *function combinators*.

Combinators are higher-order functions that can combine primitive artifacts like other functions (or other combinators) and behave as control logic. Combinators typically don't declare any variables of their own or contain any business logic; they're meant to orchestrate the flow of a functional program. In addition to `compose` and `pipe`, there's an infinite number of combinators, but we'll look at some of the most common ones:

- `identity`
- `tap`
- `alternation`
- `sequence`
- `fork` (join)

4.6.1   *Identity (I-combinator)*

The `identity` combinator is a function that returns the same value it was provided as an argument:

```
identity :: (a) -> a
```

It's used extensively when examining the mathematical properties of functions, but it has other practical applications as well:

- Supplying data to higher-order functions that expect it when evaluating a function argument, as you did earlier when writing point-free code (listing 4.12).
- Unit testing the flow of function combinators where you need a simple function result on which to make assertions (you'll see this in chapter 6). For instance, you could write a unit test for `compose` that uses identity functions.
- Extracting data functionally from encapsulated types (more on this in the next chapter).

4.6.2   *Tap (K-combinator)*

tap is extremely useful to bridge void functions (such as logging or writing a file or an HTML page) into your composition without having to any create additional code. It does this by passing itself into a function and returning itself. Here's the function signature:

```
tap :: (a -> *) -> a -> a
```

This function takes an input object a and a function that performs some action on a. It runs the given function with the supplied object and then returns the object. For instance, using R.tap, you can take a void function like debugLog

```
const debugLog = _.partial(logger, 'console', 'basic', 'MyLogger',
    'DEBUG');
```

and embed it within the composition of other functions. Here are some examples:

```
const debug = R.tap(debugLog);
const cleanInput = R.compose(normalize, debug, trim);
const isValidSsn = R.compose(debug, checkLengthSsn, debug, cleanInput);
```

Having the call to debug (based on R.tap) won't alter the result of the program in any way. In fact, this combinator throws away the result of the function passed into it (if any). This will compute the result and also perform debugging along the way:

```
isValidSsn('444-44-4444');

// output
MyLogger [DEBUG] 444-44-4444   // clean input
MyLogger [DEBUG] 444444444     // check length
MyLogger [DEBUG] true          // final result
```

4.6.3   *Alternation (OR-combinator)*

The alt combinator allows you to perform simple conditional logic when providing default behavior in response to a function call. This combinator takes two functions and returns the result of the first one if the value is defined (not false, null, or undefined); otherwise, it returns the result of the second function. Let's implement it here:

```
const alt = function (func1, func2) {
    return function (val) {
        return func1(val) || func2(val);
    }
};
```

Alternatively, you could also write this function succinctly using curry and lambdas:

```
const alt = R.curry((func1, func2, val) => func1(val) || func2(val));
```

You can use this combinator as part of the `showStudent` program to handle the case when the fetch operation returns unsuccessfully, so that you can create a new student:

```
const showStudent = R.compose(
   append('#student-info'),
   csv,
   alt(findStudent, createNewStudent));

showStudent('444-44-4444');
```

To understand what's happening, think of this code emulating a simple `if-else` statement equivalent to the imperative conditional logic:

```
var student = findStudent('444-44-4444');
if(student !== null) {
  let info = csv(student);
  append('#student-info', info);
}
else {
  let newStudent = createNewStudent('444-44-4444');
  let info = csv(newStudent);
  append('#student-info', info);
}
```

4.6.4   *Sequence (S-combinator)*

The `seq` combinator is used to loop over a sequence of functions. It takes two or more functions as parameters and returns a new function, which runs all of them in sequence against the same value. This is the implementation:

```
const seq = function(/*funcs*/) {
   const funcs = Array.prototype.slice.call(arguments);
   return function (val) {
      funcs.forEach(function (fn) {
         fn(val);
      });
   };
};
```

With it, you can perform a sequence of related, yet independent, operations. For instance, after finding the student object, you can use `seq` to both render it on the HTML page and log it to the console. All functions will run in that order against the same student object:

```
const showStudent = R.compose(
  seq(
    append('#student-info'),
    consoleLog),
  csv,
  findStudent));
```

The `seq` combinator doesn't return a value; it just performs a set of actions one after the other. If you want to inject it into the middle of a composition, you can use `R.tap` to bridge the function with the rest.

4.6.5 Fork (join) combinator

The `fork` combinator is useful in cases where you need to process a single resource in two different ways and then combine the results. This combinator takes three functions: a join function and two terminal functions that process the provided input. The result of each forked function is ultimately passed in to a `join` function of two arguments, as shown in figure 4.14.

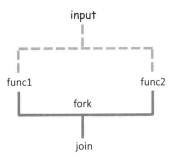

Figure 4.14 The `fork` combinator receives three functions: a `join` and two `fork` functions. The `fork` functions are executed against the supplied input, and then the final result is combined via `join`.

> **NOTE** This isn't to be confused with the Java fork-join framework, which helps with multiprocessing. This comes as a `fork` combinator implementation in Haskell and other functional toolkits.

This is the implementation:

```
const fork = function(join, func1, func2) {
    return function(val) {
        return join(func1(val), func2(val));
    };
};
```

Now let's see it in action. Let's revisit computing the average letter grade from an array of numbers. You can use `fork` to coordinate the evaluation of three utility functions:

```
const computeAverageGrade =
    R.compose(getLetterGrade, fork(R.divide, R.sum, R.length));

computeAverageGrade([99, 80, 89]); //-> 'B'
```

The next example checks whether the mean and median of a collection of grades are equal:

```
const eqMedianAverage = fork(R.equals, R.median, R.mean);
eqMedianAverage([80, 90, 100])); //-> True
eqMedianAverage([81, 90, 100])); //-> False
```

Some people view composition as restrictive, but you can see for yourself that it's quite the opposite: combinators unlock freedom and facilitate point-free programming. Because combinators are pure, they can be composed into other combinators, providing an infinite number of alternatives to express and reduce the complexity of writing any type of application. You'll see them used again in the following chapters.

Through the basic principles of immutability and purity, functional programming enables a fine level of modularity and reusability of the functions that make up your program. In chapter 2, you learned that in JavaScript, functions can also be used to implement modules. Using these same principles, you can also compose and reuse entire modules. I'll leave this idea for you to contemplate on your own.

Modular functional programs consist of abstract functions that can be understood and reused independently and whose meaning is derived from rules governing their composition. In this chapter, you learned that composing pure functions is the backbone of functional programming. These techniques take advantage of the abstraction (via currying and partial application) of pure functions with the goal of making them composable. So far, I haven't talked about error handling, which is a critical part of any robust, fault-tolerant application; that's what we'll visit next.

4.7   Summary

- Functional chains and pipelines connect reusable and modular componentized programs.
- Ramda.js is a functional library adapted for currying and composition, with a powerful arsenal of utility functions.
- Currying and partial evaluation can be used to reduce the arity of pure functions by partially evaluating a subset of a function's arguments and transforming them into unary functions.
- You can break a task into simple functions and compose them together to arrive at the entire solution.
- Using function combinators allows you to orchestrate complicated program flows to tackle any real-world problem as well as write in a point-free manner.

5
Design patterns against complexity

This chapter covers

- The issues with imperative error-handling schemes
- Using containers to prevent access to invalid data
- Implementing functors as a mechanism for data transformation
- Understanding monads as data types that facilitate composition
- Consolidating error-handling strategies with monadic types
- Interleaving and composing monadic types

Null-references … was a billion-dollar mistake.

—Tony Hoare, InfoQ

Some people mistakenly view functional programming as a paradigm devoted only to academic problems, mostly numerical in nature, that are, for the most part, oblivious to the probabilities of failure real-life systems deal with. In recent years, however, people are finding that functional programming can treat error handling more elegantly than any other development style.

Many issues can arise in software where data inadvertently becomes `null` or `undefined`, exceptions are thrown, or network connectivity is lost, to name a few. Our code needs to account for the potential of any of these issues occurring, which unavoidably creates complexity. As a result, we spend countless hours making sure our code throws and catches the proper exceptions and checks for `null` values everywhere we can think of, and what do we get? Even more complex code—code that doesn't scale and becomes harder to reason about as the size and complexity of applications increase.

We need to work smarter, not harder. In this chapter, I'll introduce the concept of *functors* as a means to create simple data types on which functions can be mapped. A functor is applied to data types called *monads* that contain specific behavior for dealing with errors in different ways. Monads are one of the hardest concepts to grasp in functional programming because the theory is deeply rooted in category theory, which I won't cover. My intention is to focus only on the practical aspects. Having said that, I'll slowly work my way into that topic, layering in some prerequisite concepts, and then show how you can use monads to create fault-tolerant function compositions in a way that imperative error-handling mechanism can't.

5.1   Shortfalls of imperative error handling

JavaScript errors can occur in many situations, especially when an application fails to communicate with a server or tries to access properties of a `null` object. Also, third-party libraries can have functions throw exceptions to signal special error conditions. Hence, we always need to be prepared for the worst and design with failure in mind, instead of letting it become an afterthought and regretting it later. In the imperative world, exceptions are handled via the `try-catch` idiom.

5.1.1   Error handling with try-catch

JavaScript's current exception-handling mechanism is geared toward throwing and catching exceptions through the popular `try-catch` structure present in most modern programming languages:

```
try {
    // code that might throw an exception in here
}
catch (e) {
    // statements to handle any exceptions
    console.log('ERROR' + e.message);
}
```

The purpose of this structure is to surround a piece of code that you deem to be unsafe. Upon throwing an exception, the JavaScript runtime abruptly halts the program's execution and creates a stack trace of all function calls leading up to the problematic instruction. As you know, specific details about the error, such as the message, line number, and filename, are populated into an object of type `Error` and passed into the catch block. The `catch` block becomes a safe haven so that you can potentially recover your program. For example, recall the `findObject` and `find-Student` functions:

```
// findObject :: DB, String -> Object
const findObject = R.curry(function (db, id) {
  const result = find(db, id)
  if(!result) {
      throw new Error('Object with ID [' + id + '] not found');
  }
  return result;
});

// findStudent :: String -> Student
const findStudent = findObject(DB('students'));
```

Because any of these functions can throw an exception, in practice you would need to enclose them in a `try-catch` block when calling them:

```
try {
    var student = findStudent('444-44-4444');
}
catch (e) {
    console.log('ERROR' + e.message);
}
```

Just as you abstracted loops and conditional statements with functions before, you need to abstract error handling. Clearly, functions that use `try-catch` as shown here can't be composed or chain together and put a great deal of pressure on the design of your code.

5.1.2 Reasons not to throw exceptions in functional programs

The structured mechanism of throwing and catching exceptions in imperative JavaScript code has many drawbacks and is incompatible with the functional design. Functions that throw exceptions

- Can't be composed or chained like other functional artifacts.
- Violate the principle of referential transparency that advocates a single, predictable value, because throwing exceptions constitutes another exit path from your function calls.
- Cause side effects to occur because an unanticipated unwinding of the stack impacts the entire system beyond the function call.

- Violate the principle of non-locality because the code used to recover from the error is distanced from the originating function call. When an error is thrown, a function leaves the local stack and environment:

```
try {
    var student = findStudent('444-44-4444');

    ... more lines of code in between
}
catch (e) {
    console.log('ERROR: not found');

    // Handle error here
}
```

- Put a great deal of responsibility on the caller to declare matching `catch` blocks to manage specific exceptions instead of just worrying about a function's single return value.
- Are hard to use when multiple error conditions create nested levels of exception-handling blocks:

```
var student = null;
try {
    student = findStudent('444-44-44444');
}
catch (e) {
    console.log('ERROR: Cannot locate students by SSN');

    try {
        student = findStudentByAddress(new Address(...));
    }
    catch (e) {
        console.log('ERROR: Student is no where to be found!');
    }
}
```

You're probably asking yourself, "Is throwing exceptions completely off the table in functional programming?" I don't believe so. In practice, they can never be off the table, because there are many factors outside of your control that you need to account for. Also, you may be writing code against a library outside of your control that implements exceptions.

Using exceptions can be effective for certain edge cases. In checkType in chapter 4, you used an exception to signal a fundamental misuse of the API. They're also useful to signal unrecoverable conditions like RangeError: Maximum call stack size exceeded, which I'll talk about in chapter 7. Throwing exceptions has a place but shouldn't be done excessively. A common scenario that occurs in JavaScript is the infamous TypeError resulting from invoking a function on a null object.

5.1.3 *Problems with null-checking*

The alternative to failing abruptly from a function call is to return `null`. That, at least, guarantees only one route that leaves a function call, but it's not any better. Functions that return `null` create a different responsibility for users: pesky `null` checks. Consider the function `getCountry`, which is in charge of reading a student's address and then country:

```
function getCountry(student) {
   let school = student.getSchool();
   if(school !== null) {
     let addr = school.getAddress();
       if(addr !== null) {
       var country = addr.getCountry();
       return country;
     }
     return null;
   }
   throw new Error('Error extracting country info');
}
```

At a glance, this function should have been simple to implement—after all, it's just extracting an object's property. I could have created a simple lens that focuses on this property; in the event of a `null` address, a lens is smart enough to return `undefined`, but it doesn't help me to print an error message.

Instead, I ended up with lots of lines of code to defend myself from unexpected behavior. Defensively wrapping code with lots of `try-catch` or `null` checks is cowardly. Wouldn't it be great to be able to handle errors effectively while avoiding all of this unnecessary boilerplate code?

5.2 *Building a better solution: functors*

Functional error handling is a radically different approach to properly cope with the adversities found in software systems. The idea, however, is somewhat similar: create a safety box (a container, if you will) around potentially hazardous code (see figure 5.1).

```
try {

    var student = findStudent('444-44-4444');

    ... more lines of code

}
catch (e) {
    console.log('ERROR: Student not found!');

    // Handle missing student
}
```

Figure 5.1 The `try-catch` structure invisibly creates a safety box around functions that can throw exceptions. This safety box is materialized into a container.

In functional programming, this notion of boxing the dangerous code still applies, but you throw away the try-catch block. Now, here's the big difference. Walling off impurity is made a first-class citizen in functional programming by the use of functional data types. Let's begin with the most basic type and move into the more advanced ones.

5.2.1 *Wrapping unsafe values*

Containerizing (or wrapping) values is a fundamental design pattern in functional programming because it guards direct access to the values so they can be manipulated safely and immutably in your programs. It's like wearing armor before going to battle. Accessing a wrapped value can only be done by *mapping an operation to its container.* In this chapter, I'll talk extensively about the concept of a *map*, but you already learned about this in chapter 3 when you used map on arrays—the array was the container of values, in that case.

It turns out you can map functions to much more than just arrays. In functional JavaScript, *a map is nothing more than a function*; this idea comes from referential transparency, where a function must always "map to" the same result given the same input. So you can also think of map as a gate that allows you to plug in a lambda expression with specific behavior that transforms an encapsulated value. In the case of arrays, you used map to create a new array with the transformed values.

Let's illustrate this concept with a simple data type called Wrapper, in the following listing. Although this type is simple, the underlying principle is extremely powerful and will pave the way for the next sections in this chapter, so it's important that you understand it.

Listing 5.1   Functional data type to wrap values

```
class Wrapper {
    constructor(value) {
        this._value = value;               ◁──┐ Simple type that stores a
    }                                            single value of any type

    // map :: (A -> B) -> A -> B
    map(f) {
      return f(this._value);               ◁──┐ Maps a function over this
    };                                           type (just like arrays)

    toString() {
      return 'Wrapper (' + this._value + ')';
    }
}
// wrap :: A -> Wrapper(A)                         Helper function that
const wrap = (val) => new Wrapper(val);       ◁── quickly creates wrappers
                                                   around values
```

You can use a wrapper object to encapsulate a potentially erroneous value. Because you won't have direct access to it, the only way to extract it is to use the identity function you learned about in chapter 4 (notice there's no explicit get method on this wrapper type). Certainly JavaScript will give you easy access to this value, but the point to understand here is that once the value enters the container, it can't be directly retrieved or transformed (like a virtual barrier); see figure 5.2.

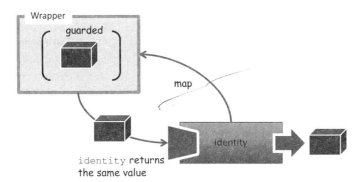

Figure 5.2 The `Wrapper` type uses `map` to safely access and manipulate values. In this case, you're mapping the identity function over the container to extract the value as is from the container.

Here's a concrete example using a valid value:

```
const wrappedValue = wrap('Get Functional');
wrappedValue.map(R.identity); //-> 'Get Functional'
```
Extracts the value

You can map any function to this container to either log to the console or manipulate it as needed:

```
wrappedValue.map(console.log);
wrappedValue.map(R.toUpper); //-> 'GET FUNCTIONAL'
```
Runs the function over the internal value

The benefit of this simple idea is that any code written against these wrappers needs to be able to "reach into the container" via `Wrapper.map` in order to use the guarded value contained within. But if the value happens to be `null` or `undefined`, the responsibility is placed on the caller, which may or may not gracefully handle this case. Later, you'll see a better alternative:

```
const wrappedNull = wrap(null);
wrappedNull.map(doWork);
```
doWork is given the burden of null-checking.

As you can see from this example, to manipulate a value within a guarded, wrapped context, you need to apply a function to it; you can't invoke a function directly. What to do in the event of an error can be delegated to concrete wrapper types. In other words, you can check for `null` before calling the function, or check for an empty string, a negative number, and so on. Hence, the semantic of `Wrapper.map` is determined by the specific implementation of the wrapping type.

Let's not get ahead of ourselves; we have some more groundwork to cover. Consider this slightly different variation of `map`, called `fmap`:

```
// fmap :: (A -> B) -> Wrapper[A] -> Wrapper[B]
fmap (f) {
  return new Wrapper(f(this._value));
}
```
Wraps the transformed value in the container before returning it to the caller ←┘

`fmap` knows how to apply functions to values wrapped in a context. It first opens the container, then applies the given function to its value, and finally closes the value back into a new container of the same type. This type of function is known as a *functor.*

5.2.2   *Functors explained*

In essence, a functor is nothing more than a data structure that you can map functions over with the purpose of lifting values into a wrapper, modifying them, and then putting them back into a wrapper. It's a design pattern that defines semantics for how `fmap` should work. Here's the general definition of `fmap`:

```
fmap :: (A -> B) -> Wrapper(A) -> Wrapper(B)
```
←┤ **Wrapper is any container type.**

The function `fmap` takes a function (from A -> B) and a functor (wrapped context) `Wrapper(A)` and returns a new functor `Wrapper(B)` containing the result of applying said function to the value and closing it once more. Figure 5.3 shows a quick example that uses the `increment` function as a mapping function from A -> B (except in this case, A and B are the same types).

Notice that because `fmap` basically returns a new copy of the container at each invocation, much as lenses (chapter 2) work, it can be considered immutable. In figure 5.3, mapping the `increment` over `Wrapper(1)` returns a completely new object,

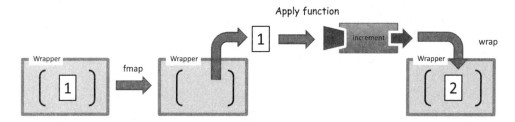

Figure 5.3   A value of 1 is contained within `Wrapper`. The functor is called with the wrapper and the `increment` function, which transforms the value internally and closes it back into a container.

`Wrapper(2)`. Let's go over a simple example before you begin applying functors to solve more-practical problems. Consider a simple 2 + 3 = 5 addition using functors. You can curry an `add` function to create a `plus3` function:

```
const plus = R.curry((a, b) => a + b);
const plus3 = plus(3);
```

Now you'll store the number 2 into a `Wrapper` functor:

```
const two = wrap(2);
```

Calling `fmap` to map `plus3` over the container performs addition:

```
const five = two.fmap(plus3); //-> Wrapper(5)          **Returns the value
five.map(R.identity); //-> 5                            in a context**
```

The outcome of `fmap` yields another context of the same type, which you can map `R.identity` over to extract its value. Notice that because the value never escapes the wrapper, you can map as many functions as you want to it and transform its value at each step of the way:

```
two.fmap(plus3).fmap(plus10); //-> Wrapper(15)
```

This can be a bit tricky to understand, so figure 5.4 shows how `fmap` works with `plus3`.

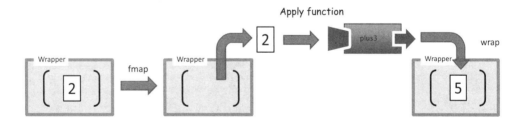

Figure 5.4   The value 2 has been added to a `Wrapper` container. The functor is used to manipulate this value by unwrapping it from the context, applying the given function to it, and rewrapping the value back into a new context.

The purpose of having `fmap` return the same type (or wrap the result again into a container of the same type) is so you can continue chaining operations. Consider the following example, which maps `plus3` on a wrapped value and logs the result.

Listing 5.2   Chaining functors to apply additional behavior to a given context

```
const two = wrap(2);
two.fmap(plus3).fmap(R.tap(infoLogger)); //-> Wrapper(5)
```

Running this code prints the following message on the console:

```
InfoLogger [INFO] 5
```

Does this pattern of chaining functions look familiar? This is intentional: you've been using functors all along without realizing it. This is exactly what the `map` and `filter` functions do for arrays (you can review sections 3.3.2 and 3.3.4 if you need to):

```
map    :: (A -> B)        -> Array(A) -> Array(B)
filter :: (A -> Boolean) -> Array(A) -> Array(A)
```

`map` and `filter` are type-preserving functors, which is what activates the chaining pattern. Consider another functor you've seen all along: `compose`. As you learned in chapter 4, it's a mapping from functions into other functions (also type-preserving):

```
compose :: (B -> C) -> (A -> B) -> (A -> C)
```

Functors, like any other functional programming artifact, are governed by some important properties:

- *They must be side effect–free.* You can map the `R.identity` function to obtain the same value over a context. This proves functors are side effect–free and preserves the structure of the wrapped value:

  ```
  wrap('Get Functional').fmap(R.identity); //-> Wrapper('Get Functional')
  ```

- *They must be composable.* This property indicates that the composition of a function applied to `fmap` should be exactly the same as chaining `fmap` functions together. As a result, the following expression is exactly equivalent to the program in listing 5.2:

  ```
  two.fmap(R.compose(plus3, R.tap(infoLogger))).map(R.identity); //-> 5
  ```

It's no surprise that functors have these requirements. As a result, they're prohibited from throwing exceptions, mutating elements, or altering a function's behavior. Their practical purpose is to create a context or an abstraction that allows you to securely manipulate and apply operations to values without changing any original values. This is evident in the way `map` transforms one array into another without altering the original array; this concept equally translates to any container type.

But functors by themselves aren't compelling, because they're not expected to know how to handle cases with `null` data. Ramda's `R.compose`, for instance, will break if a `null` function reference is passed into it. This isn't a flaw in the design; it's intentional. *Functors map functions of one type to another.* More-specialized behavior can be found in functional data types called *monads*. Among other things, monads can streamline error handling in your code, allowing you to write fluent function compositions. What's their relationship to functors? Monads are the containers that functors "reach into."

Don't let the term *monad* discourage you; if you've written jQuery code, then monads should be familiar. Behind all the complicated rules and theories, the purpose of monads is to provide an abstraction over some resource—whether it's a simple value, a DOM element, an event, or an AJAX call—so that you can safely process the data contained within it. In this respect, you can classify jQuery as a DOM monad:

```
$('#student-info').fadeIn(3000).text(student.fullname());
```

This code behaves like a monad because jQuery is taking charge of applying the `fadeIn` and `text` transformations safely. If the `student-info` panel doesn't exist, applying methods to the empty jQuery object will fail gracefully rather than throw exceptions. Monads aimed at error handling have this powerful quality: safely propagating errors so your application is fault-tolerant. Let's dive into monads next.

5.3   *Functional error handling using monads*

Monads solve all the problems of traditional error handling outlined earlier when applied to functional programs. But before diving into this topic, let's first understand a limitation in the use of functors. As you saw earlier, you can use functors to safely apply functions to values in an immutable and safe manner. But when used throughout your code, functors can easily get you into an uncomfortable situation. Consider an example of fetching a student record by SSN and then extracting its address property. For this task, you can identify two functions—`findStudent` and `getAddress`—both using functor objects to create a safe context around their returned values:

```
const findStudent = R.curry(function(db, ssn) {
   return wrap(find(db, ssn));
});

const getAddress = student =>
  wrap(student.fmap(R.prop('address')));
```

> **Wraps the fetched object to safeguard against the possibility of not finding an object**

> **Maps Ramda's R.prop() function over the object to extract its address, and then wraps the result**

Just as you've done all along, to run this program, you compose both functions together:

```
const studentAddress = R.compose(
    getAddress,
    findStudent(DB('student'))
);
```

Although you avoid all error-handling code, the result isn't what you expect. Instead of a wrapped address object, the returned value is a doubly wrapped address object:

```
studentAddress('444-44-4444'); //-> Wrapper(Wrapper(address))
```

In order to extract this value, you have to apply R.identity twice:

```
studentAddress('444-44-4444').map(R.identity).map(R.identity);    ⟵——— Ugh!
```

Certainly you don't want to access data this way in your code; just think about the case when you have three or four composed functions. You need a better solution. Enter monads.

5.3.1   Monads: from control flow to data flow

Monads are similar to functors, except that they can delegate to special logic when handling certain cases. Let's examine this idea with a quick example. Consider applying a function half :: Number -> Number to any wrapped value, as shown in figure 5.5:

```
Wrapper(2).fmap(half); //-> Wrapper(1)
Wrapper(3).fmap(half); //-> Wrapper(1.5)
```

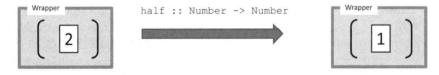

Figure 5.5   Functors apply a function to a wrapped value. In this case, the wrapped value 2 is halved, returning a wrapped value of 1.

But now suppose you want to restrict half to even numbers only. As is, the functor only knows how to apply the given function and close the result back in a wrapper; it has no additional logic. What can you do if you encounter an odd input value? You could return null or throw an exception. But a better strategy is to make this function more honest about how it handles each case and state that it returns a valid number when given the correct input value, or ignores it otherwise.

In the spirit of Wrapper, consider another container called Empty:

```
class Empty
  map(f) {                      noop. Empty doesn't store a
    return this;        ⟵——     value; it represents the concept
  }                             of "empty" or "nothing."

  toString() {
    return 'Empty ()';      ⟵——  Similarly, mapping a
  }                              function to an Empty
};                               skips the operation.

const empty = () => new Empty();
```

With this new requirement, you can implement `half` in the following way (figure 5.6):

```
const isEven = (n) => Number.isFinite(n) && (n % 2 == 0);
const half = (val) => isEven(val) ? wrap(val / 2) : empty();

half(4); //-> Wrapper(2)
half(3); //-> Empty
```

Function half only works on even numbers, returning an empty container otherwise

Helper function distinguishes between odd and even numbers

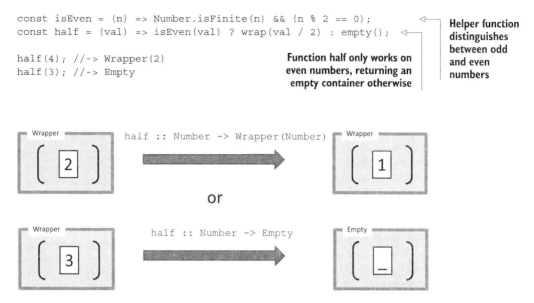

Figure 5.6 Function `half` can return either a wrapped value or an empty container, depending on the nature of the input.

A monad exists when you create a whole data type around this idea of lifting values inside containers and defining the rules of containment. Like functors, it's a design pattern used to describe computations as a sequence of steps without having any knowledge of the value they're operating on. Functors allow you to protect values, but when used with composition, monads are what let you manage data flow in a safe and side effect–free manner. In the previous example, you return an `Empty` container instead of `null` when trying to halve an odd number, which lets you apply operations on values without being concerned about errors that occur:

```
half(4).fmap(plus3); //-> Wrapper(5)
half(3).fmap(plus3); //-> Empty
```

The implicit container knows how to map functions even when input is invalid.

Monads can be targeted at a variety of problems. The ones we'll study in this chapter can be used to consolidate and control the complexity of imperative error-handling mechanisms and, thus, allow you to reason about your code more effectively.

Theoretically, monads are dependent on the type system of a language. In fact, many people advocate that you can only understand them if you have explicit types, as in Haskell. But you'll see that having a typeless language like JavaScript makes monads easy to read and frees you from having to deal with all the intricacies of a static type system.

You need to understand these two important concepts:

- *Monad*—Provides the abstract interface for monadic operations
- *Monadic type*—A particular concrete implementation of this interface

Monadic types share a lot of the same principles as the `Wrapper` object you learned about at the beginning of the chapter. But every monad is different and, depending on its purpose, can define different semantics driving its behavior (that is, for how `map` or `fmap` should work). These types define what it means to chain operations or nest functions of that type together, yet all must abide by the following interface:

- *Type constructor*—Creates monadic types (similar to the `Wrapper` constructor).
- *Unit function*—Inserts a value of a certain type into a monadic structure (similar to the `wrap` and `empty` functions you saw earlier). When implemented in the monad, though, this function is called `of`.
- *Bind function*—Chains operations together (this is a functor's `fmap`, also known as `flatMap`). From here on, I'll use the name `map`, for short. By the way, this bind function has nothing to do with the function-binding concept of chapter 4.
- *Join operation*—Flattens layers of monadic structures into one. This is especially important when you're composing multiple monad-returning functions.

Applying this new interface to the `Wrapper` type, you can refactor it in the following way.

Listing 5.3 Wrapper monad

```
class Wrapper {
  constructor(value) {                          Type
    this._value = value;                        constructor
  }

  static of(a) {                      Unit function
    return new Wrapper(a);
  }

  map(f) {                                      Bind function
    return Wrapper.of(f(this._value));          (the functor)
  }

  join() {                                      Flattens
    if(!(this._value instanceof Wrapper)) {     nested layers
      return this;
    }
    return this._value.join();
  }

  get() {
    return this._value;
  }

  toString() {                                  Returns a textual
    return `Wrapper (${this._value})`;          representation of
  }                                             this structure
}
```

Wrapper uses the functor `map` to lift data into the container so that you can manipulate it side effect–free—walled off from the outside world. Not surprisingly, the `_.iden-tity` function is used to inspect its contents:

```
Wrapper.of('Hello Monads!')
   .map(R.toUpper)
   .map(R.identity); //-> Wrapper('HELLO MONADS!')
```

The `map` operation is considered a *neutral functor* because it does nothing more than map the function and close it. Later, you'll see other monads add their own special touches to `map`. The `join` function is used to flatten nested structures—like peeling an onion. This can be used to eliminate the issues found with functors earlier, as shown next.

Listing 5.4 Flattening a monadic structure

```
// findObject :: DB -> String -> Wrapper
const findObject = R.curry((db, id) => {
   return Wrapper.of(find(db, id));
});

// getAddress :: Student -> Wrapper
const getAddress = student => {
   return Wrapper.of(student.map(R.prop('address')));
};

const studentAddress = R.compose(getAddress, findObject(DB('student')));

studentAddress('444-44-4444').join().get(); // Address
```

Because the composition in listing 5.4 returns a set of nested wrappers, the `join` operation is used to flatten out the structure into a single layer, as in this example:

```
Wrapper.of(Wrapper.of(Wrapper.of('Get Functional'))).join();

//-> Wrapper('Get Functional')
```

Figure 5.7 illustrates the join operation.

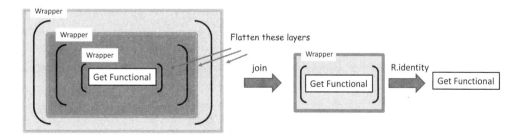

Figure 5.7   Using the `join` operation to recursively flatten a nested monad structure, like peeling an onion

With regard to arrays (which are also containers that can be mapped to), this is analogous to the `R.flatten` operation:

```
R.flatten([1, 2, [3, 4], 5, [6, [7, 8, [9, [10, 11], 12]]]]);

//=> [1, 2, 3, 4, 5, 6, 7, 8, 9, 10, 11, 12]
```

Monads typically have many more operations that support their specific behavior, and this minimal interface is merely a subset of its entire API. A monad itself, though, is abstract and lacks any real meaning. Only when implemented as a concrete type does its power begins to shine. Fortunately, most functional programming code can be implemented with just a few popular concrete types, which eliminates lots of boilerplate code while achieving an immense amount of work. Now, let's look at some full-fledged monads: `Maybe`, `Either`, and `IO`.

5.3.2 Error handling with Maybe and Either monads

In addition to wrapping valid values, monadic structures can also be used to model the absence of one—as `null` or `undefined`. Functional programming *reifies* errors (turns them into a "thing") by using the `Maybe` and `Either` types to do the following:

- Wall off impurity
- Consolidate `null`-check logic
- Avoid exception throwing
- Support compositionally of functions
- Centralize logic for providing default values

Both types provide these benefits in their own way. I'll begin with the `Maybe` monad.

CONSOLIDATING NULL CHECKS WITH MAYBE

The `Maybe` monad focuses on effectively consolidating `null`-check logic. `Maybe` is an empty type (a marker type) with two concrete subtypes:

- `Just(value)`—Represents a container that wraps a defined value.
- `Nothing()`—Represents either a container that has no value or a failure that needs no additional information. In the case of a `Nothing`, you can still apply functions over its (in this case, nonexistent) value.

These subtypes implement all the monadic properties you saw earlier, as well as some additional behavior unique to their purpose. Here's an implementation of `Maybe`.

Listing 5.5 Maybe monad with subclasses `Just` and `Nothing`

```
class Maybe {
  static just(a) {                    Container type
    return new Just(a);               (parent class)
  }

  static nothing() {
    return new Nothing();
  }
```

```
    static fromNullable(a) {
        return a !== null ? Maybe.just(a) : Maybe.nothing();
    }

    static of(a) {
        return just(a);
    }

    get isNothing() {
        return false;
    }

    get isJust() {
        return false;
    }
}

class Just extends Maybe {
    constructor(value) {
        super();
        this._value = value;
    }

    get value() {
        return this._value;
    }

    map(f) {
        return Maybe.fromNullable(f(this._value));
    }

    getOrElse() {
        return this._value;
    }

    filter(f) {
        Maybe.fromNullable(f(this._value) ? this._value : null);
    }

    chain(f) {
        return f(this._value);
    }

    toString () {
        return `Maybe.Just(${this._value})`;
    }
}

class Nothing extends Maybe {

    map(f) {
     return this;
    }

    get value()  {
      throw new TypeError("Can't extract the value
        of a Nothing.");
    }
```

Builds a Maybe from a nullable type (constructor function). If the value lifted in the monad is null, instantiates a Nothing; otherwise, stores the value in a Just subtype to handle the presence of a value.

Subtype Just to handle the presence of a value

Maps a function to Just, transforms its value, and stores it back into the container

Extracts the value from the structure or a provided default monad unity operation

Returns a textual representation of this structure

Subtype Nothing to protect against the absence of a value

Attempting to extract a value from a Nothing type generates an exception indicating a bad use of the monad (I'll discuss this shortly); otherwise, the value is returned.

```
  getOrElse(other) {
    return other;                          Ignores the value and
  }                                         returns the other

  filter(f) {
    return this._value;                    If a value is present and matches
  }                                         the given predicate, returns a
                                            Just describing the value;
  chain(f) {                               otherwise returns a Nothing
    return this;
  }

  toString() {
    return 'Maybe.Nothing';                Returns a textual
  }                                         representation of
}                                           this structure
```

Maybe explicitly abstracts working with "nullable" values (null and undefined) so you're free to worry about more important things. As you can see, Maybe is basically an abstract umbrella object for the concrete monadic structures Just and Nothing, each containing its own implementations of the monadic properties. I mentioned earlier that the implementation for the behavior of the monadic operations ultimately depends on the semantics imparted by a concrete type. For instance, map behaves differently depending on whether the type is a Nothing or a Just. Visually, a Maybe structure can store a student object as shown in figure 5.8:

```
// findStudent :: String -> Maybe(Student)
function findStudent(ssn)
```

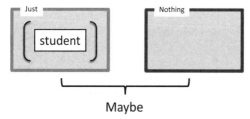

Figure 5.8 A Maybe structure has two subtypes: Just and Nothing. Calling findStudent returns its value wrapped in Just or the absence of a value in Nothing.

This monad is frequently used with calls that contain uncertainty: querying a database, looking up values in a collection, requesting data from the server, and so on. Let's continue with the example started in listing 5.4 of extracting the address property of a student object that's fetched from a local store. Because a record may or may not exist, you wrap the result of the fetch in a Maybe and add the safe prefix to these operations:

```
// safeFindObject :: DB -> String -> Maybe
const safeFindObject = R.curry((db, id) => {
    return Maybe.fromNullable(find(db, id));
});
```

```
// safeFindStudent :: String -> Maybe(Student)
const safeFindStudent = safeFindObject(DB('student'));

const address = safeFindStudent('444-44-4444').map(R.prop('address'));
address; //-> Just(Address(...)) or Nothing
```

Another benefit of wrapping results with monads is that it embellishes the function signature, making it self-documented and honest about the uncertainty of its return value. `Maybe.fromNullable` is useful because it handles the `null`-checking on your behalf. Calling `safeFindStudent` will produce a `Just(Address(...))` if it encounters a valid value or a `Nothing` otherwise. Mapping `R.prop` over the monad behaves as expected. In addition, it does a good job of detecting programmatic errors or misuses of an API call: you can use it to enforce preconditions indicating whether parameters are permitted to be invalid. If an invalid value is passed into `Maybe.fromNullable`, it produces a `Nothing` type, such that calling `get()` to open the container will throw an exception:

```
TypeError: Can't extract the value of a Nothing.
```

Monads expect you to stick to mapping functions over them instead of directly extracting their contents. Another useful operation of `Maybe` is `getOrElse` as an alternative to returning default values. Consider the example of setting the value of a form field, or a generic default in case there's no data to set:

```
const userName = findStudent('444-44-4444').map(R.prop('firstname'));

document.querySelector('#student-firstname').value =
    username.getOrElse('Enter first name');
```

If the fetch operation is successful, the student's username is displayed; otherwise, the `else` branch executes printing the default string.

Maybe in disguise

You may see `Maybe` appear in different forms such as the `Optional` or `Option` type, used in languages like Java 8 and Scala. Instead of `Just` and `Nothing`, these languages declare `Some` and `None`. Semantically, though, they do the same things.

Now let's revisit the pessimistic `null`-check anti-pattern shown earlier that rears its ugly head frequently in object-oriented software. Consider the `getCountry` function:

```
function getCountry(student) {
   let school = student.school();
   if(school !== null) {
      let addr = school.address();
      if(addr !== null) {
         return addr.country();
      }
   }
}
```

```
    return 'Country does not exist!';
}
```

What a drag. If the function returns `'Country does not exist!'`, which statement caused the failure? In this code, it's hard to discern which line is the problematic one. When you write code like this, you aren't paying attention to style and correctness; you're defensively patching function calls. Without monadic traits, you're basically stuck with `null` checks sprinkled all over the place to prevent `TypeError` exceptions. The `Maybe` structure encapsulates this behavior in a reusable manner. Consider this example:

```
const country = R.compose(getCountry, safeFindStudent);
```

Because `safeFindStudent` returns a wrapped student object, you can eliminate this defensive programming habit and safely propagate the invalid value. Here's the new `getCountry`:

```
const getCountry = (student) => student
        .map(R.prop('school'))
        .map(R.prop('address'))
        .map(R.prop('country'))
          .getOrElse('Country does not exist!');
```

If any of the steps yields a Nothing result, all subsequent operations will be skipped.

In the event that any of these properties returns `null`, this error is propagated through all the layers as a `Nothing`, so that all subsequent operations are gracefully skipped. The program is not only declarative and elegant, but also fault-tolerant.

Function lifting

Look closely at this function:

```
const safeFindObject = R.curry((db, id) => {
   return Maybe.fromNullable(find(db, id));
});
```

Notice that its name is prefixed with `safe` and it uses a monad directly to wrap its return value. This is a good practice because you make it clear to the caller that the function is housing a potentially dangerous value. Does this mean you need to instrument every function in your program with monads? Not necessarily. A technique called *function lifting* can transform any ordinary function into a function that works on a container, making it "safe." It can be a handy utility so that you aren't obligated to change your existing implementations:

```
const lift = R.curry((f, value) => {
   return Maybe.fromNullable(value).map(f);
});
```

> Instead of directly using the monad in the body of the function, you can keep it as is
>
> ```
> const findObject = R.curry((db, id) => {
>     return find(db, id);
> });
> ```
>
> and use `lift` to bring this function into the container:
>
> ```
> const safeFindObject = R.compose(lift(console.log), findObject);
> safeFindObject(DB('student'), '444-44-4444');
> ```
>
> Lifting can work with any function on any monad!

Clearly, `Maybe` excels at centrally managing checks for invalid data, but it provides `Nothing` (pun intended) with regard to what went wrong. We need a more proactive solution—one that can let us know the cause of the failure. For this, the best tool to use is the `Either` monad.

RECOVERING FROM FAILURE WITH EITHER

`Either` is slightly different from `Maybe`. `Either` is a structure that represents a logical separation between two values a and b that would never occur at the same time. This type models two cases:

- `Left(a)`—Contains a possible error message or throwable exception object
- `Right(b)`—Contains a successful value

`Either` is typically implemented with a bias on the right operand, which means mapping a function over a container is always performed on the `Right(b)` subtype. It's analogous to the `Just` branch of `Maybe`.

A common use of `Either` is to hold the results of a computation that may fail to provide additional information as to what the failure is. In unrecoverable cases, the left can contain the proper exception object to throw. The following listing shows the implementation of the `Either` monad.

Listing 5.6 Either monad with Left and Right subclasses

```
class Either {
  constructor(value) {                    ◁──┐  Constructor function for
    this._value = value;                       either type. This can hold
  }                                             an exception or a successful
                                                value (right bias).
  get value() {
    return this._value;
  }

  static left(a) {
    return new Left(a);
  }
}
```

```
  static right(a) {
    return new Right(a);
  }
```
**Takes the Left case
with an invalid value,
or else the Right**
```
  static fromNullable(val) {
    return val !== null && val !== undefined ? Either.right(val) :
    Either.left(val);
  }
```
```
  static of(a){
    return Either.right(a);
  }
}
```
**Creates a new
instance holding a
value on the Right**
```
class Left extends Either {
```
**Transforms the value on the Right
structure by mapping a function to
it; does nothing on the Left**
```
  map(_) {
   return this; // noop
  }
```
```
  get value() {
    throw new TypeError("Can't extract the
      value of a Left(a).");
  }
```
**Extracts the Right value of the
structure if it exists; otherwise,
produces a TypeError**
```
  getOrElse(other) {
    return other;
  }
```
**Extracts the Right value; if
it doesn't have one, returns
the given default**
```
  orElse(f) {
    return f(this._value);
  }
```
**Applies a given function to a Left
value; does nothing on the Right**
```
  chain(f) {
    return this;
  }
```
**Applies a function to a Right and
returns that value; does nothing on
the Left. This is the first time you
encounter chain (explained later).**
```
  getOrElseThrow(a) {
    throw new Error(a);
  }
```
**Throws an exception with the value only
on the Left structure; otherwise, ignores
the exception and returns the valid value**
```
  filter(f) {
    return this;
  }
```
**If a value is present and meets the given
predicate, returns a Right describing the
value; otherwise returns an empty Left**
```
  toString() {
   return `Either.Left(${this._value})`;
  }
 }
```
```
class Right extends Either {
   map(f) {
      return Either.of(f(this._value));
   }
```
**Transforms the value on the Right
structure by mapping a function to
it; does nothing on the Left**
```
   getOrElse(other) {
      return this._value;
   }
```
**Extracts the Right value; if
it doesn't have one, returns
the given default**

```
        orElse() {
            return this;
        }

        chain(f) {
            return f(this._value);
        }

        getOrElseThrow(_) {
            return this._value;
        }

        filter(f) {
            return Either.fromNullable(f(this._value) ? this._value : null);
        }

        toString() {
            return `Either.Right(${this._value})`;
        }
    }
```

If a value is present and meets the given predicate, returns a Right describing the value; otherwise returns an empty Left

Applies a given function to a Left value; does nothing on the Right

Applies a function to a Right and returns that value; does nothing on the Left. This is the first time you encounter chain (explained later).

Throws an exception with the value only on the Left structure; otherwise, ignores the exception and returns the valid value

Notice in both the `Maybe` and `Either` types that some operations are empty (no-op). These are deliberate and are meant to act as placeholders that allow functions to safely skip execution when the specific monad deems appropriate.

Now, let's put `Either` to use. This monad offers another alternative for the `safeFindObject` function:

```
const safeFindObject = R.curry((db, id) => {
    const obj = find(db, id);
    if(obj) {
        return Either.of(obj);
    }
    return Either.left(`Object not found with ID: ${id}`);
});
```

Could also use Either.fromNullable() to abstract the entire if-else statement. I did it this way for illustration purposes.

The Left structure can hold values as well.

If the data access operation is successful, a student object is stored in the right side (biased to the right); otherwise, an error message is provided on the left, as shown in figure 5.9.

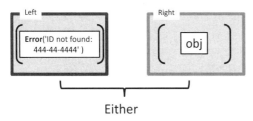

Left — Error('ID not found: 444-44-4444')

Right — obj

Either

Figure 5.9 An `Either` structure can store an object (on the right) or an `Error` (on the left) with proper stack trace information. This is useful to provide a single return value that can also contain an error message in case of failure.

Let's pause for a second. You may be wondering, "Why not use the 2-tuple (or a `Pair` type discussed in chapter 4 to capture the object and a message?" There's a subtle reason. Tuples represent what's known as a *product type*, which implies a logical AND relationship among its operands. In the case of error handling, it's more appropriate to use mutually exclusive types to model the case of a value either existing OR not; in the case of error handling, both could not exist simultaneously.

With `Either`, you can extract the result by calling `getOrElse` (providing a suitable default just in case):

```
const findStudent = safeFindObject(DB('student'));
findStudent('444-44-4444').getOrElse(new Student()); //->Right(Student)
```

Unlike the `Maybe.Nothing` structure, the `Either.Left` structure can contain values to which functions can be applied. If `findStudent` doesn't return an object, you can use the `orElse` function on the `Left` operand to log the error:

```
const errorLogger = _.partial(logger, 'console', 'basic', 'MyErrorLogger',
    'ERROR');
findStudent('444-44-4444').orElse(errorLogger);
```

This prints to the console:

```
MyErrorLogger [ERROR] Student not found with ID: 444-44-4444
```

The `Either` structure can also be used to guard your code against unpredictable functions (implemented by you or someone else) that may throw exceptions. This makes your functions more type-safe and side effect–free by eliminating the exception early on instead of propagating it. Consider an example using JavaScript's `decodeURI-Component` function, which can produce a URI error if it's invalid:

```
function decode(url) {
   try {
      const result = decodeURIComponent(url);        ◁——  Throws a
      return Either.of(result);                             URIError.
   }
   catch (uriError) {
      return Either.Left(uriError);
   }
}
```

As shown in this code, it's also customary to populate `Either.Left` with an error object that contains stack trace information as well as an error message; this object can be thrown if necessary to signal an unrecoverable operation. Suppose you want to navigate to a given URL that needs to be decoded first. Here's the function invoked with invalid and valid input:

```
const parse = (url) => url.parseUrl();                   ◁——  This function
decode('%').map(parse); //-> Left(Error('URI malformed'))     was created in
decode('http%3A%2F%2Fexample.com').map(parse);               section 4.4.1.
//-> Right(true)
```

Functional programming leads to avoiding ever having to throw exceptions. Instead, you can use this monad for lazy exception throwing by storing the exception object into the left structure. Only when the left structure is unpacked does the exception take place:

```
...

catch (uriError) {
    return Either.Left(uriError);
}
```

Now you've learned how monads help emulate a `try-catch` mechanism that contains potentially hazardous function calls. Scala implements a similar notion using a type called `Try`—the functional alternative to `try-catch`. Although not fully a monad, `Try` represents a computation they may either result in an exception or return a fully computed value. It's semantically equivalent to `Either`, and it involves two cases classes for `Success` and `Failure`.

> **Functional programming projects worth exploring**
>
> Most of the topics explored in this and the previous chapter, such as partial application, tuples, composition, functors, and monads, as well as other topics presented later, are implemented as modules in a formal specification called Fantasy Land (https://github.com/fantasyland). Fantasy Land is a reference implementation of functional concepts that defines how to implement a functional algebra in JavaScript. We've been using libraries like Lodash and Ramda for their ease of use; nevertheless, Fantasy Land and a functional library called Folktale (http://folktalejs.org/) are worth exploring if you're eager to get deep into more-functional data types.

Monads can help you cope with uncertainty and possibilities for failure in real-world software. But how do you interact with the outside world?

5.3.3 Interacting with external resources using the IO monad

Haskell is believed to be the only programming language that relies heavily on monads for IO operations: file read/writes, writing to the screen, and so on. You can translate that to JavaScript with code that looks like this:

```
IO.of('An unsafe operation').map(alert);
```

Although this is a simple example, you can see intricacies of IO tucked into lazy monadic operations that are passed to the platform to execute (in this case, a simple alert message). But JavaScript unavoidably needs to be able to interact with the ever-changing, shared, stateful DOM. As a result, any operation performed on the DOM, whether read or write, causes side effects and violates referential transparency. Let's begin with most basic IO operations:

```
const read = (document, selector) => {
   return document.querySelector(selector).innerHTML;
};

const write = (document, selector, val) => {
   document.querySelector(selector).innerHTML = val;
   return val;
};
```

Subsequent calls to read may yield different results.

Doesn't return a value, and clearly causes mutations to happen (unsafe operation).

When executed independently, the output of these standalone functions can never be guaranteed. Not only does order of execution matter, but, for instance, calling `read` multiple times can yield different responses if the DOM was modified between calls by another call to `write`. Remember, the main reason for isolating impure behavior from pure code, as you did in chapter 4 with `showStudent`, is to always guarantee a consistent result.

You can't avoid mutations or fix the problem with side effects, but you can at least work with IO operations as if they were immutable from the application point of view. This can be done by lifting IO operations into monadic chains and letting the monad drive the flow of data. To do so, you can use the IO monad.

Listing 5.7   IO monad

```
class IO {
   constructor(effect) {
      if (!_.isFunction(effect)) {
         throw 'IO Usage: function required';
      }
      this.effect = effect;
   }

   static of(a) {
      return new IO( () => a );
   }

   static from(fn) {
      return new IO(fn);
   }

   map(fn) {
      let self = this;
      return new IO(() => fn(self.effect()));
   }

   chain(fn) {
      return fn(this.effect());
   }
}
```

The IO constructor is initialized with a read/write operation (like reading or writing to the DOM). This operation is also known as the effect function.

Unit functions to lift values and functions into the IO monad

Map functor

```
    run() {
        return this.effect();
    }
}
```

> Kicks off the lazily initialized
> chain to perform the IO

This monad works differently than the others, because it wraps an *effect* function instead of a value; remember, a function can be thought of as a *lazy value*, if you will, waiting to be computed. With this monad, you can chain together any DOM operations to be executed in a single "pseudo" referentially transparent operation and ensure that side effect–causing functions don't run out of order or between calls.

Before I show you this, let's refactor `read` and `write` as manually curried functions:

```
const read = (document, selector) => {
  return () => {
    return document.querySelector(selector).innerHTML;
  };
};

const write = (document, selector) => {
  return (val) => {
    document.querySelector(selector).innerHTML = val;
    return val;
  };
};
```

And in order to avoid passing the `document` object around, make life easier and partially apply it to these functions:

```
const readDom = _.partial(read, document);
const writeDom = _.partial(write, document);
```

With this change, both `readDom` and `writeDom` become chainable (and composable) functions awaiting execution. You do this in order to chain these IO operations together later. Consider a simple example that reads a student's name from an HTML element and changes it to start-case (capitalize the first letter of each word):

```
<div id="student-name">alonzo church</div>

const changeToStartCase =
    IO.from(readDom('#student-name'))
        .map(_.startCase)
        .map(writeDom('#student-name'));
```

> You can map any
> transformation
> operation here.

Writing to the DOM, the last operation in the chain, isn't pure. So what do you expect the `changeToStartCase` output to be? The nice thing about using monads is that you preserve the requirements imposed by pure functions. Just like any other monad, the output from `map` is the monad itself, an instance of `IO`, which means at this stage nothing has been executed yet. What you have here is a declarative description of an IO operation. Finally, let's run this code:

```
changeToStartCase.run();
```

Inspecting the DOM, you'll see this:

```
<div id="student-name">Alonzo Church</div>
```

There you have it: IO operations in a referentially transparent-ish way! The most important benefit of the IO monad is that it clearly separates the pure and impure parts. As you can see in the definition of `changeToStartCase`, the transformation functions that map over the IO container are completely isolated from the logic of reading and writing to the DOM. You can transform the contents of the HTML element as needed. Also, because it all executes in one shot, you guarantee that nothing else will happen between the read and write operations, which can lead to unpredictable results.

Monads are nothing more than chainable expressions or chainable computations. This allows you to build sequences that apply additional processing at each step—like a conveyor belt in an assembly line. But chaining operations isn't the only modality where monads are used. Using monadic containers as return types creates consistent, type-safe return values for functions and preserves referential transparency. Recall from chapter 4 that this satisfies the requirement for composing function chains and compositions.

5.4 *Monadic chains and compositions*

As you can see, monads bring the world of side effects under control, so you can use them in composable structures. As you know from chapter 4, compositionality is the trick to reducing complexity in your code. But in chapter 4, you hadn't bothered to check for invalid data: if `findStudent` had returned `null`, the entire program would have failed, as shown in figure 5.10.

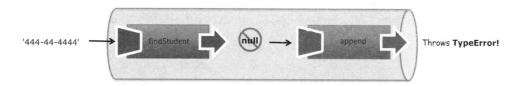

Figure 5.10 Functions `findStudent` and append are being composed. Without the proper checks, if the former produces a `null` return value, the latter will fail with a `TypeError` exception.

Fortunately, with little code, monads can also be made composable so that you can enjoy their fluent, expressive error-handling mechanism to create safe compositions. Wouldn't it be nice if functions arranged in a pipeline gracefully sidestepped null mines?

As you can see in figure 5.11, the first step is to make sure the first function to be executed wraps its result in a proper monad: both `Maybe` and `Either` work in this case.

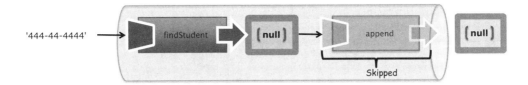

Figure 5.11 Same two functions as in figure 5.10; but this time the `null` value travels in a monad (`Either` or `Maybe`), which causes the rest of the functions in the pipeline to gracefully fail.

As you know, there are two variations for combining functions in functional programming: chain and compose. Recall that `showStudent` from the previous chapter had three parts:

1 Normalize user input
2 Find the student record
3 Add the student information to the HTML page

You're also adding input validation to the mix to make it even more complex. Hence, this program has two points of failure: a validation error and an unsuccessful student-fetch operation. You can refactor them to include the `Either` monad to supply appropriate error messages, as shown next.

Listing 5.8 Refactoring functions to use `Either`

```
// validLength :: Number, String -> Boolean
const validLength = (len, str) => str.length === len;

// checkLengthSsn :: String -> Either(String)
const checkLengthSsn = ssn => {
    return Either.of(ssn)
      .filter(R.partial(validLength, [9]));
};

// safeFindObject :: Store, string -> Either(Object)
const safeFindObject = R.curry((db, id) => {
  return Either.fromNullable(find(db, id));
});

// finStudent :: String -> Either(Student)
const findStudent = safeFindObject(DB('students'));

// csv :: Array => String
const csv = arr => arr.join(',');
```

Instead of lifting these functions into an Either, you can use the monad directly and provide specific error messages depending on the error.

Refactored csv function returns a string from an array of values

Because these functions are curried, you can partially evaluate them to create simpler ones, as you did before, as well as add some helper logging functions:

```
const debugLog = _.partial(logger, 'console', 'basic',
    'Monad Example', 'TRACE');

const errorLog = _.partial(logger, 'console', 'basic',
    'Monad Example', 'ERROR');

const trace = R.curry((msg, val) => debugLog(msg + ':' + val));
```

And that's it! The monadic operations take care of the rest and ensure that the data travels through the function calls at no additional cost. Let's look at how you can use `Either` and `Maybe` to add automatic error handling to `showStudent`.

Listing 5.9 `showStudent` using monads for automatic error handling

```
const showStudent = (ssn) =>
    Maybe.fromNullable(ssn)
        .map  (cleanInput)
        .chain(checkLengthSsn)
        .chain(findStudent)
        .map  (R.props(['ssn', 'firstname', 'lastname']))
        .map  (csv)
        .map  (append('#student-info'));
```

Methods map and chain can be used to transform the value in the monad. Map returns a monad; to avoid nesting and having to flatten the structure, weave map with chain to keep a single monad level flowing through the calls.

Extracts the selected properties from an object as an array

Listing 5.9 shows the use of the `chain` method. This is nothing more than a shortcut to avoid having to use `join` after `map` to flatten the layers resulting from combining monad-returning functions. Like `map`, `chain` applies a function to the data without wrapping the result back into the monad type.

Also, notice how both monads interleave seamlessly. This is because both `Either` and `Maybe` implement the same monadic interface. Now, calling

```
showStudent('444-44-4444').orElse(errorLog);
```

generates two results: if the student object is successfully found, it appends the student information to the HTML as expected and returns:

```
Monad Example [INFO] Either.Right('444-44-4444, Alonzo,Church')
```

Otherwise, it skips the entire operation gracefully and uses the `orElse` clause:

```
Monad Example [ERROR] Student not found with ID: 444444444
```

Chaining isn't the only pattern; you can easily introduce error-handling logic with `compose`. To do this, you perform the simple object-oriented-to-functional transform you've seen before to convert monad methods into functions that polymorphically work across any monad type (following from the Liskov Substitution Principle). In particular, you can create generalized `map` and `chain` functions, shown in the following listing.

```
// map :: (ObjectA -> ObjectB), Monad -> Monad[ObjectB]
const map = R.curry((f, container) => {
    return container.map(f);
});

// chain :: (ObjectA -> ObjectB), Monad -> ObjectB
const chain = R.curry((f, container) => {
    return container.chain(f);
});
```

You can use these functions to inject monads into a compose expression. The code in listing 5.11 produces the same results as listing 5.9. Because monads control how data flows from one expression to the next, this style of coding is also known as *programmable commas*, which is also point-free. In this case, a comma is used to delimit one expression from another in the same way a semicolon traditionally delineates one statement from the next in JavaScript. Also, using lots of `trace` statements lets you see the data flowing through the operations (logging statements are useful for debugging, as well).

```
const showStudent = R.compose(
    R.tap(trace('Student added to HTML page'))
    map(append('#student-info')),
    R.tap(trace('Student info converted to CSV')),
    map(csv),
    map(R.props(['ssn', 'firstname', 'lastname'])),
    R.tap(trace('Record fetched successfully!')),
    chain(findStudent),
    R.tap(trace('Input was valid')),
    chain(checkLengthSsn),
    lift(cleanInput));
```

Running the code prints the following log messages on the console:

```
Monad Example [TRACE] Input was valid:Either.Right(444444444)

Monad Example [TRACE] Record fetched successfully!: Either.Right(Person
[firstname: Alonzo| lastname: Church])

Monad Example [TRACE] Student converted to CSV: Either.Right(444-44-4444,
Alonzo, Church)

Monad Example [TRACE] Student added to HTML page: Either.Right(1)
```

Tracing through programs

Listing 5.11 demonstrates how easy it is to trace through functional code. Without having to drill into the body of those functions, you can demarcate an entire program with tracing statements that execute before and after function calls, which is incredibly useful for troubleshooting and debugging. If this program were written in an object-oriented style, you couldn't possibly do this without having to modify the actual functions or perhaps instrument them using aspect-oriented programming, which isn't a trivial endeavor. Functional programming gives you this for free!

Finally, let's diagram this entire flow to clearly see what's going on; see figure 5.12. Figure 5.13 shows the behavior of this same program in the event that findStudent is unsuccessful.

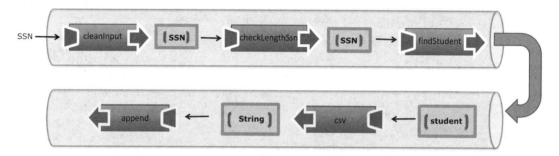

Figure 5.12 Step-by-step flow of the showStudent function in the case where findStudent successfully finds a student object by the provided SSN

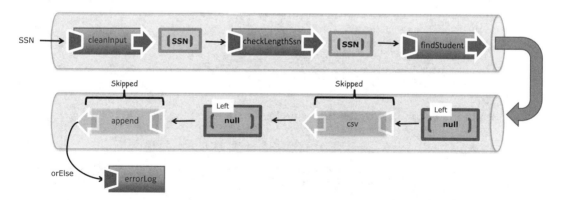

Figure 5.13 The case of an unsuccessful findStudent as it affects the rest of the composition. Regardless of the failure of any of the components in the pipeline, the program remains fault-tolerant and gracefully skips any procedures that depended on the data.

You may be wondering if you're finally done with showStudent. Not quite. From the discussion of the IO monad, now you know you can improve the code that deals with DOM reads and writes:

```
map(append('#student-info')),
```

Because append has automatic currying, it'll work well with IO. All you need to do at this point is lift the value from csv, extract its content by mapping the R.identity function into IO using IO.of, and then proceed with chaining both operations:

```
const liftIO = function (val) {
   return IO.of(val);
};
```

This produces the following program.

Listing 5.12 Complete showStudent program

```
const showStudent = R.compose(
   map(append('#student-info')),
   liftIO,
   map(csv),
   map(R.props(['ssn', 'firstname', 'lastname'])),
   chain(findStudent),
   chain(checkLengthSsn),
   lift(cleanInput));
```

Incorporating the IO monad allows you to achieve something truly amazing. You see, running showStudent(ssn) now runs through all the logic of validating and fetching the student record, as it should. Once this completes, the program waits on you to write this data to the screen. Because you've lifted the data into an IO monad, you need to call its run function for the data that's lazily contained within it (in its closure) to be flushed out to the screen:

```
showStudent(studentId).run(); //-> 444-44-4444, Alonzo, Church
```

A common pattern that occurs with IO is to tuck the impure operation toward the end of the composition. This lets you build programs one step at a time, perform all the necessary business logic, and finally deliver the data on a silver platter for the IO monad to finish the job, declaratively and side effect–free.

   Just to show how functional programming makes code easier to reason about, for the sake of comparison (apologies for reviving some ugly code), let's bring back the equivalent nonfunctional version of showStudent:

```
function showStudent(ssn) {
    if(ssn != null) {
        ssn = ssn.replace(/^\s*|\-|\s*$/g, '');
        if(ssn.length !== 9) {
            throw new Error('Invalid Input');
        }
```

```
        let student = db.get(ssn);
        if (student) {
            document.querySelector(`#${elementId}`).innerHTML =
                `${student.ssn},
                 ${student.firstname},
                 ${student.lastname}`;
        }
        else {
            throw new Error('Student not found!');
        }
    }
    else {
        throw new Error('Invalid SSN!');
    }
}
```

Due to side effects, lack of modularity, and imperative error handling, this program is difficult to use and test; we'll examine this more closely in the next chapter. Whereas composition controls program flow, monads control data flow. Both are possibly the most important concepts in the functional programming ecosystem.

This chapter completes part 2 of the book. Your developer toolbox is equipped with all the functional concepts you need to take on real-world solutions.

5.5   *Summary*

- Exception-throwing mechanisms in object-oriented code result in impure functions that impose a great deal of responsibility on the caller to provide adequate try-catch logic.
- The pattern of value containerization is used to create side effect–free code by wrapping possible mutations under a single referentially transparent process.
- Use functors to map functions to containers in order to access and modify objects in a side effect–free and immutable manner.
- Monads are a functional programming design pattern used to reduce an application's complexity by orchestrating a secure flow of data through functions.
- Resilient and robust function compositions interleave monadic types such as Maybe, Either, and IO.

Part 3

Enhancing your functional skills

Parts 1 and 2 of this book taught you about the tools you need to apply functional programming to solve real-world scenarios. You learned new techniques and design patterns, all targeted at eliminating side effects so you can write code that's modular, extensible, and easy to reason about. In this part of the book, you'll use this learning to tackle the challenges of unit testing JavaScript applications, optimizing your code under the functional umbrella, and handling the complexities of dealing with asynchronous events and data.

Chapter 6 focuses on unit testing imperative applications and why FP is inherently testable and less complex. Achieving referential transparency also leads to an automated testing modality called *property-based testing*.

Chapter 7 explores the inner workings of JavaScript's function context as well as the performance considerations that must be taken into account when using deeply nested function closures and recursion. To improve overall application performance, you'll learn about lazy evaluation, memoization, and tail-call optimization.

Finally, in chapter 8, you'll learn more monadic design patterns to combat the increasing complexity of applications. This chapter focuses specifically on two frequent JavaScript tasks: fetching data asynchronously from a server or a database using promises, and cutting down on traditional function callbacks of event-driven programs by approaching them from a reactive mindset using RxJS.

After reading through this entire book, you should be equipped to become successful at applying functional programming techniques during your professional endeavors.

Bulletproofing your code

6

Good fences make good neighbors

—Robert Frost, "Mending Wall"

Welcome to part 3 of this book. Having read parts 1 and 2, you'll have noticed a central theme: functional programming makes your code easier to understand, read, and maintain. You can even say its declarative nature makes your code self-documented.

Now that you've written functional code, how do you prove that it works? In other words, how do you ensure that it meets the specifications laid out by your customers? The only way is to write code that tests whether the resulting behavior is as expected. Thinking functionally has a deep impact on application-level code and, through it, directly influences the way you design your tests.

You create unit tests to ensure that code meets a problem specification and builds fences around all possible boundary conditions that may cause it to fail. I assume you've written unit tests before; you've likely experienced that testing imperative programs can be a daunting effort, especially in large code bases. Due to side effects, imperative code is susceptible to errors originating from false assumptions about the global state of the system. Likewise, tests can't run independently of others, as they should, making it difficult to guarantee consistent results regardless of the order in which they're called. This is unfortunate and is the main reason testing is often left until the end or, in most cases, skipped.

In this chapter, we'll look at why functional code is by definition inherently testable, whereas in most other paradigms, you must intentionally design your code to make it easy to test. Most of the best practices associated with proper testing—eliminating external dependencies, making functions predictable, and others—are core principles embedded in functional design. Pure, referentially transparent functions have this quality built into them for free and lend themselves to a more advanced method such as property-based testing. Before we begin, let's take a moment to understand the influence FP has on the different types of tests and focus on where it will help you be the most productive: unit tests.

6.1   *Functional programming's influence on unit tests*

Generally, there are three testing categories: unit tests, integration tests, and acceptance tests. The testing pyramid in figure 6.1 shows that the influence of FP on your code is greater as you move from acceptance tests (top) to unit tests (bottom). This is evident because functional programming is a software-development paradigm that focuses on the design of functions and modules as well as the integration among its constituent parts.

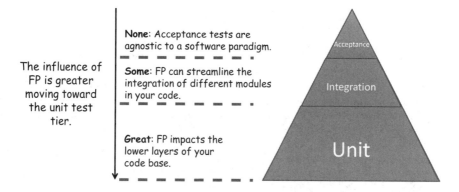

Figure 6.1   Because functional programming is a software paradigm with focus on code, its influence mostly impacts the design of unit tests, with little effect on integration tests. It's completely agnostic to acceptance testing.

Although important, testing the user's acceptance criteria with regard to look and feel, usability, and navigability of your web application is distanced from the code and thus has little or nothing to do with whether your program is written functionally or imperatively. This task is better suited to test-automation frameworks. With regard to integration tests, as you saw in chapter 4, FP cedes control of the orchestration of the different components of your application to composition, which you know to work without question. So part of the time spent in integration tests is given back to you for free just by adopting FP as a paradigm.

The real focus of functional programming is on functions—the units of modularity in your code—and the interactions among them. The test-runner library of choice for this book is the popular QUnit. I won't cover setting up testing libraries; if you've set up any unit test library before, QUnit will be simple to get up and running. See this book's appendix for more details.

Here's the basic structure of a single unit test:

```
QUnit.test('Test Find Person', function(assert) {
  const ssn = '444-44-4444';
  const p = findPerson(ssn);
  assert.equal(p.ssn, ssn);
});
```

The test code lives in a JavaScript file that's not part of the main application code but imports all the functions that will be tested. Unit testing imperative programs is extremely challenging due to the presence of side effects and mutations. Let's examine some of the downfalls of testing imperative code.

6.2 Challenges of testing imperative programs

Imperative tests suffer from the same challenges as imperative code. Because imperative code is based on global state and mutations, rather than contained data flow and joined computations, testing is a real challenge. One of the main principles to follow when designing unit tests is *isolation*. A unit test should run as if in a vacuum and ignorant of any other data or tests around it; but side effects in the code severely limit the extent to which you can test functions.

Imperative code is

- Difficult to identify and decompose into simple tasks
- Dependent on shared resources that make test results inconsistent
- Forced to a predefined order of evaluation

Let's examine some of these challenges more closely.

6.2.1 Difficulty identifying and decomposing tasks

Unit tests are designed to test the smallest parts of your application. In procedural programs, it's much harder to identify the *units of modularity* because there's no intuitive way to slice the different sections of a single, monolithic program that wasn't designed with that mindset to begin with. In this case, the *units are functions* that encapsulate your business logic. For example, recall the imperative version of show-Student that you've been working on throughout the book. Figure 6.2 shows a good attempt to slice it into its constituent parts.

```
function showStudent(ssn) {
   if(ssn !== null) {
      ssn = ssn.replace(/^\s*|\-|\s*$/g, '');
      if(ssn.length !== 9) {
         throw new Error('Invalid input');          1| Validation
      }

      var student = db.get(ssn);                     2| Storage IO write

      if (student !== null) {
         var info =
            `${student.ssn},
             ${student.firstname},
             ${student.lastname}`;
         document.querySelector(`\#${elementId}`)    3| DOM IO
            .innerHTML = info;
         return info;
      }
      else {
         throw new Error('Student not found!');       4| Error handling
      }
   }
   else {
      return null;
   }
}
```

Figure 6.2 The functional sections of the monolithic function showStudent. To simplify writing tests, these sections should be split into separate functions that deal with validation, IO, and error handling.

As you can see, this program is made up of tightly coupled business logic that's concerned with different aspects of a program, all in a single monolithic function. But there's no real reason to couple data validation with fetching student records and appending elements to the DOM; those can be separate testable business units that are assembled via composition. In addition, as you learned in chapter 5, you should factor out error-handling logic and allow monads to handle it.

Monads and error handling

In chapter 5, you learned about a few design patterns that you can apply to consolidate and remove error-handling code from your main functions while still keeping them fault-tolerant. By using the monads Maybe and Either, you can write point-free code that knows how to properly propagate errors through the components while making sure your program remains responsive.

In order to widen the testable scope of this function, you need to find ways to split it into loosely coupled components that segregate the pure from the impure. Impure code is difficult to test due to the presence of side effects that can occur when reading and writing to external resources such as the DOM or external storage.

6.2.2 *Dependency on shared resources leads to inconsistent results*

In chapter 2, I talked about JavaScript's unwieldy freedom to access globally shared data. Testing programs with side effects requires extreme care and discipline because you're responsible for managing the state around the function under test. I've seen too many cases where adding a new test to a working test suite causes other unrelated tests to inadvertently fail. Why is this? In order for tests to be reliable, they must be self-contained or independent from the rest, which means each unit test essentially runs in its own sandbox, leaving the system in exactly the same state as it was found. Tests that break this rule can never consistently produce the same outcomes.

I'll use a simple example to illustrate. Recall the imperative `increment` function:

```
var counter = 0;  // (global)

function increment() {
    return ++counter;
}
```

You can write a simple unit test to ensure that incrementing a number from 0 equals 1; this result should hold whether you run it once or 100 times. But because the function modifies and reads from external data (see figure 6.3), this isn't the case.

Repeating same test

```
QUnit.test("Increment with zero", function (assert) {
    assert.equal(increment(), 1)
});                                                              ✓

QUnit.test("Increment with zero (again)", function (assert) {
    assert.equal(increment(), 1)
});                                                              ✗
```

Figure 6.3 Repeating a unit test for the imperative `increment` function is impossible due to the function's dependency on the external counter variable.

The second iteration fails because the first modified the external `counter` variable to 1, preempting the global context for the second run of the same code and causing it to fail in its assertion. By the same token, functions with side effects are also prone to bugs originating from order of evaluation. Let's examine this next.

6.2.3   *Predefined order of execution*

Along the same lines as consistency, unit tests should be designed to be *commutative*, which means changing the order in which they run shouldn't affect their outcome. For the same reasons as before, this principle doesn't work with impure functions. To work around this problem, unit testing libraries like QUnit contain out-of-the-box mechanisms to set up and tear down the global testing environment in order for subsequent tests to run; but the setup of one test may be completely different than another, so you're forced to set up preconditions at the beginning of each test. This also implies that for each test, you're responsible for identifying all the side effects (external dependencies) of the code under test.

To illustrate, let's create simple tests around `increment` to verify its behavior against negative numbers, zero, and positive numbers (see figure 6.4). In the first run (left), all tests pass. Shuffling the order of the tests (right), with no additional changes, causes the second test to fail. This is because tests with side effects run based on the assumption that you've adequately set up the surrounding state.

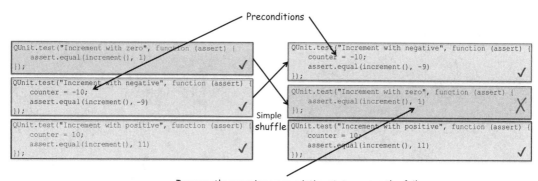

Figure 6.4   Falsely making assumptions about the global state of the system causes simple tests to fail. The left side shows that all tests executed perfectly, because each test correctly prepared its surrounding state before executing. But shuffling the tests (right) invalidates all assumptions about the state.

As you can see from this simple exercise, even if you manage to successfully run multiple unit tests for a particular function by manipulating the global context within each test, you can't guarantee they'll work if you move them around. A simple shift in sequence is enough to invalidate all your assertions.

Thinking functionally can also help you build reliable test suites. And if your code is written in a functional style, you'll get this for free. Instead of hopelessly shoehorning functional principles into your test code, why not write functionally from the beginning and recover the invested time in the test phase? Let's look at the benefits of functional code for testing.

6.3   *Testing functional code*

Whether you're testing imperative or functional code, many of the best practices surrounding the development of unit tests, such as isolation, predictability, and repeatability, are reciprocated in FP. Because every function clearly defines all of its input parameters, it's straightforward to supply multiple sets of boundary conditions to perform a thorough examination of all paths in your code. With respect to side effects, recall from previous chapters that all of the functions are simple and clearly defined, and all of the impure code can be safely wrapped in monads.

In addition, the impurity found in manual looping constructs has also been addressed by ceding control to higher-order operations like `map`, `reduce`, `filter`, and recursion, as well as using functional libraries that are side effect–free. These techniques and design patterns allow you to effectively abstract the complexity of your code so that you can test more productively and worry only about the main pieces of your business logic. This section discusses benefits of testing functional code, including the following:

- Treating a function as a black box
- Focusing on business logic instead of control flow
- Separating the pure from the impure with monadic isolation
- Mocking external dependencies

6.3.1   *Treating a function as a black box*

Functional programming encourages you to write independent functions that know how to work on a set of inputs in a loosely coupled manner, regardless of the rest of the application. These functions are also side effect–free and referentially transparent, which results in predictable test runs whose outcome is the same regardless of how many times they're invoked and in what order. This allows you to treat a function as a black box and only focus on the inputs that assert the corresponding outputs. Testing a function like `showStudent`, for example, requires the same level of effort as testing the functional `increment` function shown in figure 6.5.

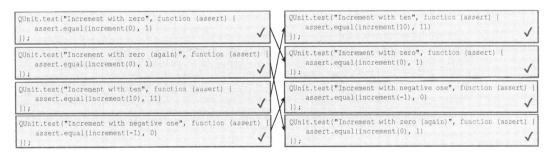

Can be run in any order.

Figure 6.5   Tests against the functional `increment` function, which can be repeated or run in a different order without altering their outcome

Recall from chapter 1 that declaring all function parameters explicitly in the function signature makes functions more configurable. This simplifies testing significantly because nothing is hidden from the caller at the moment of supplying proper arguments and creating expectations of what the functions are supposed to do. Simple functions typically declare one or two parameters that are put together via composition to create richer functions.

6.3.2 *Focusing on business logic instead of control flow*

The theme of decomposing tasks into simple functions has been a pattern throughout this book. I mentioned in chapter 1 that when writing functional code, you'll spend most of your time decomposing your problem into smaller parts. This is the challenging step; the rest of the time is spent gluing them together. Fortunately, libraries like Lodash and Ramda fill in the functional gaps in the JavaScript by providing glue points with functions like curry and compose. Together with the functional combinators you learned about in section 4.6, the upfront time spent designing and decomposing is given back to you in the testing phase. Your only responsibility is to test the individual functions that make up the main logic of your program. As an example, let's begin writing some tests for the functional version of computeAverageGrade (here's the code again for quick reference).

Listing 6.1 Testing the computeAverageGrade program

```
const fork = (join, func1, func2) => {
   return (val) => {
      return join(func1(val), func2(val));
   };
};

const toLetterGrade = (grade) => {
   if (grade >= 90) return 'A';
   if (grade >= 80) return 'B';
   if (grade >= 70) return 'C';
   if (grade >= 60) return 'D';
   return 'F';
};

const computeAverageGrade =
    R.compose(toLetterGrade, fork (R.divide, R.sum, R.length));

QUnit.test('Compute Average Grade', function(assert) {

   assert.equal(computeAverageGrade([80, 90, 100]), 'A');
});
```

This program uses many simple functions, such as Ramda's R.divide, R.sum, and R.length, combined using a custom functional combinator fork, the result of which is composed with toLetterGrade. The functions provided in Ramda have already been thoroughly tested for you, so there's no need to reinvent the wheel. This is the benefit of using functional libraries whenever possible. All that's left for you to do is write a unit test for `toLetterGrade`:

```
QUnit.test('Compute Average Grade: toLetterGrade', function (assert) {

    assert.equal(toLetterGrade(90), 'A');
    assert.equal(toLetterGrade(200),'A');
    assert.equal(toLetterGrade(80), 'B');
    assert.equal(toLetterGrade(89), 'B');
    assert.equal(toLetterGrade(70), 'C');
    assert.equal(toLetterGrade(60), 'D');
    assert.equal(toLetterGrade(59), 'F');
    assert.equal(toLetterGrade(-10),'F');
});
```

Because `toLetterGrade` is pure, you can run it several times against different inputs to test many of its boundary conditions. Because it's referentially transparent, you can also shift the order of these test cases without altering the result of the test. Later, you'll learn an automated way of generating proper sample input; but for now, you'll do this manually to see that the function works correctly against a comprehensive set of input. Now that all the individual pieces of the program have been tested, you can safely assume the program as a whole works, because it's driven by the power of composition and functional combinators.

Along the same lines, what about `fork`? Functional combinators don't require much testing, because they contain no business logic other than orchestrating function calls in your application's control flow. Recall from section 4.6 that combinators are useful for substituting standard control artifacts like `if-else` (alternation) and loops (sequence).

Some libraries implement combinators out of the box, like `R.tap`; but when using custom ones (like `fork`), you can test them independent of the rest of the application and apart from the business logic. For the sake of completeness, let's write a quick test for `fork` that showcases another good use of `R.identity`:

```
QUnit.test('Functional Combinator: fork', function (assert) {

    const timesTwo = fork((x) => x + x, R.identity, R.identity);
    assert.equal(timesTwo(1), 2);
    assert.equal(timesTwo(2), 4);
});
```

Again, testing with a simple function is sufficient, because combinators are completely agnostic when it comes to the arguments provided. Using functional libraries, composition, and combinators makes development and testing trivial; but things can get messy when you're dealing with impure behavior.

6.3.3 *Separating the pure from the impure with monadic isolation*

In previous chapters, you learned that most programs have pure and impure parts. This is especially true in client-side JavaScript, because interacting with the DOM is what the language was meant for. On the server, you'll have other requirements such as reading from a database or file. You learned how to use composition to combine the pure and impure functions that make up your programs. But this still made them impure; you relied on the IO monad to push the line of purity even further away so that you could obtain referential transparency from the application's perspective, making it more declarative and easier to reason about. In addition to IO, you used other monads like Maybe and Either to create a surefire way to run programs that are still responsive in the event of failure. With all these techniques, you can control most side effects. But when your JavaScript code needs to read and write to the DOM, how can you guarantee that your tests remain isolated and repeatable?

Recall that the nonfunctional version of showStudent makes no effort to separate its impure parts: it's all mixed together, so it will run as a whole on each and every test. This is utterly inefficient and unproductive because you would need to run the entire program every time even when you only wanted to validate, say, that db.get(ssn) worked with different combinations of Social Security numbers. Another disadvantage is that you can't test it thoroughly because all statements are tightly coupled. For instance, the first block of code will exit the function early with an exception and prevent you from testing db.get(ssn) against invalid input.

On the other hand, functional programming is aimed at reducing the involvement of operations that cause side effects (like IO) to minimal functions (simple reads and writes) so that you can increase the testable scope of your application logic while decoupling the boundaries of IO testing you aren't responsible for. Let's revisit the functional version of showStudent:

```
const showStudent = R.compose(
    map(append('#student-info')),
    liftIO,
    map(csv),
    map(R.props(['ssn', 'firstname', 'lastname'])),
    chain(findStudent),
    chain(checkLengthSsn),
    lift(cleanInput));
```

Looking closely at both programs, you can see how the functional version is essentially taking the imperative version apart and bolting it together with composition and monads. As a result, you dramatically increase the testable scope of showStudent and clearly recognize and isolate the pure functions from the impure (see figure 6.6).

Let's analyze the testability of the components of showStudent. Of the five functions, only three can be tested reliably: cleanInput, checkLengthSsn, and csv. Although findStudent has side effects when reading data from external resources, you'll see ways to get around this in a later section. The remaining function, append, has no real business logic because it's been reduced to appending to the DOM whatever data is given to it. It's not in your best interest, and it isn't the best use of your time, to test DOM APIs; leave that to browser manufacturers. With functional programming, you can take a hard-to-test program and split it into highly testable pieces.

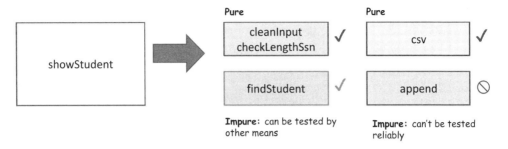

Figure 6.6 Identifying the testable areas of the `showStudent` program. The components that perform IO are impure and can't be tested reliably because they contain side effects. Other than having impure parts, the scope of the entire program remains highly testable.

Now, let's compare this against the nonfunctional, tightly coupled code in listing 6.2. In the functional version, you're able to test roughly 90% of the program reliably, whereas the imperative version has the same fate as the procedural `increment` function—it fails on subsequent or out-of-order runs.

The following listing shows the unit tests for each testable component in figure 6.6.

Listing 6.2 Unit testing pure components of `showStudent`

```
QUnit.test('showStudent: cleanInput', function (assert) {

    const input = ['', '-44-44-', '44444', '    4    ', '  4-4  '];       ◁─┐
    const assertions = ['', '4444', '44444', '4', '44'];

    expect(input.length);                                        Using inputs of
    input.forEach(function (val, key) {                          varying lengths
        assert.equal(cleanInput(val), assertions[key]);          and containing
    });                                                          whitespace
});

QUnit.test('showStudent: checkLengthSsn', function (assert) {

    assert.ok(checkLengthSsn('444444444').isRight);              ◁─┐
    assert.ok(checkLengthSsn('').isLeft);
    assert.ok(checkLengthSsn('44444444').isLeft);                ◁─
    assert.equal(checkLengthSsn('444444444').chain(R.length), 9);
});

QUnit.test('showStudent: csv', function (assert) {

    assert.equal(csv(['']), '');
    assert.equal(csv(['Alonzo']), 'Alonzo');
    assert.equal(csv(['Alonzo', 'Church']), 'Alonzo,Church');
    assert.equal(csv(['Alonzo', '', 'Church']), 'Alonzo,,Church');
});
```

Using Either.isLeft or Either.isRight to make assertions about the contents of the monad

Because these functions are isolated and thoroughly tested on their own (again, later I'll show you an automated mechanism for generating input data), you can safely refactor them without fear of breaking things in other places.

You have one last function to test: `findStudent`. This function originates from the impure `safeFindObject`, which queries an external object storage to look up student records. But the side effects in this function are manageable by using a technique called *mock objects*.

6.3.4   *Mocking external dependencies*

Mocking is a popular testing technique used to simulate the behavior of a function's external dependencies in a controlled, assertable manner, so it's good for dealing with some types of side effects. Mock objects will cause your test to fail if its expectations aren't met. They're like programmable dummy methods (or stubs) that you can use to define up front the expected behavior of an object that interact with your functions. In this case, mocking the call to the `DB` object gives you complete control over this external resource in order to create more predictable and consistent tests. For this task, you'll use a QUnit mock plug-in called Sinon.JS (see the appendix for details on how to set up this plug-in).

Sinon.JS enhances the test environment with a `sinon` object used to create mock versions of any object, all accessible in a mock context. In this case, you populate the context with the `DB` object, which will serve as the acting stub for this dependency:

```
const studentStore = DB('students');
const mockContext = sinon.mock(studentStore);
```

Using this mock context, you can set many expectations for the behavior of the mocked object to assert things like how many times it's called, what arguments it receives, as well as what its return value should be. To validate the behavior of the `Either` monad that wraps the return value of the `safeFindObject`, you'll create two unit tests: one that exercises the `Either.Right` type and another that triggers an `Either.Left`. You'll take advantage of the curried nature of `findStudent` that lets you easily inject any storage implementation to be used to perform the lookups, similar to what you did in chapter 4 with the factory method pattern. As you've seen in the code listings, this function invokes the `get` method on the storage object; now that you have full control of this object via the mock context, you can easily control the desired return value, as shown next.

Listing 6.3   Mocking the external dependency of `findStudent`

```
var studentStore, mockContext;

QUnit.module('CH06',
{
  beforeEach: function() {
    studentStore = DB('students');
```

Prepares the
mock context for
all unit tests

```
      mockContext = sinon.mock(studentStore);
    },
    afterEach: function() {
      mockContext.verify();
      mockContext.restore();
    }
});
```

Cleans up after each test

Verifies the assertions set forth in the mock configuration

On the first unit test, the mock object simulates a call to its query method (strictly once) that returns null.

```
QUnit.test('showStudent: findStudent returning null',
  function (assert) {

    mockContext.expects('find').once().returns(null);

    const findStudent = safefetchRecord(studentStore);

    assert.ok(findStudent('xxx-xx-xxxx').isLeft);
});
```

Asserting the returned value is wrapped in an Either.Left

```
QUnit.test('showStudent: findStudent returning valid object',
  function (assert) {

    mockContext.expects('get').once().returns(
        new Student('Alonzo', 'Church', 'Princeton').
            setSsn('444-44-4444'));

    const findStudent = safefetchRecord(studentStore);

    assert.ok(findStudent('444-44-4444').isRight);
});
```

On the second unit test, the mock object simulates a call to query with a valid result.

Asserting the valid response is wrapped inside an Either.Right

Figure 6.7 shows the result of running the tests with QUnit and Sinon.JS for the testable parts of showStudent.

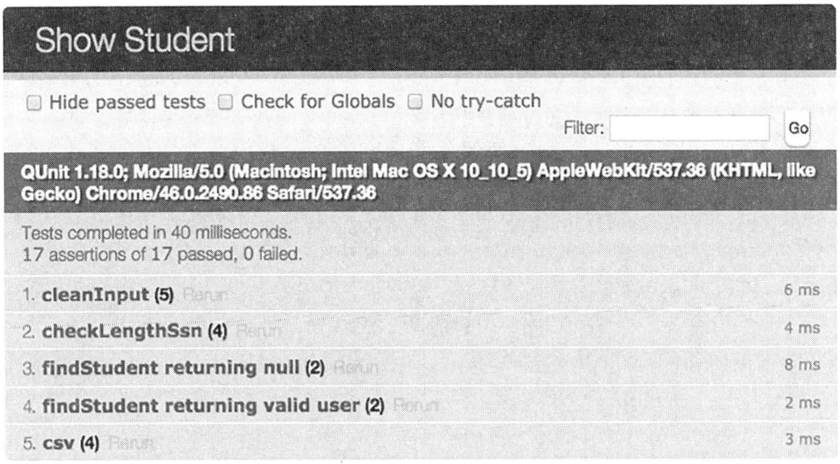

Figure 6.7 Execution of all unit tests for the showStudent program. Tests 3 and 4 use QUnit with Sinon.JS because they require mocked dependencies to simulate the functionality of fetching a student record.

The fact that functional code is orders of magnitude more testable than imperative code boils down to one principle: referential transparency. The essence of an assertion is verifying that referential transparency always holds:

```
assert.equal(computeAverageGrade([80, 90, 100]), 'A');
```

There's a lot more to referential transparency than meets the eye. This concept can extend into other realms of software development, such as program specifications. After all, the sole purpose of tests is to verify that the specifications of the system are met.

6.4   *Capturing specifications with property-based testing*

Unit tests can be used as artifacts to document and capture the runtime specification of a function. In the case of computeAverageGrade, for example

```
QUnit.test('Compute Average Grade', function (assert) {
    assert.equal(computeAverageGrade([80, 90, 100]),'A');
    assert.equal(computeAverageGrade([80, 85, 89]), 'B');
    assert.equal(computeAverageGrade([70, 75, 79]), 'C');
    assert.equal(computeAverageGrade([60, 65, 69]), 'D');
    assert.equal(computeAverageGrade([50, 55, 59]), 'F');
    assert.equal(computeAverageGrade([-10]),        'F');
});
```

you can come up with a simple document that states the following:

- "If the student's average is 90 or above, the student is awarded an A."
- "If the student's average is between 80 and 89, the student is awarded a B."
- … And so on

Natural language is often used as a means to capture the requirements a system shall fulfill; but natural languages express meaning in a certain context, often not known by all parties, and this generates ambiguity when you try to translate requirements to code. This is why you have to constantly bug product owners or team leads to clarify ambiguities present in task specifications. One of the main causes of ambiguity is a result of adopting an imperative style of documentation when using if-then cases: *if* case A, *then* the system should do B. The downside of this approach is that it doesn't describe the totality of the task to account for all boundary conditions. What if case A doesn't occur? What is the system expected to do then?

Good specifications shouldn't be case-based; they should be generic and universal. Look at the slight difference in wording in these two statements:

- "If the student's average is 90 or above, the student is awarded an A."
- "Only an average of 90 or above will award the student an A."

By removing the imperative-case clauses, the second statement is much more complete. Not only does it express what happens when the student reaches 90 or above, but it also places the restriction that no other numerical range will result in an A. You can derive from the second statement that, at the least, any other computed average won't result in the student being awarded an A, which you couldn't intuit from the first.

Universal requirements are much easier to work with, because they aren't dependent on the status of the system at any point in time. For this reason, like unit tests, good specifications don't have side effects or make assumptions about their surrounding context.

Referentially transparent specifications increase our understanding of what functions are supposed to do and give us a clear picture of the input conditions they must satisfy. Because referentially transparent functions are consistent and have clear input parameters, they lend themselves to being easily tested with automated mechanisms that can push them to the limit. This brings us into a much more compelling testing modality called *property-based testing*. A property-based test makes a statement about what the output of a function should be when executed against a definite set of inputs. The canonical framework or reference implementation is Haskell's QuickCheck.

QuickCheck: Property-based test for Haskell

QuickCheck is a Haskell library for randomized property-based testing of a program's specification or properties. You design a specification of a pure program in the form of properties the program should fulfill, and QuickCheck generates a large permutation of test cases against your program and produces a report. You can find more information at https://hackage.haskell.org/package/QuickCheck.

By the same token, JavaScript emulates QuickCheck with a library called JSCheck (see the appendix for setup information), by none other than Douglas Crockford,[1] author of *JavaScript: The Good Parts* (O'Reilly, 2008). JSCheck can be used to create a technical response to a matching referentially transparent specification of a function or program. Hence, proving the properties of a function is done by generating a large number of random test cases aimed at rigorously exercising all possible output paths of your function.

Also, property-based tests control and manage the evolution of your program as it's being refactored to ensure that new code doesn't introduce unintentional bugs into the system. The main advantage of using a tool like JSCheck is that its algorithm generates abnormal datasets to test with. Some of the edge cases it generates would most likely be overlooked if you had to manually write them.

The JSCheck module is nicely encapsulated into a global JSC object:

```
JSC.claim(name, predicate, specifiers, classifier)
```

---

[1] Douglas Crockford is a popular computer programmer, writer, and speaker best known for his ongoing involvement in the evolution of the JavaScript language, popularizing JSON, and creating several JavaScript libraries like JSLint, JSMin, and JSCheck, among others. He's also the author of the must-read *JavaScript: The Good Parts*.

At the heart of this library is the creation of *claims* and *verdicts*. A claim is made up of the following:

- *Name*—Description of the claim (similar to QUnit's test description).
- *Predicate*—Function that returns a verdict of `true` when the claim is satisfied or `false` otherwise.
- *Specifiers*—Array describing the type of the input parameters and the specification with which to generate random datasets.
- *Classifier (optional)*—Function associated with each test case that can be used to reject non-applicable cases

Claims are passed into `JSCheck.check` to run random test cases. This library wraps creating a claim and feeding it into the engine in a single call to `JSCheck.test`, so you'll use this shortcut method in the example tests. Let's look at an example of writing a simple JSCheck specification for `computeAverageGrade` that captures the following specification: "Only an average of 90 or above will award the student an A."

Listing 6.4   Property-based test for `computeAverageGrade`

```
JSC.clear();                                          ◁─── I always like to start with
JSC.on_report((str) => console.log(str));                  JSC.clear to initialize and
                                                           start a fresh testing context.

JSC.test(
                                                                      Passes the predicate
    'Compute Average Grade',                                          function the verdict
    function (verdict, grades, grade) {               ◁───            object that defines the
        return verdict(computeAverageGrade(grades) === grade);        condition to verify
    },
    [
      JSC.array(JSC.integer(20), JSC.number(90,100)),
      'A'
    ],
    function (grades, grade) {
        return 'Testing for an ' + grade + ' on grades: ' + grades;   ◁───
    }
);
```

Name of the claim (points to `'Compute Average Grade'`)

Signature or specifier array describing the contract for generating averages that deserve an A (points to the specifier array)

Classifier function runs on each test, so you can use it to append data to the report

As you can see in listing 6.5, you use declarative specifiers to capture the properties of this program:

- `JSC.array`—Describes that the function expects inputs of `Array` type.
- `JSC.integer(20)`—Indicates the maximum length this function is expected to work with. In this case, it's arbitrary, so any number from 1 to 20 will suffice.

- `JSC.number(90, 100)`—Describes the types of elements in the input array. In this case, they're numeric (including integers and floating-point numbers) in the range from 90 to 100.

The predicate function is a bit tricky to understand. The predicate returns a `true` verdict when a claim holds, but what happens in the body of the predicate is for you to determine depending on your specific program and what you want it to verify. In addition to the verdict function used to announce the result of the test case, you're also given the generated random input and the expected output. In this case, the result you want to announce is the check to validate that `computeAverageGrade` returns the expected grade: A. This example uses a few specifiers, but there are many more you can read about on the project's website, and you can also create your own.

Now that you understand the main pieces of the program, let's go ahead and run it. The report can be lengthy, because JSCheck will generate by default 100 random test cases based on the specification provided. I've trimmed it, but you can still follow what's happening:

```
Compute Average Grade: 100 classifications, 100 cases tested, 100 pass

Testing for an A on grades:
    90.042,98.828,99.359,90.309,99.175,95.569,97.101,92.24 pass 1
Testing for an A on grades:
    90.084,93.199, pass 1

// and so on 98 more times

Total pass 100, fail 0
```

JSCheck programs are self-documented; you can easily describe the contract for your function's inputs and outputs to a level regular unit tests can't. You can also see the significant level of detail that a JSCheck report contains. JSCheck programs can run as standalone scripts or embedded into QUnit tests; that way, they can be included as part of your test suites. The interaction between these libraries is shown in figure 6.8.

In the next example, you'll use JSCheck to test the `checkLengthSsn` program, which has the following specification:

- A valid Social Security number must satisfy these conditions:
  - Contains no spaces
  - Contains no dashes
  - Is nine characters long
  - Follows the format outlined by ssa.gov, composed of three parts:
    1 The first set of three digits is called the Area Number.
    2 The second set of two digits is called the Group Number.
    3 The final set of four digits is called the Serial Number.

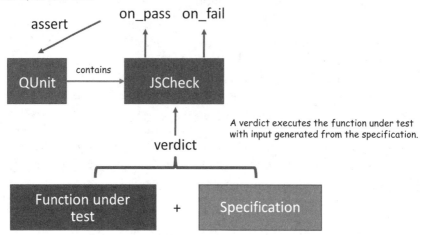

Figure 6.8 The integration of the main components: JSCheck and QUnit. A QUnit test encapsulates a JSCheck test specification. The specification and the function being tested are supplied to the `verdict` function, which is run through the JSCheck engine to invoke the pass/fail callbacks. These callbacks can be used to trigger QUnit assertions.

The following listing shows the code; then I explain the relevant parts.

Listing 6.5 JSCheck test for `checkLengthSsn`

```
QUnit.test('JSCheck Custom Specifier for SSN', function (assert) {
    JSC.clear();

    JSC.on_report((report) => trace('Report'+ str));
        JSC.on_pass((object) => assert.ok(object.pass));

    JSC.on_fail((object) =>
        assert.ok(object.pass || object.args.length === 9,
            'Test failed for: ' + object.args));

        JSC.test(
         'Check Length SSN',
         function (verdict, ssn) {
            return verdict(checkLengthSsn(ssn));
         },
         [
            JSC.SSN(JSC.integer(100, 999), JSC.integer(10, 99),
                JSC.integer(1000,9999))
         ],
         function (ssn) {
            return 'Testing Custom SSN:  ' + ssn;
         }
     );
)};
```

Uses JSC.on_fail to ensure that the test fails on arguments with length not equal to 9

Because the function is Boolean, you can feed the result of the validation in to the verdict.

Uses a custom specifier JSC.SSN (defined in the text), composed of JSC.integer specifiers. JSC.integer picks a random number in the specified range.

This program joins the forces of JSCheck and QUnit through the `JSC.on_fail` and `JSC.on_pass` functions, which report to QUnit about any assertions that are fulfilled or that violate the specification provided. Because the specifier

```
JSC.SSN(JSC.integer(100, 999), JSC.integer(10, 99), JSC.integer(1000,9999))
```

describes the contract for valid SSNs, this program is expected to always output the correct results for any combination of SSN of the form XXX-XX-XXXX:

```
Check Length SSN:
100 classifications, 100 cases tested, 100 pass

Testing Custom SSN:    121-76-4808 pass 1
Testing Custom SSN:    122-87-7833 pass 1
Testing Custom SSN:    134-44-6044 pass 1
Testing Custom SSN:    139-47-6224 pass 1
...
Testing Custom SSN:    992-52-3288 pass 1
Testing Custom SSN:    995-12-1487 pass 1
Testing Custom SSN:    998-46-2523 pass 1

Total pass 100
```

Nothing out of the ordinary here. But you can tweak the specification to also include invalid input with a three-digit Group Number and see how the program behaves:

```
JSC.SSN(JSC.integer(100, 999),JSC.integer(10, 999),JSC.integer(1000,9999))
```

Running QUnit with JSCheck flags failures as expected. Figure 6.9 shows the output of a single failure, for brevity.

Figure 6.9   **A failure detected as a result of an invalid property check with QUnit. When you randomize the input to include invalid inputs, the JSCheck algorithm has enough entropy that 89 of 90 tests fail.**

Where did `JSC.SSN` come from? JSCheck specifiers behave just like functional combinators that can be composed to create more-specialized specifiers. This case uses a custom `JSC.SSN` made from the combination of three `JSC.integer` specifiers describing the properties of each SSN group, as shown next.

Listing 6.6 Custom JSC.SSN specifier

```
/**
  * Produces a valid social security string (with dashes)
  * @param param1 Area Number    -> JSC.integer(100, 999)
  * @param param2 Group Number   -> JSC.integer(10, 99)
  * @param param3 Serial Number -> JSC.integer(1000,9999)
  * @returns {Function} Specifier function
  */
JSC.SSN = function (param1, param2, param3) {
   return function generator() {
      const part1 = typeof param1 === 'function'
         ? param1(): param1;

      const part2 = typeof param2 === 'function'
         ? param2(): param2;

      const part3 = typeof param3 === 'function'
         ? param3(): param3;

      return [part1 , part2, part3].join('-');
   };
};
```

> Added as part of the JSC object so the code looks consistent

> Each part of the SSN number is made up of either a constant or a function that JSCheck uses to inject random inputs.

> All three data points are combined into a valid SSN syntax.

JSCheck works only with pure programs, which means you can't test the showStudent program entirely, but you can use it to test each component in isolation. I leave that to you as an exercise. Property-based testing is compelling because it exercises functions to the limit. Its best quality, in my opinion, is that it can be used to verify whether code is indeed referentially transparent, because it's expected to work consistently against the same contract and verdict. But why submit your code to such a heavy procedure? The answer is simple: to make your tests effective.

6.5 *Measuring effectiveness through code coverage*

Measuring a unit test's effectiveness is an arduous task if not done with the proper tools in place, because it involves studying the test's code coverage through the functions under test. Getting coverage information involves traversing all unique paths belonging to a program's control flow; one way to achieve this is by studying the flow of code against a function's boundary conditions.

Certainly, code coverage alone isn't an indicator of quality, but it does describe the degree to which your functions are tested, which correlates to better quality. Would you want code that's never seen the light of day deployed to production? I didn't think so.

Code-coverage analysis can find areas in your code that haven't been tested, allowing you to create additional tests to uncover them. Normally, this includes code for error handling that you let slip through the cracks and forget to come back to. You can use code coverage to measure the percentage of lines of code that are executed when invoking a program via unit tests. To compute this information, you can use a library called Blanket.js, which is a code-coverage tool for JavaScript. It's designed to complement your existing JavaScript unit tests with code-coverage statistics. It works in three phases:

1   Load source files
2   Instrument the code by adding tracker lines
3   Connect the hooks in the test runner to output coverage details

Blanket collects coverage information with the help of an instrumentation phase during which it captures meta-information regarding statement execution, which you can display nicely in a QUnit report. Details for setting up Blanket can be found in the appendix. You can instrument any JavaScript module or program via the custom `data-covered` attribute in the script `include` line. By analyzing the statement-coverage percentage, you can see that functional code is much more testable than imperative code.

6.5.1   *Measuring the effectiveness of testing functional code*

Throughout this chapter, you've seen that functional programs are more testable due to the ease with which tasks can be broken apart to become atomic, verifiable units. But don't take my word for it; you can measure it empirically by performing a statement-by-statement percentage-coverage analysis on the `showStudent` program. First, let's look at the simplest test case: a positive test.

MEASURING EFFECTIVENESS OF IMPERATIVE AND FUNCTIONAL CODE WITH VALID INPUTS

First let's look at code-coverage statistics against a successful run of the imperative version of `showStudent`, shown in listing 6.2. Using Blanket with QUnit, mark this program to be instrumented:

```
<script src="imperative-show-student-program.js" data-cover></script>
```

Now, running the following test

```
QUnit.test('Imperative showStudent with valid user', function (assert) {
    const result = showStudent('444-44-4444');
    assert.equal(result, '444-44-4444, Alonzo, Church');
});
```

produces an 80% total statement-coverage percentage, as shown in the QUnit/Blanket output in figure 6.10.

This shouldn't surprise you, because the error-handling code was all skipped. For imperative programs, 75–80% code coverage is considered to be very good. What you can take from this run is that 80% is the best coverage you can get with a single unit test execution. On the other hand, let's instrument and run a positive test against the functional version:

```
<script src="functional-show-student-program.js" data-cover></script>
```

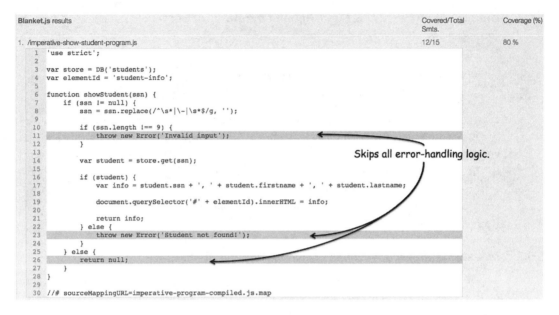

```
 1  'use strict';
 2
 3  var store = DB('students');
 4  var elementId = 'student-info';
 5
 6  function showStudent(ssn) {
 7      if (ssn != null) {
 8          ssn = ssn.replace(/^\s*|\-|\s*$/g, '');
 9
10          if (ssn.length !== 9) {
11              throw new Error('Invalid input');
12          }
13
14          var student = store.get(ssn);
15
16          if (student) {
17              var info = student.ssn + ', ' + student.firstname + ', ' + student.lastname;
18
19              document.querySelector('#' + elementId).innerHTML = info;
20
21              return info;
22          } else {
23              throw new Error('Student not found!');
24          }
25      } else {
26          return null;
27      }
28  }
29
30  //# sourceMappingURL=imperative-program-compiled.js.map
```

Skips all error-handling logic.

Figure 6.10   QUnit/Blanket output running the imperative `showStudent` with valid input. The highlighted lines represent statements that never ran. Because 12 of 15 lines ran, this registers only 80% of total coverage information on this function.

Again, running the "happy path" test runs the program with a valid SSN, but this time producing a whopping figure of 100% coverage (see figure 6.11)!

Blanket.js results	Covered/Total Smts.	Coverage (%)
1. /functional-show-student-program.js	29/29	100 %

Figure 6.11   A positive unit test against the functional `showStudent` generates a 100% line-percentage coverage. Every line of the testable business logic is executed!

But wait: if the input was valid, why didn't it skip the error-handling logic? This is the work of monads in the code, which can propagate the concept of an empty value, or nothingness (in the form of an `Either.Left` or a `Maybe.Nothing`) seamlessly throughout the entire program; thus, every function is run, yet logic encapsulated in mapping functions is skipped.

It's remarkable how functional code is so robust and flexible. Now, let's run a negative test with invalid input.

Blanket.js results	Covered/Total Smts.	Coverage (%)
1. /imperative-show-student-program.js	6/15	40 %

```
 1  'use strict';
 2
 3  var store = DB('students');
 4  var elementId = 'student-info';
 5
 6  function showStudent(ssn) {
 7      if (ssn != null) {
 8          ssn = ssn.replace(/^\s*|\-|\s*$/g, '');
 9
10          if (ssn.length !== 9) {
11              throw new Error('Invalid input');
12          }
13
14          var student = store.get(ssn);
15
16          if (student) {
17              var info = student.ssn + ', ' + student.firstname + ', ' + student.lastname;
18
19              document.querySelector('#' + elementId).innerHTML = info;
20
21              return info;
22          } else {
23              throw new Error('Student not found!');
24          }
25      } else {
26          return null;
27      }
28  }
```

Skips all error-handling & business logic

Figure 6.12 The imperative version of `showStudent` skips the positive path of execution, which translates to only a few lines being executed and a low 40% coverage.

MEASURING EFFECTIVENESS OF IMPERATIVE AND FUNCTIONAL CODE WITH INVALID INPUTS

Let's measure the effectiveness of both programs when run with invalid conditions, such as when the input is `null`. As you can see from figure 6.12, the imperative code reports (not surprisingly) a mediocre coverage value:

```
QUnit.test('Imperative Show Student with null', function (assert) {
    const result = showStudent(null);
    assert.equal(result, null);
});
```

This result is due to the presence of `if-else` blocks that create divergent control flow that branches in different directions. As you'll see shortly, this also leads to complex functions.

In contrast, the functional program handles the `null` case much more gracefully, because it only skips logic that would manipulate the invalid input (now `null`) directly. But the entire structure of the program (the interaction among functions) stays put and is successfully invoked and tested from start to finish. Recall that because there's an error, the output of the functional code is a `Nothing`. You don't have to check for a `null` output—the following test case is sufficient:

```
QUnit.test('Functional Show Student with null', function (assert) {
    const result = showStudent(null).run();
    assert.ok(result.isNothing);
});
```

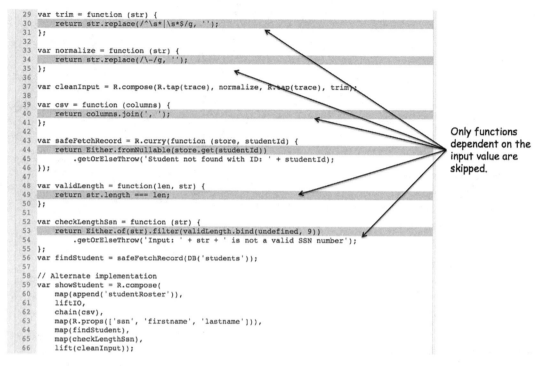

Figure 6.13   The functional version of `showStudent` skips lines related only to manipulating the data that would have originated from an otherwise valid input.

Figure 6.13 shows the areas that were left untouched due to the skipped logic.

Even in the presence of invalid data, the functional program doesn't just skip execution of entire sections of code. It gracefully and safely propagates the invalid condition in monads, outputting a decent 80% (twice as much as the imperative counterpart); see figure 6.14.

Blanket.js results	Covered/Total Smts.	Coverage (%)
1. /functional-show-student-program.js	23/29	79.31 %

Figure 6.14   The functional `showStudent` continues to yield great coverage results even against invalid inputs.

Because it's a lot more testable, the functional code should give you a sense of security and comfort to deploy it to your production systems—in case immutability and elimination of side effects hasn't done the trick. As mentioned earlier, the presence of conditional and loop blocks in imperative code not only makes it hard to test and hard to reason about, but also further increases the complexity of the function in question. How can you measure complexity?

6.5.2 *Measuring the complexity of functional code*

You can measure a program's complexity by closely examining its control flow. At a glance, you determine that a block of code is complex when it's visually difficult to follow. Functional programming presents a nice declarative view of the code that makes it visually appealing. This equates to reduced complexity from the developer's point of view. In this section, you'll see that functional code is also less complex from an algorithmic point of view.

Many factors can contribute to complex code, including conditional blocks and loops, which can also be nested in other structures. Branching logic, for instance, is mutually exclusive and splits the control-flow logic into two independent branches according to a Boolean condition. Multiple if-else blocks in your code can be hard to trace; the process is even harder when their conditions are based on external factors—side effects dictating the path the code should follow. The higher the number of conditional blocks and nested conditional blocks, the harder functions are to test, which is why it's important to keep your functions as simple as possible. This is deeply rooted in FP's philosophy of reducing all functions to simple lambda expressions whenever possible and combining them using composition and monads.

Cyclomatic complexity (CC) is a quantitative software metric used to measure the number of linearly independent paths that functions take. From this concept comes the idea of verifying a function's boundary conditions, to ensure that all possible paths through the functions are tested. This is accomplished with some simple graph theory of nodes and edges (as shown in figure 6.15):

- Nodes correspond to indivisible blocks of code.
- Directed edges connect two blocks of code if the second block can be possibly executed after the first.

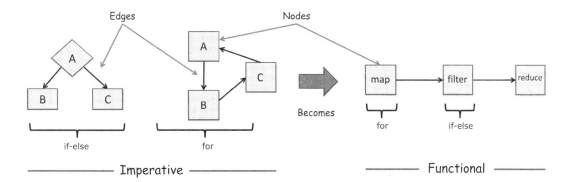

Figure 6.15 Imperative if-else blocks and for loops in imperative code are translated into the use of map, filter, and reduce in functional programs.

In chapter 3, we studied the difference between an imperative control-flow graph and a functional one, and how functional cedes all branching and iteration logic to higher-order operations like `map` and `filter`.

What contributes to CC? Mathematically, the complexity of any program can be computed as $M = E - N + P$, where

- E = Number of edges in the flow
- N = Number of nodes or blocks
- P = Number of nodes that have exit points

All control structures contribute to CC; the lower the value, the better. A conditional block affects complexity the most because it bifurcates the program's control flow into two linearly independent paths. So, naturally, the greater the number of control artifacts, the larger the CC metric will be, and, thus, the harder the program is to test.

Let's revisit the control flow of the imperative `showStudent`. To easily delineate the flow, I've annotated the statements that translate to nodes in the graph and then generated a flowchart, shown in figure 6.16. Applying the CC formula to this graph with 11 edges, 10 nodes, and 3 exit points yields $M = E - N + P = 11 - 10 + 3 = 4$.

On the other hand, measuring CC in functional programs is much simpler because FP tends to avoid both loops and conditional statements as much as possible in favor of higher-order functions, functional combinators, and other abstractions. All this translates to fewer nodes and edges and all paths in the function being linearly independent. Hence, functional programs tend to have a *cyclomatic complexity value near 1.* This is exactly what happens with the functional `showStudent`, because it's composed

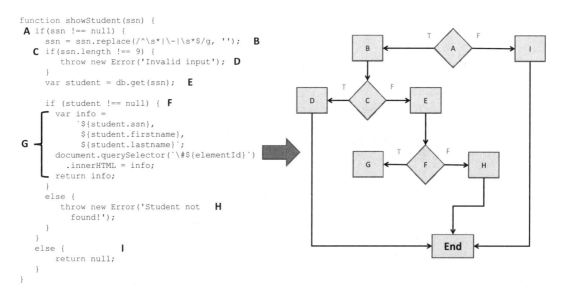

```
function showStudent(ssn) {
A  if(ssn !== null) {
       ssn = ssn.replace(/^\s*|\-|\s*$/g, '');   B
C      if(ssn.length !== 9) {
           throw new Error('Invalid input');   D
       }
       var student = db.get(ssn);   E

       if (student !== null) {  F
         var info =
           `${student.ssn},
            ${student.firstname},
            ${student.lastname}`;
G        document.querySelector(`\#${elementId}`)
           .innerHTML = info;
         return info;
       }
       else {
           throw new Error('Student not   H
             found!');
       }
   }
   else {                       I
       return null;
   }
}
```

Figure 6.16   Potential nodes in the imperative version of `showStudent`. These labels have been converted into a flowchart of nodes and edges, which illustrates the number of different linearly independent paths through the code caused by the presence of conditional statements.

of many functions that don't contain nodes and edges (just single exit points), making its cyclomatic complexity value $M = E - N + P = 0 - 0 + 1 = 1$. In the realm of complexity, some other related metrics extrapolated from both programs are worth noting (see table 6.1). You can measure them with the help of the website at http://jscomplexity.org.

Table 6.1 Other important static code metrics comparing the imperative to the functional solutions

Imperative	Functional
▪ Cyclomatic complexity: 4 ▪ Cyclomatic complexity density: 29% ▪ Maintainability index: 100	▪ Cyclomatic complexity: 1 ▪ Cyclomatic complexity density: 3% ▪ Maintainability index: 148

The cyclomatic complexity density reexpresses the original CC value as a percentage based on the number of imperative lines of code, which is also substantially lower in functional programs. The degree to which a program is testable is directly proportional to how well the program is designed. Simply put, the more modular your code is, the easier it is to test. Functional programs easily take the lead because they embrace the modularity of your units, which are the functions themselves.

Because functional programming is heavily rooted in eliminating manual loops in favor of higher-order functions; composition instead of imperative; sequential evaluation of code; and higher levels of abstractions with currying, it's not senseless to think that all this could affect performance. Can we have our cake, and eat it too?

6.6   *Summary*

- Programs that rely on abstractions to join very simple functions are modular.
- Modular code based on pure functions is easy to test and leads the way for more-rigorous types of testing methodology such as property-based testing.
- Testable code must have a straightforward control flow.
- A simple control flow reduces the complexity of your program as a whole. This can be measured quantitatively via complexity metrics.
- Reduced complexity leads to programs that are easy to reason about.

Functional optimizations 7

This chapter covers

- Indicating where functional code is performant
- Examining the internals of JavaScript function execution
- Implications of nesting function contexts and recursion
- Optimizing function evaluation with lazy evaluation
- Speeding up program execution with memoization
- Unwinding recursive calls with tail recursive functions

We should forget about small efficiencies, say about 97% of the time … premature optimization is the root of all evil. Yet we should not pass up our opportunities in that critical 3%.

—Donald Knuth, *The Art of Computer Programming*

Always optimize last, or so they say. In previous chapters, you learned how to write and test your functional code; and now, nearing the end of this wonderful journey, we look at ways to optimize it. No single programming paradigm is the Holy Grail, and each has its share of trade-offs: performance versus abstraction, for example. Functional programming provides layers of abstractions around your code to achieve its high level of fluency and declarativeness. With all of this internal currying, recursion, and monadic wrapping composed together to solve even the simplest types of problems, you may wonder, "Is functional code as performant as imperative code?"

It's true that with most modern web applications nowadays, excluding games, there's nothing to be gained from cutting milliseconds of execution time from your programs. Computers have become incredibly fast and compiler technology amazingly smart, which guarantees fast performance of correct code. FP isn't any less performant than imperative code, as you may think; it just shines in different ways.

It's not wise to begin using a new paradigm without understanding its implications for the environment in which it's running. So, in this chapter, I'll explain some aspects of functional JavaScript code that you need to be aware of, especially when processing large amounts of data. I'll be talking about core JavaScript features, like closures, so make sure you've read and understood chapter 2. I'll also discuss some interesting optimization techniques such as lazy evaluation, memoization, and recursive call optimizations.

Functional programming won't speed up the evaluation times of individual functions; rather, its strategy is based on avoiding duplicated function calls and delaying calling code until it's absolutely needed, which may speed up your application overall. In pure functional languages, these optimizations are built into the platform and can be used without any involvement from you. In JavaScript, though, you'll need to manually plug in these optimizations via custom code or functional libraries. But before we dive in, I'll briefly show you the challenges of using JavaScript functionally and why these optimizations are important.

7.1 Under the hood of function execution

Because FP relies on evaluating functions for everything you do, when learning about performance and optimizations, it's important to understand what goes on in each function call. Every function call in JavaScript internally creates a record (a frame) in the function context stack.

> **NOTE** A *stack* is a basic data structure that contains objects such that insertion and removal follow a last-in first-out (LIFO) approach. Consider the analogy of a pile of dishes stacked one on top of another: all operations on the stack are performed at the top.

The context stack is a component of the JavaScript programming model responsible for managing the execution of a function and the variables it closes over (if you don't know what this means, please revisit closures in section 2.4). The stack always starts with the global execution context frame, which contains all global data, as shown in figure 7.1.

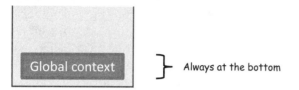

Figure 7.1   JavaScript's execution context stack on initialization. Depending on how many scripts are loaded on the page, the global context can keep track of lots of variables and functions.

The global context frame always resides at the bottom of the stack. Each function context frame takes up a certain amount of memory depending on the number of local variables contained within it. Without any local variables, an empty frame is approximately 48 bytes. Local variables and parameters like numbers and Booleans require 8 bytes each. Intuitively, the more variables the function body declares, the larger the stack frame. Each frame contains roughly the following information:[1]

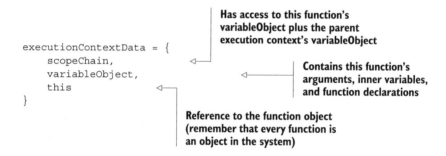

From this structure, we can extract a few important insights. First, the `variable-Object` property is what primarily determines the size of the stack frame, because it has references to a function's arguments, the actual array-like `arguments` object (covered in chapter 2), as well as any local variables and functions. Second, the function's scope chain is what links or references this function's context with its parent execution context (I'll talk more about the scope chain later). Whether directly or indirectly, every function's scope chain eventually links to the global context.

> **NOTE**   A function's scope chain is different from a JavaScript object's prototype chain. Although both behave in similar ways, the latter refers to the link established in object inheritance through the `prototype` property. The scope chain refers particularly to the access an inner function has to its outer function's closure.

---

[1]   Information taken from David Shariff's excellent blog post "What Is the Execution Context & Stack in JavaScript?" June 19, 2012, http://mng.bz/mqTu.

The behavior of the stack is determined by the following important rules:

- JavaScript is single-threaded, which means it has synchronous execution.
- There is one and only one global context (shared among all function contexts).
- You can have an unlimited number of function contexts (for client-side code, different browsers can impose different limits).
- Each function call creates a new execution context, even when calling itself recursively.

As you know, functional programming exploits the use of functions to the maximum degree, and you're encouraged to decompose problems into as many functions as possible as well as curry them for additional flexibility and reuse. But using lots of curried functions has its own implications on the context stack.

7.1.1 *Currying and the function context stack*

Personally, I am a huge fan of currying. In fact, I'd like for JavaScript to automatically curry all function evaluations. But this additional level of abstraction can cause some context overhead compared to a regular function evaluation. To understand this better, let's explore what happens under the hood of a curried function call in JavaScript.

Recall from chapter 4 that when you curry a function, you internally transform its evaluation mechanism from a single-shot call with all parameters, to multiple one-at-a-time inner function executions. In other words, the `logger` function from chapter 4

```
const logger = function (appender, layout, name, level, message)
```

when curried, becomes this nested structure:

```
const logger =
   function (appender) {
      return function (layout)  {
         return function (name)   {
            return function (level) {
               return function (message) {
         . . .
```

A nested structure uses the function stack more heavily than a straight call. First I'll explain the non-curried execution of `logger`. Due to JavaScript's synchronous execution, a call to `logger` results in pausing execution of the global context to make way for `logger` to run, becoming the new active context and creating a reference to the global context for purposes of variable resolution. This is shown in figure 7.2.

Internally, the logger function makes calls to other Log4js operations, which create new function contexts that are put on the stack (if you haven't done so, you can visit the appendix for an introduction to Log4js). Due to closures in JavaScript, the function contexts resulting from inner function calls are stacked one on top of the other, each taking up its fair share of allocated memory and linked via the `scopeChain` reference (see figure 7.3).

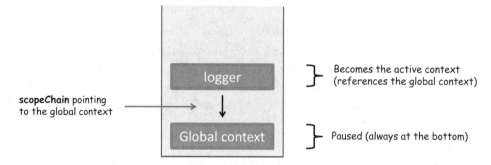

Figure 7.2   When invoking any function, like `logger` in this case, the single-threaded JavaScript runtime pauses the current global context and activates the context for the new function to run. At this point, a link is created between the global context and the function context, traversable via the `scopeChain`. Once `logger` returns, its execution context is popped off the stack, and the global context resumes.

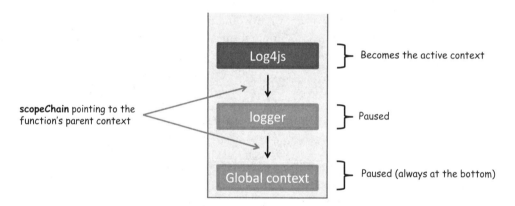

Figure 7.3   How the function context grows when running nested functions. Because each function produces a new stack frame, the stack grows in proportion to the level of nesting in functions. Both currying and recursion rely on nested function calls.

Finally, once the Log4js code completes, it gets popped off the stack; the `logger` function follows suit, leaving the runtime back in its original state—with only the single global context running (refer back to figure 7.1). This is the magic behind closures in JavaScript.

Although this approach is powerful, deeply nested functions can consume large amounts of memory. In chapter 8, I'll introduce you to RxJS, a functional library used to handle asynchronous code. The latest release, RxJS 5, is a complete revamp of the

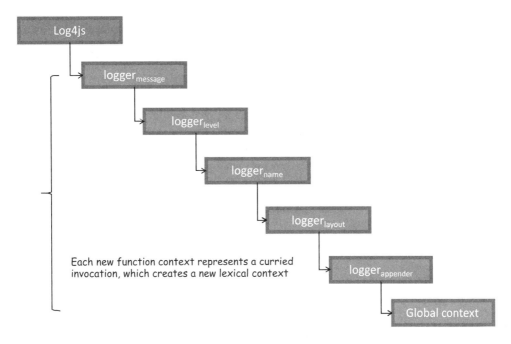

Figure 7.4 With currying, each parameter of the curried function is internally transformed to a nested call. This flexibility of being able to supply parameters sequentially has the downside of occupying additional stack frames.

code from the previous version with focus on performance; reducing the number of closures was a top priority.

Now let's look at the curried version of the `logger` function, illustrated in figure 7.4.

Currying all functions might seem like a good idea, but overdoing it can lead to programs that take up larger chunks of memory and run significantly slower. You can run this simple benchmark program to prove it:

```
const add = function (a, b) {
    return a + b;
};

const c_add = curry2(add);

const input = _.range(80000);

addAll(input, add);   //->511993600000000
addAll(input, c_add); //-> browser halts

function addAll(arr, fn) {
    let result= 0;
    for(let i = 0; i < arr.length; i++) {
        for(let j = 0; j < arr.length; j++) {
            result += fn(arr[i], arr[j]);
```

```
        }
    }
    return result;
}
```

This program creates an array of 80,000 numbers and compares the non-curried version to the curried function. The non-curried version returns the correct result in a few seconds, whereas the curried function causes the browser to halt. Undoubtedly, there's a price to pay with currying, but having to process such large datasets in most applications is highly unlikely.

This isn't the only situation that can cause the stack to grow. Inefficient or incorrect recursive solutions are the leading cases where the stack overflows.

7.1.2   *Challenges of recursive code*

New function contexts are created even when functions call themselves. An incorrect recursive call—one where the base case is never reached—can easily cause the stack to overflow. Luckily, recursion is one of those cases where it either works or it doesn't, and when it doesn't, it's not shy about letting you know. If you've ever had the pleasure of seeing the dreaded Range Error: Maximum Call Stack Exceeded or too much recursion error, you know what I mean. You can benchmark your browser with this simple script to get an approximate function stack size:

```
function increment(i) {
    console.log(i);
    increment(++i);
}
increment(1);
```

Different browsers implement stack errors differently: on my machine, Chrome fires the exception after approximately 17,500 iterations, whereas Firefox will goes much longer, to about 213,000 iterations. Don't use these numbers as upper bounds below which to write your functions! These are superfluous numbers meant to show you that there are limits you can't exceed. Your code should be far below these thresholds, or you likely have a bug somewhere in your recursion.

If you happen to deal with an unusually large amount of data using recursion, you may cause the stack to grow proportionally to the size of the array. Consider this example to find the longest string in an array:

```
function longest(str, arr) {
    if(R.isEmpty(arr)) {
      return str;
    else {
        let currentStr = R.head(arr).length >= str.length
            ? R.head(arr): str;
        return longest(currentStr, R.tail(arr));
    }
}
```

Running `longest` against all 192 countries in the world isn't a problem, but using it to find the longest city name out of 2.5 million can cause the application to fail; see figure 7.5. (Actually, this particular algorithm won't fail with large arrays in ES6 JavaScript; more on this later.)

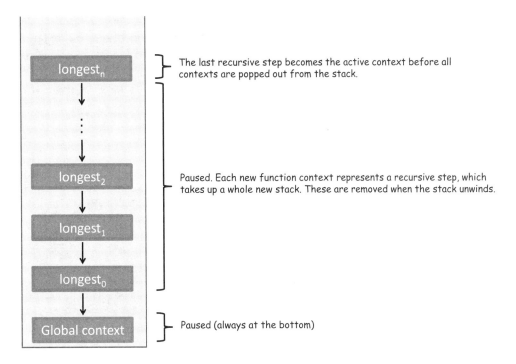

Figure 7.5 The `longest` function, in order to find the longest string in an array of size *n*, grows proportionally to the size of the input, inserting *n* frames into the context stack.

An alternative to keep in mind when traversing lists this way, especially with unusually large arrays, is to resort to using higher-order functions you learned about in chapter 3, such as `map`, `filter`, and `reduce`. Using these functions doesn't generate nested function calls, and the stack size is recycled at each iteration.

Although currying and recursion lead to functions that take up more memory than their otherwise imperative counterparts, think of what you gain in terms of the flexibility and reuse that come with currying, as well as the correctness inherent in recursive solutions. These definitely make the extra memory requirements worth it.

On the bright side, functional programming provides optimizations that other paradigms don't. Placing lots of functions on the stack can increase your program's memory footprint, so why not avoid making some calls altogether?

7.2   *Deferring execution using lazy evaluation*

You can experience many performance benefits when avoiding unnecessary function calls and large inputs when only a subset is sufficient. Functional languages like Haskell have *lazy function evaluation* built into every function expression. There are different types of lazy-evaluation schemes, all with the same goal of delaying the execution of a function as much as possible, or until a dependent expression is called.

But the more mainstream function-evaluation strategy, as used in JavaScript, is eager evaluation. In eager evaluation, an expression is evaluated as soon as it's bound to a variable, regardless of whether the result of this function is needed; this is also known as *greedy evaluation*. Consider the sample case of taking a subset of elements from an array, shown in figure 7.6.

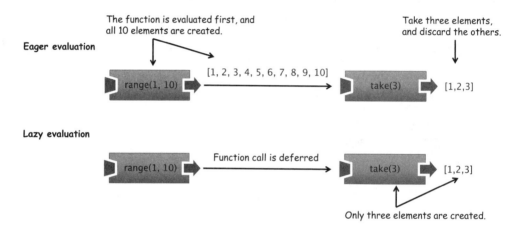

Figure 7.6   The composition of the function `range` (returns a list of numbers from beginning to end) with `take` (reads the first *n* elements). In eager evaluation, the `range` function executes completely, feeding its result to `take`. With lazy evaluation, the result of `range` never executes until the dependent operation, `take`, is called.

As you can see, in the eager-evaluation scheme, the `range` function is executed first; its result is passed to `take`, which only requires a subset of the output, discarding the rest. Think of how wasteful this would be if you were generating a larger number of elements. With lazy evaluation, on the other hand, the execution of `range` is deferred until the dependent operation, `take`, demands it. Now, with more knowledge about the function's purpose, the `range` function only produces the required number of elements. Consider another example involving the `Maybe` monad:

```
Maybe.of(student).getOrElse(createNewStudent());
```

At a glance, using `Maybe` may lead you to think this expression behaves like this:

```
if(!student) {
    return createNewStudent();
}
else {
    return student;
}
```

But due to JavaScript's eager-evaluation scheme, this code will execute the create-NewStudent function regardless of whether the `student` object is `null`. Under lazy evaluation, the expression would have behaved like the earlier snippet and never called `createNewStudent` if the student object were invalid. So how can you take advantage of lazy evaluation? This section looks at a couple of tips and tricks:

- Avoiding needless computations
- Using shortcut fusion in functional libraries

7.2.1 Avoiding computations with the alternation functional combinator

Not surprisingly, you can do certain things to emulate lazy evaluation and still reap some of the benefits of pure functional languages. In the simplest case, you can avoid a needless computation by passing functions by reference (or by name) and conditionally invoking one or the other. In chapter 4, you saw the `alt` functional combinator that takes advantage of the `||` (OR) operator to evaluate `func1` first and only call `func2` in the event `func1` produces a value of `false`, `null`, or `undefined`. Here it is again, with an example:

```
const alt = R.curry((func1, func2, val) => func1(val) || func2(val));

const showStudent = R.compose(append('#student-info'),
    alt(findStudent, createNewStudent));

showStudent('444-44-4444');
```

No functions are prematurely called, because they're passed as references for the combinator to coordinate their invocations.

Because the functional combinator takes care of orchestrating the calls, this code is equivalent to the imperative conditional logic:

```
var student = findStudent('444-44-4444');
if(student !== null) {
    append('#student-info', student);
}
else {
    append('#student-info', createNewStudent('444-44-4444'));
}
```

This is a very simple way of avoiding computing functions unnecessarily with far less duplication; I'll show you a more powerful strategy later in this chapter when we get to *memoization*. Alternatively, defining the entire program ahead of time, before it's run, can allow functional libraries to perform an optimization called *shortcut fusion*.

7.2.2 *Taking advantage of shortcut fusion*

In chapter 3, you learned about Lodash's `_.chain` function, which is used to wrap and execute an entire sequence of functions that you can trigger via the terminating `value()` function. This not only allows you to separate a program's description from its execution, but also lets Lodash infer places for optimizations such as consolidating the execution of some functions for more-efficient storage use. Here's an example that produces a sorted list of people's country by count:

```
_.chain([p1, p2, p3, p4, p5, p6, p7])
   .filter(isValid)
   .map(_.property('address.country'))    .reduce(gatherStats, {})
   .values()
   .sortBy('count')
   .reverse()
   .first()
   .value()
```

This declarative mode of programming means you don't have to worry about how the functions work, just what needs to be done, by defining what it is you want to accomplish ahead of time. On some occasions, this allows Lodash to internally optimize the execution of your program using shortcut fusion. It's a function-level optimization that can merge the execution of some functions into one and condense the number of internal data structures used to compute intermediate results. Creating fewer data structures lowers the excess memory needed when processing large collections.

This is possible due to functional programming's strict rules about referential transparency, which give it this unique mathematical or algebraic correctness. For instance, the execution `compose(map(f), map(g))` can be replaced by the expression `map(compose(f, g))` without altering the meaning. Similarly, `compose(filter(p1), filter(p2))` equates to `filter((x) => p1(x) && p2(x))`. This is exactly what happens in the `filter` and `map` pair beginning the previous chain. Again, manipulating the sequence of operations in this mathematical way is only possible with pure functions. Let's go over another example in the following listing to see this clearly.

Listing 7.1 Lodash's lazy evaluation and shortcut fusion

```
const square = (x) => Math.pow(x, 2);
const isEven = (x) => x % 2 === 0;
const numbers = _.range(200);              ◁——  Generates an array of
                                                  numbers 1–200
const result =
   _.chain(numbers)
    .map(square)
```

```
    .filter(isEven)
    .take(3)
    .value();   //-> [0,4,16]
result.length; //-> 5
```

> Processes only the first three
> numbers that pass the criteria
> imposed by filter(map)

Listing 7.1 has a couple of optimizations: First, the call to take(3) advises Lodash to only worry about the first three values that pass the mapping and filtering criteria instead of wasting precious cycles on the remaining 195 elements. Second, shortcut fusion allows the subsequent calls to map and filter to fuse into compose(filter(isEven), map(square)). You can easily proof this by augmenting the square and isEven functions with trace logs (using Ramda to effectively compose the tap combinator for logging purposes):

```
square = R.compose(R.tap(() => trace('Mapping')), square);
isEven= R.compose(R.tap(() => trace('then filtering')), isEven);
```

The console will show the following pair of messages repeated five times:

```
Mapping
then filtering
```

which confirms the merging of map and filter. Using functional libraries not only simplifies your tests but also improves the runtime of your code. Other functions in Lodash that benefit from shortcut-fusion are _.drop, _.dropRight, _.dropRightWhile, _.dropWhile, _.first, _.initial, _.last, _.pluck, _.reject, _.rest, _.reverse, _.slice, _.takeRight, _.takeRightWhile, _.takeWhile, and _.where.

Along the same lines of avoiding computations until they're needed is another powerful optimization feature of functional programs called *memoization*.

7.3   *Implementing a call-when-needed strategy*

One way to speed up the execution of applications is to avoid computing repetitive values, especially when these computations are expensive. In traditional object-oriented systems, this is accomplished by placing a cache or proxy layer that's checked before a function is called. Upon return, the result of the function is given a key that references it uniquely, and this key-value pair is persisted in the cache. A *cache* is an intermediary repository, or memory, that's queried before an expensive operation. In web applications, it's used for images, documents, compiled code, HTML pages, query results, and so on. Consider this code snippet that implements a simple caching layer for any function:

> Formulates a key value to identify
> the result of this function based on
> the function name and arguments

> Checks the cache first
> to see if the provided
> function was executed
> previously

```
function cachedFn (cache, fn, args) {
    let key = fn.name + JSON.stringify(args);
    if(contains(cache, key)) {
```

```
        return get(cache, key);
    }
    else {
        let result = fn.apply(this, args);
        put(cache, key, result);
        return result;
    }
}
```

If so, the value in the cache is returned (cache hit).

Otherwise, the function is run (cache miss).

Its result is stored in the cache.

You can use this to wrap the execution of findStudent:

```
var cache = {};
cachedFn(cache, findStudent, '444-44-4444');
cachedFn(cache, findStudent, '444-44-4444');
```

The first time results in a cache miss, so findStudent runs.

The second time, the value is read straight from the cache.

This cachedFn function acts as a proxy between the function execution and its result to ensure that the same function isn't invoked twice. But writing code with this wrapper to serve every function call in your code is tedious and makes it hard to read. What's even worse is that this function has a side effect because it depends on a globally shared cache object. What we need is a ubiquitous solution that lets us enjoy the benefits of caching while keeping our code and tests agnostic to this mechanism. In functional languages, this mechanism is called *memoization*.

7.3.1 *Understanding memoization*

The caching scheme behind memoization, similar to the previous code, makes use of the function's arguments to create a unique key with which to store the function's result, so that on subsequent invocations of the function with the same arguments, the stored result can be returned immediately. Relating the function's result with its input, or shall we say, equating the computation of a function's input to a value, is achieved due to a certain functional principle. You guessed it: referential transparency. First, let's study the benefits of memoization with a simple function call.

7.3.2 *Memoizing computationally intensive functions*

Pure functional languages implement memoization automatically; others, like JavaScript and Python, give you the option to choose when to memoize a function. Naturally, functions that are computationally intensive can benefit from interlacing a caching layer. Consider the example of computing a rot13 function, which encodes strings into ROT13 format (rotation of the 26 ASCII characters of the alphabet by 13 positions). Although this is a weak algorithm, it's practical in web applications for hiding puzzle solutions and discount codes, muddling offensive material, and so on:

```
var discountCode = 'functional_js_50_off';

rot13(discountCode); //-> shapgvbany_wf_50_bss
```

Here are the details of the ROT13 algorithm:

```
var rot13 = s =>
   s.replace(/[a-zA-Z]/g, c =>
      String.fromCharCode((c <= 'Z' ? 90 : 122)
         >= (c = c.charCodeAt(0) + 13) ? c : c - 26));
         (c = c.charCodeAt(0) + 13) ? c : c - 26);
   });
};
```

Understanding it isn't relevant to this discussion; the important thing to know is that the computed message is always the same for the same input string (a referentially transparent function), which means you can gain extraordinary performance benefits by memoizing it. Before I show you the code for the `memoize` function, I want to show that you can apply it in two ways:

- By invoking a method on a function object:

  ```
  var rot13 = rot13.memoize();
  ```

- By wrapping the function definition shown earlier:

  ```
  var rot13 = (s =>
     s.replace(/[a-zA-Z]/g, c =>
        String.fromCharCode((c <= 'Z' ? 90 : 122)
           >= (c = c.charCodeAt(0) + 13) ? c : c - 26))).memoize();
  ```

With memoization, you expect a subsequent call of a function with the same input to trigger the internal cache hit and return immediately. To illustrate this, let's use JavaScript's High Resolution Time API (also known as Performance API) to produce more-accurate timestamps than traditional JavaScript functions like `Date.now()` and `console.time()`, and measure the elapsed time of a function call. You'll use the `IO` monad to inject time-capturing statements before and after the function under test. The entire program involves creating simple `start` and `end` functions that wrap the side effects in `performance.now()`, and tapping a simple function used to run the function under test. The following listing shows the time-measuring code; I'll omit it in later examples to make the programs shorter.

Listing 7.2 Using `tap` to add performance timing calls

```
const start = () => performance.now();          Uses start and end functions
                                                to measure time
const end = function (start) {
    let end = performance.now();
    return (end - start).toFixed(3);            Uses the Performance API to
};                                              measure time in milliseconds
                                                to three decimal digits
const test = function (fn, input) {
    return () => fn(input);
};
```

```
const testRot13 =
    IO.of(start)
      .map(R.tap(start('rot13')))
      .map(R.tap(test(
          rot13,
            'functional_js_50_off'
      )))
      .map(end);

testRot13.run(); // 0.733 ms
testRot13.run(); // second time: 0.021 ms
```

Uses the tap combinator to let start-time information propagate through the monad (you do this because you don't care about the result of the function, only the time it takes to run)

As you can see, the second call to `rot13` on the same string returns in a blink of an eye. Although JavaScript has no built-in automatic memoization, you can add it to the language by augmenting the `Function` object as shown next.

Listing 7.3   Adding memoization to function calls

Internal helper method responsible for performing the caching logic for this specific function instance

Stringifies the set of inputs to obtain an identifier for this function. This can be made more robust by detecting the type of input and applying a key-generation scheme accordingly. But for these examples, this is sufficient.

```
Function.prototype.memoized = function () {

    let key = JSON.stringify(arguments);

    this._cache = this._cache || {};

    this._cache[key] = this._cache[key] ||
            this.apply(this, arguments);

    return this._cache[key];
};

Function.prototype.memoize = function () {
    let fn = this;
    if (fn.length === 0 || fn.length > 1) {
        return fn;
    }

    return function () {
      return fn.memoized.apply(fn, arguments);
    };
};
```

Creates an internal local cache for this function instance

Attempts to read the cache first to see if the set of inputs had been computed before. If the value is found, skips the function and returns its result; otherwise, runs the computation.

Enables memoization of this function

Only attempts to memoize unary functions

Wraps this function instance into a memoized function

By extending the `Function` object, this implementation makes memoization ubiquitous and also removes any observable side effects of accessing a globally shared cache. In addition, abstracting the function's internal caching mechanism makes it completely test-agnostic, which means you aren't responsible for sprinkling caching statements all over your code or for testing the caching functionality; you only worry about what the function is supposed to do.

To get a clearer picture, look at the detailed sequence diagram of the memoization of rot13 in figure 7.7. The first call to the memoized function results in a cache miss and the ROT13 message being computed. On completion, the result of the computation is stored with a key generated from the input arguments so that the result can be reused and skip all computations on the next invocation.

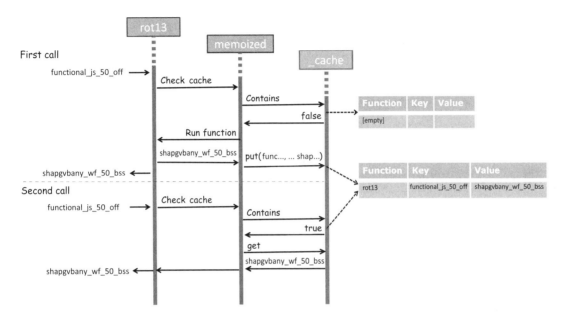

Figure 7.7   A detailed view of two calls to the rot13 function with the message "functional_js_50_off." The first time around, with an empty cache, the ROT13 code of the provided discount code is computed. This result is stored in the internal cache with a key generated from this input. The second call results in a cache hit: the value is directly returned without the hash being computed again.

NOTE   The examples in this book memoize functions of one argument. But how would you handle functions of multiple arguments? I won't cover this, and instead leave it to you as an exercise to research, but there are two strategies you can follow: you can create a multidimensional cache (an array of arrays), or you can create a unique key by combining the string representation of the arguments.

If you closer at the code in listing 7.3, you'll notice that memoization is limited to unary functions. I did it this way to simplify the key-generation step in the caching logic. If you need to memoize functions that take multiple arguments, the logic for formulating a proper cache key can get complicated and expensive. In some cases, though, currying can help you work around this issue.

7.3.3 *Taking advantage of currying and memoization*

More-complex functions, or functions involving multiple arguments, are harder to cache, even if they're pure. This is due to the increased complexity in generating a proper key value—an operation that needs to be simple and quick in order to avoid incurring additional overhead in the caching layer. One way to mitigate this is through currying. Recall from chapter 4 that currying is used to transform a multivariate function into a unary function. Currying allows you to memoize a function like safeFindObject through findStudent:

```
const safeFindObject = R.curry(function (db, ssn) {     ◁——
  // expensive IO lookup operation
});
```

This function isn't referentially transparent, but in practice it's customary to cache the results of expensive lookups and remote HTTP requests.

```
const findStudent = safeFindObject(DB('students')).memoize();
findStudent('444-44-4444');
```

This works because the DB object is used only for data access and doesn't contribute to uniquely distinguishing the purpose of findStudent, which is to find a student by a unique ID. The emphasis on making functions unary is not only to make them easier to work with and compose, but also so that memoization can take advantage of finer-grained decomposition and implement caching across the components that make up the entire program. Let's discuss this next.

7.3.4 *Decomposing to maximize memoization*

The relationship of memoization and decomposition can be understood with a simple chemical analogy that will take you on a stroll down memory lane (bear with me!). You may have learned in high school chemistry, when studying the principles of solubility, that a solution is composed of a solute and a solvent. A solute is the substance that dissolves in the solvent. The rate of solution, which is how quickly a solute dissolves, is determined by many factors, one of which is *surface area*. For instance, if you prepare two solutions of sugar and water, one with powdered sugar and the other with chunks of sugar, which one dissolves faster? When sugar dissolves, only its surface comes in contact with the water. Therefore, the greater the surface area of the solute, the faster it dissolves.

This same analogy can be applied to breaking up problems into tiny, memoizable functions. The more fine-grained your code is, the greater the benefits obtained via memoization will be. Each and every function's internal caching mechanism is playing a role in speeding up evaluation of your programs—there's more surface contact, if you will.

In the case of showStudent, for example, if you've previously validated certain inputs, why bother to validate them again? Similarly, if you've fetched student objects by SSN from a local store, with cookies, or even via a server-side call, and you don't expect them to have changed, why waste precious time doing the lookup again? What's remarkable is that in the case of findStudent, memoization can serve as a small query cache, retaining already-fetched objects for quick access. Memoization puts the icing on the cake in terms of reasoning about functions as just values—lazily computed values. To illustrate, let's replace some of the functions in showStudent with their memoized counterparts (just for illustration purposes, the memoized functions are prefixed with m_—this isn't a general convention):

```
const m_cleanInput = cleanInput.memoize();
const m_checkLengthSsn = checkLengthSsn.memoize();
const m_findStudent = findStudent.memoize();

const showStudent = R.compose(
    map(append('#student-info')),
    liftIO,
    chain(csv),
    map(R.props(['ssn', 'firstname', 'lastname'])),
    map(m_findStudent),
    map(m_checkLengthSsn),
    lift(m_cleanInput));

showStudent('444-44-4444').run(); //-> 9.2 ms on average (no memoization)

showStudent('444-44-4444').run(); //-> 2.5 ms on average (with memoization)
```

Because this function is decomposed into smaller tasks, the speed improvements are compounded, creating a program that runs 75% faster the second time around!

Recursion is another type of decomposition, where a program is split into self-similar smaller tasks—memoizable, self-similar subtasks. Likewise, memoization can turn a slow-performing recursive algorithm into a really fast one.

7.3.5 *Applying memoization to recursive calls*

Recursion can cause a browser to grind to a halt or throw nasty exceptions. This tends to happen when the stack grows out of control, such as when processing very large input. In some cases, memoization can help mitigate the issue. As you learned in chapter 3, recursion is a mechanism of decomposing a task into smaller versions of itself. Typically, a recursive call solves "the same problem," or a subset of the bigger problem, many times until it reaches the base case, which finally causes the stack to unwind and the result to be returned. If you could cache the results of the subtasks, you could improve the performance of invoking this same function on bigger input.

To illustrate, you'll use a simple function that computes the factorial of a number *n*. The factorial of *n* (denoted *n*!) is the product of all positive integers less than or equal to *n*:

$$n! = n * (n - 1) * (n - 2) * \ldots * 3 * 2 * 1$$

For example:

$$3! = 3 * 2 * 1 = 6$$
$$4! = 4 * 3 * 2 * 1 = 4 * 3! = 24$$

> Notice that factorial numbers can also be recursively defined in terms of smaller factorials, such as $4! = 4 \times 3!$.

The program for this task can be nicely expressed as a memoized recursive solution:

```
const factorial = ((n) => (n === 0) ? 1
               : (n * factorial(n - 1))).memoize();

factorial(100); //-> Takes .299 ms
factorial(101); //-> Second time, takes .021 ms
```

> Runs through the entire computation $100 \times 99 \times 98 \times \ldots \times 3 \times 2 \times 1$

> Uses the previously cached value to shortcut the computation, stopping at $101 \times 100!$

Because memoization uses the mathematical principles of factorials, you obtain remarkable throughput in the second iteration of the function. In the second run, the function "remembers" to use the formula $101! = 101 \times 100!$ and can reuse the value of `factorial(100)`, causing the entire algorithm to short-circuit and return instantly. This has other benefits in terms of stack frame management and avoiding stack pollution; see figure 7.8.

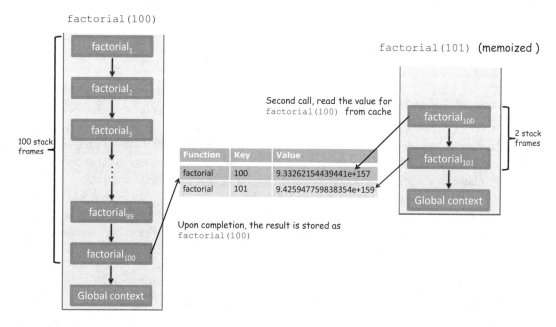

Figure 7.8 Running the memoized `factorial(100)` the first time creates 100 stack frames because it needs to compute 100! by multiplying every single number. On the second call to `factorial` with 101, via memoization it's able to reuse the result of `factorial(100)` and create only 2 stack frames.

As you can see, the first run of `factorial(100)` runs through the entire algorithm, creating 100 frames on the function stack. This is the downfall of some recursive solutions: they tend to be careless with stack space, especially in cases such as `factorial` that use frames proportional to the input received. But with memoization, you can significantly reduce the number of stack frames required to compute the next number.

Memoization isn't the only method to optimize recursive calls. There are other ways to benefit performance by using compiler-level instrumentation.

7.4 *Recursion and tail-call optimization (TCO)*

All along, you've seen that programs with recursion use the stack much more heavily than ones that don't. Some functional languages don't even have built-in looping mechanisms and rely on recursion and memoization to implement efficient iteration. But there are cases where even memoization won't help much, such as when the nature of the input to the functions is always changing; then, nothing is gained from having an internal caching layer. Can recursion be optimized to run as efficiently as standard loops? It turns out that you can write recursive algorithms in such a way that compilers help you achieve this with *tail-call optimization* (TCO). In this section, you'll learn that this recursive factorial function

```
const factorial = (n, current = 1) =>
   (n === 1) ? current
      : factorial(n - 1, n * current);
```

The recursive step is now the last statement in this function (said to be in tail position).

which is slightly different than the previous one because it places the recursive step in tail position, runs as fast as the imperative version:

```
var factorial = function (n) {
   let result = 1;
   for(let x = n; x > 1; x--) {
      result *= x;
   }
   return result;
}
```

TCO, also known as *tail-call elimination*, is a compiler enhancement added to ES6 that flattens the execution of a recursive call into a single frame. But this can only occur when the last act of the recursive solution is to invoke another function (typically itself); this last invocation is said to be in *tail position* (hence the name).

Why is this an optimization? Having a function call as the last thing to run in a recursive function allows the JavaScript runtime to realize it doesn't need to hold on to the current stack frame any longer, because it doesn't have any more work to do; so it discards the stack frame. In most cases, you achieve this by transferring all the necessary state from one function context to the next as part of the function's arguments (as you saw in the recursive factorial function). This way, the recursive iteration tends to happen with a new frame every time, recycled from the previous one, instead of frames stacked one after the other. Because `factorial` is in tail form, the execution of `factorial(4)` goes from the typical recursive pyramid of calls

```
factorial(4)
  4 * factorial(3)
    4 * 3 * factorial(2)
      4 * 3 * 2 * factorial(1)
        4 * 3 * 2 * 1 * factorial(0)
          4 * 3 * 2 * 1 * 1
        4 * 3 * 2 * 1
      4 * 3 * 2
    4 * 6
return 24
```

to the following flat structure, as shown in figure 7.9, with respect to the context stack:

```
factorial(4)
  factorial(3, 4)
  factorial(2, 12)
  factorial(1, 24)
  factorial(0, 24)
  return 24
return 24
```

As you can see, this flatter structure makes more efficient use of the stack, which no longer needs to unwind *n* frames. Let's step through the process of converting the non-tail `factorial` function into the tail-recursive function.

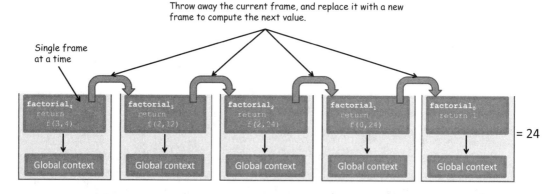

Figure 7.9 A detailed view of tail-recursive `factorial(4)` evaluation. As you can see, the function uses a single frame. TCO is in charge of throwing the current function frame to give way for a new one, as if `factorial` was being evaluated in a loop.

7.4.1 *Converting non-tail calls to tail calls*

Let's optimize `factorial` to take advantage of JavaScript's TCO mechanism. The recursive implementation of `factorial` that you started with

```
const factorial = (n) =>
   (n === 1) ? 1
    : (n * factorial(n - 1));
```

wasn't in tail position because the last return expression multiplies a number times the value of the recursive step: `n * factorial(n - 1)`. Remember that for TCO to occur, the last step needs to be the recursive step, which is what allows the runtime to convert `factorial` into a loop. You'll do this in two steps:

1 Move the multiplication as an additional parameter to the function, to keep track of the current multiplication.
2 Use ES6 default parameters to preset a default value for this argument (you could also partially apply them, but with default arguments it will look much cleaner):

```
const factorial = (n, current = 1) =>
   (n === 1) ? current :
      factorial(n - 1, n * current);
```

Now this factorial function will run as if it were implemented with standard looping, with no additional stack frames created, while still preserving some of the declarative and mathematical feel it originally had. This transformation takes place because a tail-recursive function shares common features with a standard loop, as shown in figure 7.10.

```
var factorial = function (n) {        var factorial = (n, current = 1)
   let result = 1;         ─ Base case ─→     => (n === 1) ? current :
   for(let x = n; x > 1; x--) {           factorial(n - 1, n * current);
     result *= x;
   }
   return result;
}
                                    Afterthought

                              Result
```

Figure 7.10 The similarities between a standard loop (left) and its equivalent tail-recursive function. In both code samples, you can easily see the base case, the afterthought or accumulated parameter, and the result.

Let's examine another example. In chapter 3, you saw a small recursive solution to sum up all the elements in an array:

```
function sum(arr) {
   if(_.isEmpty(arr)) {
      return 0;
   }
   return _.first(arr) + sum(_.rest(arr));
}
```

Again, you can see that the last action this function performs, `_.first(arr) + sum(_.rest(arr))`, isn't in tail form. Let's refactor this code and optimize it for memory consumption. Again, any data that needs to be shared with subsequent invocations is now added as part of the function arguments:

```
function sum(arr, acc = 0) {
   if(_.isEmpty(arr)) {
      return 0;
   }
   return sum(_.rest(arr), acc + _.first(arr));
}
```

Tail recursion brings the performance of a recursive loop closer to that of a manual loop. So in languages that have it, as ES6 JavaScript does, it can be used as a replacement for manual loops when performance is of upmost priority, while keeping the correctness of the algorithm and controlling mutations. But tail calls aren't limited to recursion. They can be used with any function whose last action is to invoke another function, which tends to happen quite a bit in JavaScript applications. The caveat when using TCO, however, is that this new JavaScript standard, which began to be drafted with ES4, is not yet widely adopted by browsers. In fact, as of this writing, none of the browsers have TCO natively implemented, which is why I've been using the Babel transpiler.

Emulating tail-recursive calls in ES5

The current mainstream JavaScript implementation, ES5, doesn't have support for tail-call optimization. This was added to the language with the ES6 proposal known as *proper tail calls* (section 14.6 of the ECMA-262 specification). Recall from chapter 2 that the examples work due to the use of the Babel transpiler, a source-to-source compiler, which is an excellent way to test out the future features of the language.

But you can work around this through a process called *trampolining*. Trampolining is a way to simulate tail recursion in an iterative way, which is ideal for controlling function stack growth in stack-based languages like JavaScript.

A trampoline is a function combinator that takes another function as input and invokes it repeatedly (or bounces a function, if you will) until a certain condition occurs. The function that bounces or repeats is encapsulated in a structure called a *thunk.* A thunk is nothing more than a function wrapper used to assist a call to another function. In the context of functional JavaScript, thunks lazily wrap an argument expression in an anonymous function that has no parameters of its own, delaying its evaluation until a receiving function invokes the anonymous function.

The topics of trampolining and thunks are outside of the scope of this book, so if you're desperately seeking to optimize your recursive functions now, I recommend you begin your research here.

To check for the compatibility of TCO and other ES6 features, you can check out the following website: https://kangax.github.io/compat-table/es6/.

If you're writing a tight graphics-rendering loop or you need to process large datasets in a short time, then performance becomes a key requirement. In these cases, you're ready to make the necessary trade-offs, and you aren't looking to write elegant, extensible code—you need to get the job done fast. For this, I recommend sticking to standard loops. But for most application needs, functional programming remains a very performant way to write code. Always optimize last; and, in certain edge cases that require extra milliseconds of performance, you can always use any of the performance enhancements provided in this chapter.

Every software decision has an equal opposing force; but for most applications, sacrificing efficiency in favor of maintainability is a valid trade-off, in my opinion. I'd much rather write code that is easy to read and debug, even if it's not the fastest. As Knuth said, "In 97% of the code you write, a few extra milliseconds make no difference, especially compared to the value of writing maintainable code."

Functional programming is a complete paradigm. It provides a rich level of abstraction and redirection while crafting interesting ways to make it efficient. Until now, you've learned how to create functional programs with linear data flows through chaining or composition. But as you're well aware, JavaScript programs mix in lots of nonlinear or asynchronous behavior, such as when handling user input or making remote HTTP requests. In chapter 8, you'll take on these challenges and learn about reactive programming, a paradigm built on the principles of functional programming.

7.5   *Summary*

- In certain cases, functional code can be slower or consume more memory than its equivalent imperative counterpart.
- You can implement a deferred strategy using lazy evaluation by taking advantage of the alternation combinator and the support provided in functional libraries like Lodash.
- Memoization, an internal function-level caching strategy, can be used to avoid duplicating the evaluation of potentially expensive functions.

- Decomposing programs into simple functions can not only create extensible code, but also make it more efficient via memoization.
- Decomposition also extends into recursion as a method to solve a problem in terms of self-similar simpler problems, fully utilizing memoization to optimize the use of the context stack.
- Converting functions to tail-recursive form allows you to take advantage of a compiler enhancement known as tail-call elimination.

Managing asynchronous
events and data

8

This chapter covers

- Identifying the challenges of writing asynchronous code
- Avoiding the use of nested callbacks through functional techniques
- Streamlining asynchronous code using promises
- Generating data lazily with function generators
- Introducing reactive programming
- Applying reactive programming to tackle event-driven code

Functional programmers argue that there are great material benefits— that a functional programmer is an order of magnitude more productive than his conventional counterpart, because functional programs are an order of magnitude shorter.

—John Hughes, "Why Functional Programming Matters"[1]

---

[1] From *Research Topics in Functional Programming*," ed. D. Turner (Addison-Wesley, 1990), 17–42, http://mng.bz/Zr02.

Until now, you've been learning how to think functionally and using functional techniques to write, test, and optimize your JavaScript code. All of these techniques are designed to tame the complexities intrinsic to mid- and large-scale web applications, which can easily become increasingly difficult to maintain. Many years ago, interaction with web applications was limited to submitting large forms and rendering entire pages at once. Applications have evolved, and with them the demands of users. Nowadays, we all expect pages to behave more like native applications that respond and react in real time.

In the world of client-side JavaScript, the number of challenges we face is greater than in any other environment. This is directly influenced by the emergence of bulky client code that not only shares the burden associated with conventional web middleware, but also needs to effectively interact with user input, communicate with remote servers (via AJAX), and display data on the screen, all at once. The proposed solution in this book is functional programming, which is ideal for systems that need to maintain a high level of integrity despite all of these concerns.

In this chapter, you'll apply functional programming to tackle real-world JavaScript programming challenges related to asynchronous data flows where code isn't linear to the program's execution. Some of the examples feature browser technology like AJAX and local storage requests. The goal is to use functional programming in conjunction with ES6 promises, as well as introduce reactive programming, both of which are used to turn messy callback code into elegant, fluent expressions. Reactive programming will seem familiar because it's a way of thinking about problems that follows closely from functional programming.

Asynchronous behavior is tricky to get right. Unlike normal functions, asynchronous functions can't just return data to the caller. Instead, you rely on the infamous callback pattern that notifies you when long-running computations, database fetches, or remote HTTP calls have been computed. You also use callbacks to handle browser events like clicks, key presses, and mobile gestures in response to user interaction. You need to build code that responds to these events happening after your program is run, which poses many challenges for a functional design that instead expects data to come in predictably and at the right time. After all, how you can compose or chain functions for behavior that will happen in the future?

8.1 Challenges of asynchronous code

Modern JavaScript programs are seldom loaded in a single request; most often, data is progressively loaded on the page by multiple asynchronous requests that respond to a user's needs. A simple use case is an email client. Your inbox can have thousands of long email threads, yet you see and interact only with the recent ones. It doesn't make sense for you to have to wait a few seconds (or even minutes) for your entire inbox to load. As JavaScript developers, we deal with problems of this nature frequently, and they all involve implementing some form of nonblocking asynchronous calls, which can present the following challenges:

- The creation of temporal dependencies among your functions
- The inevitable fall into a callback pyramid
- An incompatible mix of synchronous and asynchronous code

8.1.1 *Creating temporal dependencies among functions*

Consider a function used to perform an AJAX request to fetch a list of student objects from the server. In figure 8.1, because getJSON is asynchronous, the function returns as soon as the request is sent and gives control back to the program, which subsequently invokes showStudents. But at this point in time, the students object is still null because the slower remote request hasn't yet completed. The only way to ensure that the right order of events transpires is to create a *temporal dependency* between the asynchronous code and the action to take next. This involves including showStudents in the callback function so that it's executed at the right time.

```
var students = null;
getJSON('/students', function(studentObjs) {
    students = studentObjs;
  },
  function (errorObj) {
    console.log(errorObj.message);
  }
);

showStudents(students);
```

This flow is temporally broken because the student object won't be initialized in time.

Figure 8.1 **This code has a big problem. Can you spot it? Because you need to fetch data asynchronously, the students object will never be populated in time to be added to the roster table.**

Temporal coupling or *temporal cohesion* occurs when the execution of certain functions is logically grouped together. This is done when functions need to wait for data to be available or need to wait for other functions to run. Whether you're depending on data or, in this case, time, both can cause side effects.

Because performing remote IO operations is noticeably slower than the rest of your code, you delegate them to nonblocking processes that can request data and "wait" for it to come back. When data is received, the user-provided callback function is invoked. This is precisely what getJSON does; the following listing shows the details.

Listing 8.1   Function `getJSON` using the native `XMLHttpRequest`

```
const getJSON = function (url, success, error) {
    let req = new XMLHttpRequest();
    req.responseType = 'json';
    req.open('GET', url);
    req.onload = function() {
        if(req.status == 200) {
            let data = JSON.parse(req.responseText);
            success(data);
        }
        else {
            req.onerror();
        }
    }
    req.onerror = function () {
        if(error) {
            error(new Error(req.statusText));
        }
    };
    req.send();
};
```

Callback functions are commonly used in JavaScript. But they're hard to scale when you need to load more data sequentially, which leads to the popular callback pattern.

8.1.2   *Falling into a callback pyramid*

The main use of callbacks is to avoid blocking the UI to wait for long-running processes to complete. Functions that accept a callback instead of returning values implement a form of *inversion of control*: "Don't call me, I'll call you." As soon as an event happens, such as data being available or a user clicking a button, the callback function is invoked with the requested data to allow your synchronous code to run:

```
var students = null;
getJSON('/students',
    function(students) {
        showStudents(students);
    },
    function (error) {
        console.log(error.message);
    }
);
```

In the event of an error, the corresponding error callback function is called, giving you the chance to report the error and recover. But this inversion of control works against the design of functional programs, where functions are supposed to be independent of one another and are expected to return values to the caller immediately. As I said earlier, this situation worsens if you need to add more asynchronous logic into already-nested callbacks.

To show this, consider a slightly more complicated scenario. Suppose that after fetching a list of students from the server, you also need to fetch grades—but only for students residing in the United States. This data is then sorted by SSN and displayed on an HTML page, as shown in the next listing.

Listing 8.2 Nested JSON calls, each with its own success and error callbacks

```
getJSON('/students',
    function (students) {                          First level of nesting on the
        students.sort(function(a, b){              first AJAX request with
            if(a.ssn < b.ssn) return -1;           success and error callbacks
            if(a.ssn > b.ssn) return 1;
            return 0;
        });
        for (let i = 0; i < students.length; i++) {
            let student = students[i];
            if (student.address.country === 'US') {
                getJSON(`/students/${student.ssn}/grades`,    Second level of
                    function (grades) {                       nesting to fetch grade
                        showStudents(student, average(grades));   data for each student
                    },                                        with its own success
                    function (error) {                        and error callbacks
                        console.log(error.message);
                    });
            }
        }
    },
    function (error) {                             First level of nesting on the
        console.log(error.message);                first AJAX request with
    }                                              success and error callbacks
);
```

You receive grades for each student, so you change this function to add each student to the table with the respective grade, one at a time.

Before you read this book, this code would've looked acceptable to you; but to a functional programmer such as yourself, it looks messy and tangled (later, I'll show you a complete functional version of this code). The same effect occurs when handling events. Listing 8.3 interleaves AJAX calls with user-input handling. It listens for clicks and mouse events, fetches multiple pieces of data from the server, and renders the data on the DOM.

Listing 8.3 Retrieving student records from the server by SSN

```
var _selector = document.querySelector;
_selector('#search-button').addEventListener('click',
    function (event) {
        event.preventDefault();

        let ssn = _selector('#student-ssn').value;
        if(!ssn) {
            console.log('WARN: Valid SSN needed!');
            return;
        }
```

```
    else {
       getJSON(`/students/${ssn}`, function (info) {
           _selector('#student-info').innerHTML = info;
           _selector('#student-info').addEventListener('mouseover',
               function () {
                   getJSON(`/students/${info.ssn}/grades`,
                       function (grades) {
                           // ... process list of grades for this
                           //     student...
                       });
               });
       })
       .fail(function() {
           console.log('Error occurred!');
       });
    }
});
```

Again, this code is hard to follow. As you can see, nesting a sequence of callbacks quickly makes the code resemble a horizontal pyramid like the one shown in figure 8.2. This is known casually as "callback hell" or the "Christmas tree of doom," characteristic of programs dealing with lots of asynchronous code and user/DOM behavior.

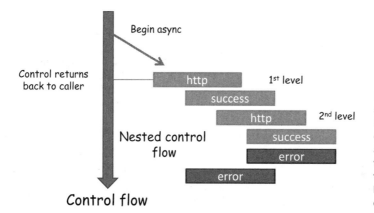

Figure 8.2 A program's simple linear control flow breaks down on a remote call and degenerates into a waterfall of nested function calls—a pyramid that grows horizontally like a "Christmas tree of doom."

When a program begins taking this form, you find yourself relying on spacing and syntactic organization, such as grouping statements just to improve readability. But this is just putting lipstick on a pig. Let's see how thinking functionally can help in this situation.

8.1.3   *Using continuation-passing style*

Listing 8.3 is another example of a program that hasn't been properly decomposed. The nested callback functions not only are hard to read, but also create closures that enclose their own scope plus the variable scope of the functions in which they're nested. The only reason to nest a function in another is when it needs direct access to its outer variables in order to fulfill its purpose. But in this case, the inner callback function that processes all the grades still keeps references to unnecessary external data. One solution that makes this code better is to unravel it by using *continuation-passing style* (CPS). In the following listing, I refactored listing 8.3 using CPS.

Listing 8.4   Refactoring student retrieval using continuation-passing style

```
var _selector = document.querySelector;

_selector('#search-button').addEventListener('click', handleMouseMovement);

var processGrades = function (grades) {
    // ... process list of grades for this student...
};

var handleMouseMovement = () =>
    getJSON(`/students/${info.ssn}/grades`, processGrades);

var showStudent = function (info) {
    _selector('#student-info').innerHTML = info;
    _selector('#student-info').addEventListener(
        'mouseover', handleMouseMovement);
};

var handleError = error =>
    console.log('Error occurred' + error.message);

var handleClickEvent = function (event) {
    event.preventDefault();

    let ssn = _selector('#student-ssn').value;
    if(!ssn) {
        alert('Valid SSN needed!');
        return;
    }
    else {
        getJSON(`/students/${ssn}`, showStudent).fail(handleError);
    }
};
```

All I did was separate the inner callbacks into separate functions or lambda expressions. CPS is a style of programming used for nonblocking programs that encourages you to separate pieces of a program into individual components; for this reason, it's an intermediate form of functional programming. In this case, the callback functions are known as the *current continuations,* which are provided by its callers on the return value. An important advantage of CPS is its efficiency in terms of the context stack (revisit chapter 7 for information on JavaScript's function stack). If your program is completely in CPS (like listing 8.4), continuing into other functions will clean up the current function's context and prepare a new one to support the function that continues the flow of the program—every function is essentially in tail form.

Using continuations also fixes a problem in listing 8.2 that occurs when interlacing synchronous and asynchronous behavior. The problematic section of code is the nested loop that makes AJAX requests to retrieve each student's grades and compute their average:

```
for (let i = 0; i < students.length; i++) {
    let student = students[i];
    if (student.address.country === 'US') {
        getJSON(`/students/${student.ssn}/grades`,
            function (grades) {
                showStudents(student, average(grades));
            },
            function (error) {
              console.log(error.message);
            }
        );
    }
}
```

At a glance, this code looks like it should work and print the names of students Alonzo Church and Haskell Curry with their respective information (the code uses an HTML table to append all data for each student, but it could also be a file or a database insert). Running it, however, produces the result shown in figure 8.3.

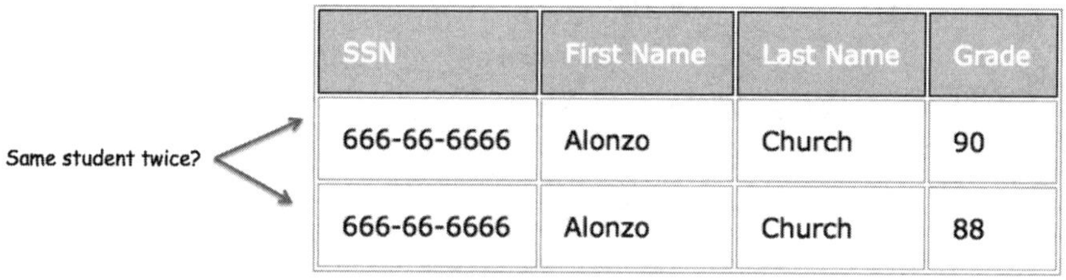

SSN	First Name	Last Name	Grade
666-66-6666	Alonzo	Church	90
666-66-6666	Alonzo	Church	88

Same student twice?

Figure 8.3   Results from running the buggy imperative code that mixes asynchronous functions with a synchronous loop. While fetching the remote data, the function call will always refer to the last iterated student record (in its closure) and print it several times.

Certainly not what you expected. Why is the same student printed twice? The error is due to using a synchronous artifact—a loop, in this case—to execute an asynchronous function, getJSON. The loop doesn't understand that it needs to wait for getJSON to complete. Regardless of using the block-scoped keyword let, all the inner calls to showStudents(student, average(grades)) see the last student object reference in its closure, displaying the same student record. We discussed this in chapter 2 when we looked at the ambiguous loop problem, and it's a testimony that a function's closure isn't a copy of its enclosing environment but an actual reference to it. Notice that the grade column is still correct, though. This is because the fetched value is properly passed into the callback by coupling the right value to the function's parameter.

As you learned in chapter 2, the solution to this problem is to properly scope the student object into a function that makes the AJAX request. Using CPS in this case is not as straightforward as before, because the nested callback function to handle the grades depends on the student object as well. Remember, this is a side effect. Restoring the continuation requires you to think about what you learned in chapter 4 on currying, to help link function inputs and outputs:

```
const showStudentsGrades = R.curry(function (student, grades) {          Currying lets you to
    appendData(student, average(grades));                                convert this into a
});                                                                      unary function.

const handleError = error => console.log(error.message);                 Function appendData
                                                                         appends the rows on
const processStudent = function (student) {                              the HTML table.
    if (student.address.country === 'US') {
        getJSON(`/students/${student.ssn}/grades`,
            showStudentsGrades(student), handleError);                   The curried function
    }                                                                    showStudentsGrades(student)
};                                                                       is eventually called back with
                                                                         the grade data.
for (let i = 0; i < students.length; i++) {
    processStudent(students[i]);                                         Passing the looped object into
}                                                                        the function effectively captures
                                                                         the student into its closure.
```

This new code computes the correct results shown in figure 8.4.

Correct results

SSN	First Name	Last Name	Grade
444-44-4444	Haskell	Curry	90
666-66-6666	Alonzo	Church	88

Figure 8.4 Passing the current student object as a parameter properly sets the function's closure and solves the ambiguity resulting from executing remote calls in a loop.

Adopting a continuation passing style helps to break the temporal dependency in your code, as well as disguise the asynchronous flow into a linear evaluation of functions—both good things. But someone else reading this code, who isn't familiar with it, may be confused as to why the functions aren't executing at the right times. You need to make these long-running operations first-class objects in your programs.

8.2 *First-class asynchronous behavior with promises*

The previous code example is definitely an improvement over the imperative asynchronous programs you saw at the beginning of the chapter, but it's far from being functional. As with any functional program, you also seek other qualities like these:

- Using composition and point-free programming
- Flattening the nested structure into a more linear flow
- Abstracting the notion of temporal coupling so that you don't need to be concerned with it
- Consolidating error handling to a single function rather than multiple error callbacks so that it's not in the way of the code

Whenever I talk about flattening structures, composition, and consolidating behavior, a design pattern should come to mind; this sounds like the job for a monad. Let's explore the `Promise` monad. Just to give you a rough idea, imagine a monad that wraps a long computation (this isn't the actual `Promise` interface, but a close analogy):

```
Promise.of(<long computation>).map(fun1).map(fun2);//-> Promise(result)
```

Unlike the other monads you learned about in this book, promises know to "wait" for the long-running computation to complete before the mapped functions are run. In this manner, this data type tackles head-on the problem of latency present in asynchronous calls. Just like `Maybe` and `Either` document functions with uncertain return values, promises make the notion of waiting for data honest and transparent; they also have the benefit of providing a simpler alternative for executing, composing, and managing asynchronous operations when compared to traditional callback-based approaches.

You can use promises to wrap a value or a function to be processed in the future (if you have some Java experience, this is similar to the `Future<V>` object). A long-running operation can be a complex calculation, fetching data from a database or a server, reading a file, and so on. In the event of a failure, promises allow you to consolidate error-handling logic using approaches with a look and feel much like that used with `Maybe` and `Either`. In a similar fashion, a promise can provide information about the state of the work being done, so you can ask questions such as these: Has data been fetched successfully? And were there any errors during the operation?

As you can see in figure 8.5, at any point in time a promise can be in any of these states: pending, fulfilled, rejected, or settled. It begins with a status of *pending* (also called *unresolved*). Depending on the outcome of the long-running operation, the promise can move into either *fulfilled* (in case `resolve` is called) or *rejected* (in case `reject` is called). Once a promise has been fulfilled, it can notify other objects (continuations or callbacks) that its data has arrived; or, in the case of errors, it can invoke

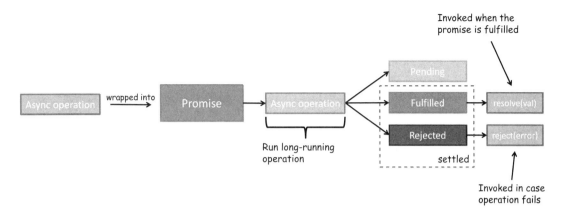

Figure 8.5 How an async operation is wrapped in a `Promise` and provided with two callbacks: one for `resolve` and another for `reject`. The promise begins with a status of pending and then is either fulfilled or rejected, invoking the function `resolve` or `reject`, respectively, before moving into the settled state.

any failure callback function that you registered with it. At this point, the promise is said to be in the *settled* state.

Promises allow you to reason about your programs more effectively and to cut through tangled and tightly coupled callbacks. Just as `Maybe` was used to eliminate the number of nested `if-else` conditions resulting from `null`-checks in your code, `Promise` can be used to convert a series of nested callback functions into a sequence of actions, similar to a monad's `map` functor.

ES6 has adopted the Promises/A+ standard, which is an open standard for the interoperability of JavaScript promises across browser manufacturers. The reference document can be found at https://promisesaplus.com; I encourage you to read it to learn more about the intricacies of this protocol as well as the terminology. At a basic level, here's how you can construct a `Promise` object:

```
var fetchData = new Promise(function (resolve, reject) {

   // fetch data async or run long-running computation

   if (<success>) {
      resolve(result);
   }
   else {
      reject(new Error('Error performing this operation!'));
   }
});
```

The promise constructor takes a single function (called the *action* function) that wraps the asynchronous operation; it takes two callbacks (you can think of them as continuations), `resolve` and `reject`, to be invoked in cases where the promise is either fulfilled or rejected, respectively. Notice the strong influence of the `Either` design pattern as well. Let's look at a quick example using promises in conjunction with the simple `Scheduler` from chapter 4:

```
var Scheduler = (function () {
   let delayedFn = _.bind(setTimeout, undefined, _, _);

   return {
     delay5:  _.partial(delayedFn, _, 5000),
     delay10: _.partial(delayedFn, _, 10000),
     delay:   _.partial(delayedFn, _, _)
   };
})();

var promiseDemo = new Promise(function(resolve, reject) {   ⟵  Schedules a delayed
   Scheduler.delay5(function () {                                function to simulate a
      resolve('Done!');            ⟵  Resolves                  long-running operation
   });                                 the promise
});

promiseDemo.then(function(status) {                            The promise is
   console.log('After 5 seconds, the status is: ' + status);  ⟵  resolved after
});                                                            5 seconds.
```

Just like a monad's `map`, promises provide a mechanism to apply transformations against a value that doesn't exist yet—a value in the future.

8.2.1 Future method chains

The `Promise` object defines a `then` method (analogous to a functor's `fmap`), which applies an operation on a value returned in a promise and closes it back into a `Promise`. Similar to `Maybe.map(f)`, `Promise.then(f)` can be used for chaining data transformations as well as joining functions in time, abstracting the use of temporal coupling among your functions. With this, you can chain multiple levels of dependent asynchronous behavior linearly without creating new nested levels, as seen in figure 8.6.

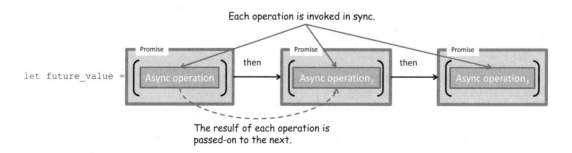

Figure 8.6 A sequence of chained promises joined via the `then` method. Each `then` clause is executed serially with one promise value after the next as soon as each is fulfilled.

The `then` method takes two optional arguments: a callback for success and another for error. Providing error callbacks into each `then` block is ideal for reporting detailed errors, but you can also use a series of success callbacks and defer all error-handling logic to a single `catch` method at the end. Before you begin chaining promises, let's refactor `getJSON` to take advantage of `Promise`—known as *promisifying* a function.

Listing 8.5 Promisifying `getJSON`

```
var getJSON = function (url) {
    return new Promise(function(resolve, reject) {
        let req = new XMLHttpRequest();
        req.responseType = 'json';
        req.open('GET', url);
        req.onload = function() {                    // Called when the
                                                     // AJAX function
                                                     // returns
            if(req.status == 200) {
                let data = JSON.parse(req.responseText);
                resolve(data);                       // If the response is
            }                                        // successful (200
                                                     // response code),
                                                     // resolves the promise
            else {
                reject(new Error(req.statusText));   // Rejects the promise if the
            }                                        // response code is different
        };                                           // than 200 or there was an
        req.onerror = function () {                  // error with establishing a
            if(reject) {                             // connection
                reject(new Error('IO Error'));
            }
        };
        req.send();                    // Sends a remote
    });                                // request
};
```

Promisifying your APIs is good practice. It makes working with your code a lot easier than with traditional callbacks. Because promises are designed to wrap any type of long-running operation, not just fetching data, they can be used with any object that implements a `then` method (known as a *thenable*). Soon, all JavaScript libraries will incorporate promises into their functions.

Promises with jQuery

If you're a jQuery user, you've probably interacted with promises already. jQuery's `$.getJSON` operation (and any variation of the JQuery `$.ajax` calls) returns its own `Deferred` object (a nonstandard version of a `Promise`), which implements the `Promise` interface and has a `then` method. Hence, you can use `Promise.resolve()` to treat the `Deferred` object as a `Promise`:

```
Promise.resolve($.getJSON('/students')).then(function () ...);
```

This object is now a *thenable* and used just like any promisified object. I chose to implement my own `getJSON` in listing 8.5 to illustrate the process of refactoring an API call to use promises.

First let's go over a simple example that fetches student data from the server using this new promise-based `getJSON`, and then you'll incorporate the call to fetch grades so that you can see the chained promises:

```
getJSON('/students').then(
    function(students) {
        console.log(R.map(student => student.name, students));
    },
    function (error) {
        console.log(error.message);
    }
);
```

Now, instead of continuation passing, you'll refactor listing 8.2 with a superior solution based on promises. Here's the code from listing 8.2 once more:

```
getJSON('/students',
    function (students) {
        students.sort(function(a, b){
                if(a.ssn < b.ssn) return -1;
                if(a.ssn > b.ssn) return 1;
                return 0;
        });
        for (let i = 0; i < students.length; i++) {
            let student = students[i];
            if (student.address.country === 'US') {
                getJSON(`/students/${student.ssn}/grades`,
                    function (grades) {
                      showStudents(student, average(grades));
                    },
                    function (error) {
                       console.log(error.message);
                    });
            }
        }
    },
    function (error) {
        console.log(error.message);
    }
);
```

The functional approach in listing 8.6 makes the following changes:

- Instead of nesting asynchronous calls, chain them together using `then` and use the `Promise` monad to abstract out asynchronous parts of the code.
- Remove all variable declarations and mutations in favor of lambda functions.
- Take advantage of Ramda's curried functions to create succinct data-transformation steps like sorting, filtering, and mapping.
- Consolidate error-handling logic into a final catchall function.
- Lift the data into an `IO` monad to write data to the DOM in a side effect–free manner.

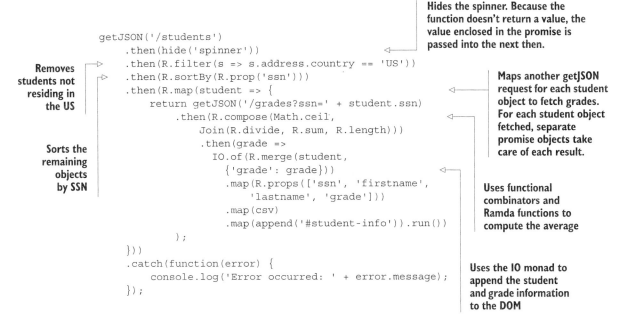

Hides the spinner. Because the function doesn't return a value, the value enclosed in the promise is passed into the next then.

Removes students not residing in the US

Sorts the remaining objects by SSN

```
getJSON('/students')
    .then(hide('spinner'))
    .then(R.filter(s => s.address.country == 'US'))
    .then(R.sortBy(R.prop('ssn')))
    .then(R.map(student => {
        return getJSON('/grades?ssn=' + student.ssn)
            .then(R.compose(Math.ceil,
                Join(R.divide, R.sum, R.length)))
            .then(grade =>
                IO.of(R.merge(student,
                    {'grade': grade}))
                .map(R.props(['ssn', 'firstname',
                    'lastname', 'grade']))
                .map(csv)
                .map(append('#student-info')).run())
            );
    }))
    .catch(function(error) {
        console.log('Error occurred: ' + error.message);
    });
```

Maps another getJSON request for each student object to fetch grades. For each student object fetched, separate promise objects take care of each result.

Uses functional combinators and Ramda functions to compute the average

Uses the IO monad to append the student and grade information to the DOM

Because promises remove the details of handling asynchronous calls, you can create programs that feel as if every function executes one after the other, without any wait time or knowledge that you're requesting data from an external server; promises hide the asynchronous flow but emphasize the notion of time with `then`. In other words, you could just as easily swap `getJSON(url)` with a promisified local storage call, say `getJSON(db)`, and your code would work exactly the same. This level of flexibility is known as *location transparency*. Also notice that the code has a point-free style. Figure 8.7 illustrates the behavior of this program.

The code in listing 8.6 fetches each student and appends them to the DOM one at a time. But by serializing operations to fetch grades, you're losing some precious time. `Promise` also has the ability to take advantage of the browser's multiple connections to fetch multiple items at once. Consider a slight variation to this problem. Suppose that for the same set of students, you want to compute their total average grade. In this case, it doesn't matter in which order you fetch the data or which requests arrive first, so you can do it concurrently. For this, you use `Promise.all()` as shown next.

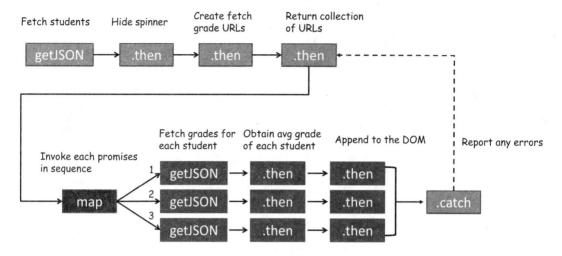

Figure 8.7   The flow of behavior through the chained use of promises. Each thenable block contains a function that transforms the data passed through it. Although this program is bug-free and has all the desired functional qualities, it's inefficient because it uses a waterfall sequence of getJSON requests to fetch each student's grades.

Listing 8.7   Fetching multiple items at once with Promise.all()

```
const average = R.compose(Math.ceil,
    Join(R.divide, R.sum, R.length));
```
Average is pulled into a separate function because it's used more than once.

Computes the average grade for each student

Uses the IO monad to write the values to the console

```
getJSON('/students')
    .then(hide('spinner'))
    .then(R.map(student => '/grades?ssn=' + student.ssn))
    .then(gradeUrls =>
      Promise.all(R.map(getJSON, gradeUrls)))
    .then(R.map(average))
    .then(average)
    .then(grade => IO.of(grade).map(console.log).run())
    .catch(error => console.log('Error occurred: ' + error.message));
```
Downloads all student URLs concurrently

Computes the total average of the class

Using Promise.all takes advantage of the browser's ability to download multiple things at once. The resulting promise resolves as soon as all promises in the iterable argument have resolved. Listing 8.7 brings together two basic components of functional code: splitting a program into simple functions and then composing them together via a monadic data type that orchestrates the program's entire execution. Figure 8.8 illustrates what's happening.

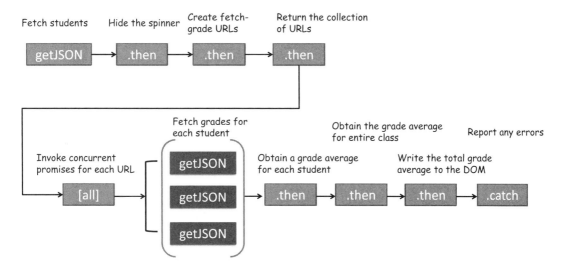

Figure 8.8 The flow of behavior through the chained use of linear as well as concurrent promises with `Promise.all()`. Each thenable block contains a function that transforms the data passed through it. This program is efficient because it can spawn several parallel connections to fetch all the data at once.

But monads aren't effective only for forming method chains. As you learned in previous chapters, they're also effective when used with composition.

8.2.2   Composing synchronous and asynchronous behavior

When you think of the way inputs and outputs of composed functions are linked together, your intuition tells you that these functions must be executing linearly one after the other. But using promises, you can execute functions that are separated in time, while still preserving the look of an otherwise synchronous program made up of functions that compose. This concept is a bit mind-bending to grasp, so I'll explain with an example.

Throughout the code examples in the book, you've used a synchronous version of `find(db, ssn)` to implement `showStudent`. To make things easier, you assumed `find` was synchronous. Now you'll implement the actual asynchronous version that relies on the browser's local store using `IndexedDB`, which can be to used to store objects mapped by a certain key (SSN). If you've never used this API, don't worry. Because you use promises to implement `find`, as shown in the following listing, the important thing to understand here is that if a `student` object exists, the promise will resolve with that object; otherwise, it will be rejected.

Listing 8.8   `find` function using the browser's local store

```
// find :: DB, String -> Promise(Student)
const find = function (db, ssn) {
    let trans = db.transaction(['students'], 'readonly');
    const store = trans.objectStore('students');
    return new Promise(function(resolve, reject) {
        let request = store.get(ssn);
        request.onerror = function() {
            if(reject) {
                reject(new Error('Student not found!'));
            }
        };
        request.onsuccess = function() {
            resolve(request.result);
        };
    });
};
```

Wraps the result of the fetch task into a promise

In the event of a failure finding the object in the store, rejects it

If the object is found, resolves it and passes the matching student object

---

I've omitted the details of setting up the db object because they're not relevant to this discussion. You can learn how to initialize and use the indexed local store API here: https://developer.mozilla.org/en-US/docs/Web/API/IndexedDB_API. What you'll learn from reading this document is that the APIs are all asynchronous—rely on callback passing—for reading and writing to storage. But how can you compose functions together that execute at different moments in time? Until now, the find function has always been synchronous. Luckily, promises abstract the execution of asynchronous code so that composing functions with promises is equivalent to composing functions in the future, with not much change to the code. Before you implement the code, let's create a few helper functions:

```
// fetchStudentDBAsync :: DB -> String -> Promise(Student)
const fetchStudentDBAsync = R.curry(function (db, ssn) {
    return find(db, ssn);
});
```

Curries the datastore object so you can include this function into the composition

```
// findStudentAsync :: String -> Promise
const findStudentAsync = fetchStudentDBAsync(db);
```

```
// then :: f -> Thenable -> Thenable
const then = R.curry(function (f, thenable) {
    return thenable.then(f);
});
```

Enables chaining operations on thenable types (objects that implement a then method, such as Promise)

```
// catchP :: f -> Promise -> Promise
const catchP = R.curry(function (f, promise) {
    return promise.catch(f);
});
```

Provides error logic for a Promise object

```
// errorLog :: Error -> void
const errorLog = _.partial(logger, 'console', 'basic',
    'ShowStudentAsync', 'ERROR');
```

Creates a console error logger

Using these functions with R.compose produces the code in the next listing.

Listing 8.9　Asynchronous version of `showStudent`

```
const showStudentAsync = R.compose(
    catchP(errorLog),
    then(append('#student-info')),
    then(csv),
    then(R.props(['ssn', 'firstname', 'lastname'])),
    chain(findStudentAsync),
    map(checkLengthSsn),
    lift(cleanInput));
```

Catch-all clause in case of errors

Using then is equivalent to a monad's map function.

Point of inflexion where you chain the synchronous to the asynchronous code (explained later)

Here you can really see the power of composition with promises. As figure 8.9 shows, when findStudentAsync runs, the entire program waits for the asynchronous function to return to the caller with data, in order to proceed to execute the rest of the functions. The promise in this case acts as a gateway into the asynchronous part. It's also declarative in that nothing in this program reveals the internal behavior of the asynchronous nature of the function or that callbacks are being used. Thus, compose can still be used to orchestrate point-free programs that glue together functions that won't execute at the same time, but rather in the future, showing its true color as a functional combinator.

I added error-handling logic as well; running this program with an existing SSN showStudentAsync('444-44-4444') successfully appends the student record to the

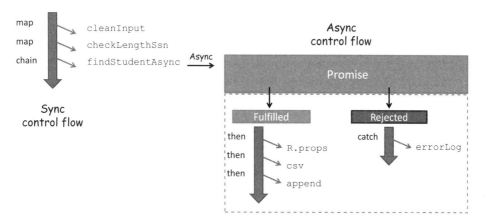

Figure 8.9　When composing synchronous code with asynchronous behavior, there's a point of inflexion in the program where the code shifts into a time-bound adjacent sequence of events that happen within the confines of the promise type.

page. Otherwise, if the promise is rejected, the error is safely propagated throughout the program until the `catch` clause prints the following:

```
[ERROR] Error: Student not found!
```

This program is certainly complex, yet you were able to preserve its functional style by combining many concepts learned throughout this book: composition, higher-order functions, monads, containerization, mapping, chaining, and others. Furthermore, this notion of a program waiting or *yielding* for data to become available is such a compelling concept that it has been introduced as a first-class citizen in ES6 JavaScript, as you'll see next.

8.3 *Lazy data generation*

One of ES6's most powerful features is the ability of functions to cooperate with others by pausing to provide data without necessarily running to completion. This brings many (possibly infinite) opportunities for functions to become vehicles for lazily producing data instead of having to process massive data structures all at once.

On one hand, you can have large collections of objects that are transformed according to business rules (you've done this all along with `map`, `filter`, `reduce`, and others); on the other, you can specify rules that govern how data should be created. For instance, the function x => x * x, in the mathematical sense, is nothing more than a specification for all squared numbers (1, 4, 9, 16, 25, and so on). With some special syntax, this is known as a *generator.*

A generator function is a language-level artifact defined with the `function*` notation (yes, a function with an asterisk). This new type of function has the unique quality that it can be exited using the new keyword `yield` and later reentered having its context (all local variable bindings) saved across reentrances. If you're not familiar with a function's execution context, see chapter 7 for more information. Unlike typical function calls, the ability to reenter a generator is possible because the execution context of a generator function can be temporarily paused and then resumed at will.

Lazily evaluated languages can generate lists of arbitrary size as required by the program. If JavaScript were lazily evaluated, you could theoretically do something like the following:

```
R.range(1, Infinity).take(1); //-> [1]
R.range(1, Infinity).take(3); //-> [1,2,3]
```

This is conceptual, of course. As you learned in chapter 7, JavaScript evaluates functions eagerly, so the calls to `R.range(1, Infinity)` will fail to complete and will overflow the browser's function stack. Generators provide lazy behavior through an internal `iterator` object that's created when the generator function is called. The iterator serves data to the caller on demand on every call to `yield`, as shown in figure 8.10.

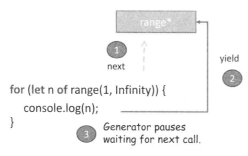

for (let n of range(1, Infinity)) {
    console.log(n);
}

next

yield

Generator pauses
waiting for next call.

Figure 8.10 Executing the `range` generator in a `for..of` loop. Every iteration of the loop prompts the generator to pause and yield new data. Hence, generators have semantics similar to those of an iterator.

Let's go over a quick example that the takes the first three elements without attempting to produce an infinite list of numbers:

```
function *range(start = 0, finish = Number.POSITIVE_INFINITY) {
  for(let i = start; i < finish; i++) {
    yield i;
  }
}
```

Returns back to the caller but remembers the state of any local variable bindings

```
const num = range(1);
num.next().value; //-> 1
num.next().value; //-> 2
num.next().value; //-> 3

// or
```

A generator is an iterable type, meaning it can be placed in loop blocks just like any array (more on this later). ES6 introduces a new looping construct, for..of, to be used with generators.

```
for (let n of range(1)) {
  console.log(n);
  if(n === threshold) {
    break;
  }
}// -> 1,2,3,...
```

Checks a threshold so the program doesn't loop infinitely

With generators, you can implement the lazy program to `take` a certain number of elements from an infinite set:

```
function take(amount, generator) {
  let result = [];
  for (let n of generator) {
    result.push(n);
    if(n === amount) {
      break;
    }
  }
  return result;
}
take(3, range(1, Infinity)); //-> [1, 2, 3]
```

With a few limitations, generators behave much like any standard function call. You can pass arguments to them, and perhaps a function, to drive the nature of the generated values:

```
function *range(specification, start = 0,
    finish = Number.POSITIVE_INFINITY) {
  for(let i = start; i < finish; i++) {
    yield specification(i);
  }
}
for (let n of range(x => x * x, 1, 4)) {
  console.log(n);
}// -> 1,4,9,16
```

Applies the specification function to each value generated

A generator behaves like any higher-order function that can receive arguments to apply specialized behavior. In this case, you tell the generator to produce squared numbers.

Another quality of generator functions is that they can be used recursively.

8.3.1 *Generators and recursion*

Just like any function call, generators can be called from other generators. This is useful in cases where you want to create a flattened view of a nested set of objects, which is ideal when iterating over trees. Because generators can be looped over with for..of, delegating to another generator is similar to merging two collections and iterating over the entire thing. Recall the apprentice graph from chapter 3, shown again in figure 8.11.

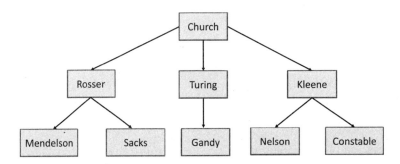

Figure 8.11   Revisiting the apprentice graph from chapter 3, where each node represents a student object and each line represents a "student-of" relationship

You can easily model the data included in the branches of this tree using simple generators like so (I'll show the printed result of running this program later):

```
function* AllStudentsGenerator(){
    yield 'Church';

    yield 'Rosser';
    yield* RosserStudentGenerator();
```

Uses yield to delegate to another generator*

```
        yield 'Turing';
        yield* TuringStudentGenerator();

        yield 'Kleene';
        yield* KleeneStudentGenerator();
}

function* RosserStudentGenerator(){
        yield 'Mendelson';
        yield 'Sacks';
}

function* TuringStudentGenerator(){
        yield 'Gandy';
        yield 'Sacks';
}

function* KleeneStudentGenerator(){
        yield 'Nelson';
        yield 'Constable';
}

for(let student of AllStudentsGenerator()){
        console.log(student);
}
```

You can interleave other generator data with this.

The looping mechanism iterates just as if it were one big generator.

Because recursion is such an integral part of functional programming, I also want to demonstrate that despite the special semantics behind generators, they behave much like standard function calls, which can delegate to themselves. Here's a simple traversal of the same tree (recall that each node contains a `Person` object), this time using recursion:

```
function* TreeTraversal(node) {
        yield node.value;
        if (node.hasChildren()) {
            for(let child of node.children) {
                yield* TreeTraversal(child);
            }
        }
}

var root = node(new Person('Alonzo', 'Church', '111-11-1231'));

for(let person of TreeTraversal(root)) {
    console.log(person.lastname);
}
```

Uses yield* to delegate back to itself

Recall that the tree root object from chapter 3 starts at the Church node.

Running this code produces the same output as previous: Church, Rosser, Mendelson, Sacks, Turing, Gandy, Kleene, Nelson, Constable. As you can see, control is given to the other generators and then, once completed, returned to the caller in the exact same spot where it left off. From the `for..of` loop point of view, however, it just calls an internal *iterator* until it runs out of data and doesn't know recursion is even taking place.

8.3.2 *The Iterator protocol*

Generators are closely tied to another ES6 artifact called *iterators*, which is the reason you can loop over generators like any other data structure (such as arrays). Behind the scenes, a generator function returns a `Generator` object that conforms to the iterator protocol; this means it implements a method called `next()` that returns a value resulting from using the `yield` keyword. This object has the following properties:

- `done`—Has the value `true` if the iterator is passed the end of the sequence. Otherwise, a value of `false` means the iterator was able to produce another value in the sequence.
- `value`—Any value returned by the iterator.

This is enough for you to understand how generators work behind the scenes. Let's look at the `range` generator again, implemented in a raw format:

```
function range(start, end) {

  return {
    [Symbol.iterator]() {                              Indicates that the returned
      return this;                                     object is iterable (implements
    },                                                 the Iterator protocol)
    next() {
      if(start < end) {                                         Implements the main logic for
        return { value: start++, done:false };                  this generator. If there's any
      }                                                         more data to generate,
      return { done: true, value:end };                         returns an object with the
    }                                                           yielded value and sets the
  };                                                            done flag to false; otherwise,
}                                                               sets the done flag to true.
```

With this implementation, you can create generators to produce any kind of data that governs a certain pattern or specification. Here's the `squares` generator, for instance:

```
function squares() {
  let n = 1;
  return {
    [Symbol.iterator]() {
      return this;
    },
    next() {
      return { value: n * n++ };
    }
  };
}
```

For more details about working with iterators and iterables, please visit https://developer.mozilla.org/en-US/docs/Web/JavaScript/Reference/Iteration_protocols. With the internal `@@iterator` property, many things in JavaScript can be treated as iterable objects. You already expect arrays to work this way:

```
var iter = ['S', 't', 'r', 'e', 'a', 'm'][Symbol.iterator]();
iter.next().value; // S
iter.next().value; // t
```

But even strings can be iterated over:

```
var iter = 'Stream'[Symbol.iterator]();
iter.next().value// -> S
iter.next().value// -> t
```

I want to call out the idea of thinking about data as streams that, when probed, produce discrete sequences of events or values. As you've seen all along, these values flow into a sequence of pure higher-order functions and transform into your desired output. This way of thinking is vitally important and gives rise to another programming paradigm (based on functional programming) called *reactive programming*.

8.4 Functional and reactive programming with RxJS

I've mentioned before that the nature of web applications has changed drastically, mostly influenced by the AJAX revolution. As we push the limits of the web, users' expectations become increasingly demanding of not just more data, but also more interactivity. Applications need to be able to process user input coming from different sources like button presses, text fields, mouse movements, finger gestures, voice commands, and others, and it's important to be able to interact with all of these in a consistent manner.

In this section, I'll introduce a reactive library called Reactive Extensions for JavaScript (RxJS) that you can use to elegantly combine asynchronous and event-based programs (refer to the appendix for installation information). RxJS works in ways similar to the functional promise-based examples you saw earlier in this chapter, but it provides a higher degree of abstraction and many more powerful operations. Before we get started, you must understand the concept of *observables*.

8.4.1 Data as observable sequences

An observable is any data object that you can *subscribe* to. Applications can subscribe to asynchronous events emitted from reading a file, a web service call, querying a database, pushing system notifications, handling user input, traversing a collection of elements, or even parsing a simple string. Reactive programming unifies all of these data providers into a single concept called an *observable stream*, using the `Rx.Observable` object. A stream is a *sequence of ordered events happening over time.* To extract its value, you must subscribe to it. Let's look at some examples:

```
Rx.Observable.range(1, 3)
    .subscribe(
        x => console.log(`Next: ${x}`),
        err => console.log(`Error: ${err}`),
        () => console.log('Completed')
    );
```

The subscribe method expects three callback functions: handle each element in the sequence, exceptional termination, and graceful termination.

Running this code creates an observable sequence from a range of numbers that will emit the values 1, 2, 3. Finally, it flags the completion of the stream:

```
Next: 1
Next: 2
Next: 3
Completed
```

Consider another example using the earlier `squares` generator function to populate the stream of values (you add a parameter to generate a finite number of squares):

```
const squares = Rx.Observable.wrap(function* (n) {
  for(let i = 1; i <= n; i++) {
     return yield Observable.just(i * i);
  }
});

squares(3).subscribe(x => console.log(`Next: ${x}`));
```

```
Next: 1
Next: 4
Next: 9
```

As you can see from these examples, you can work with any type of data in the exact same manner using `Rx.Observable`, because it converts this data into a stream. `Rx.Observable` wraps or lifts any observable object so that you can map and apply different functions to transform the observed values into the desired output. Hence, it's a monad.

8.4.2 Functional and reactive programming

The `Rx.Observable` object unites the world of functional and reactive programming. It implements the equivalent of the minimal monadic interface you learned about in chapter 5 (map, of, and join) as well as many methods specific to stream manipulation. Here's a quick example:

```
Rx.Observable.of(1,2,3,4,5)
  .filter(x => x%2 !== 0)
  .map(x => x * x)
  .subscribe(x => console.log(`Next: ${x}`));

//-> Next: 1
    Next: 9
    Next: 25
```

Filters out even numbers

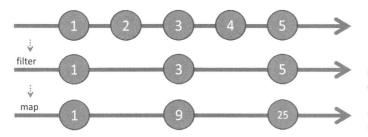

Figure 8.12   The process of applying functions `filter` and `map` from an observable sequence of numbers

To illustrate what's happening behind the scenes, the diagram in figure 8.12 shows the transformation.

If you hadn't just read a functional programming book, you would've felt that the hardest part about reactive programming is learning to "think reactively." But thinking reactively isn't that different from thinking functionally, just with a different set of tools; so half the battle is won. In fact, there's so much overlap, that most of the documentation on reactive programming found on the web begins by teaching functional programming techniques. Streams bring declarativeness and chained computations into your code. Hence, reactive programming tends to resemble functional programming, giving rise to the term *functional reactive programming* (FRP).

Suggested reading

Reactive programming has been on the rise since 2013, so a sizeable amount of content is available related to it and FRP. My goal isn't to teach you reactive programming, but to demonstrate that reactive programming is really functional programming applied to asynchronous and event-based problems.

If you wish to learn more about reactive programming and the FRP world, you can check out *Functional Reactive Programming* (Manning 2016) by Stephen Blackheath and Anthony Jones, which you can obtain at https://www.manning.com/books/functional-reactive-programming. If you're interested in learning about using RxJS with functional programming, I recommend that you read *RxJS in Action* (Manning, forthcoming 2017) by Paul Daniels and Luis Atencio, which you can begin reading using the Manning Early Access Program (MEAP) at https://www.manning.com/books/rxjs-in-action.

Now that you understand observables, let's use RxJS to handle user input. When you need to interact with and capture events from many different sources, you can easily get into code that's tangled and hard to read. Consider a simple example of reading and validating an SSN field:

```
document.querySelector('#student-ssn')
    .addEventListener('change', function (event) {
        let value = event.target.value;
```

```
      value = value.replace(/^\s*|\-|\s*$/g, '');
      console.log(value.length !== 9 ? 'Invalid' : 'Valid'));
});
//-> 444          Invalid
//-> 444-44-4444  Valid
```

Because the change event happens asynchronously, you're forced to write all the business logic in a single callback function. As you saw earlier in the chapter, this doesn't scale if you continue to pile on more event-handling code for every button, field, and link on the page. Your only opportunity for reuse will be to refactor and pull out core logic from the callback. How can you scale this so that your code's complexity doesn't grow in proportion to adding more logic?

Just as with asynchronous code, you can't force functional programming to cooperate nicely with traditional event-based functions—both paradigms are diverse. The same way promises solved the impedance mismatch between functional and asynchronous functions, you need the layer of abstraction provided by Rx.Observable to bridge the world of events to the functional world. This example code that listens for change events fired over time as the user updates a student SSN input field can be modeled as a stream (see figure 8.13).

Figure 8.13 Shows the event values for SSN treated as an observable stream created from subscribing to the change event of the student SSN input field

With that in mind, you can refactor the previous imperative event-based code using FRP, which means subscribing to the event and using pure functions to implement all the business logic:

```
Rx.Observable.fromEvent(
  document.querySelector('#student-ssn'), 'change')

    .map(x => x.target.value)

    .map(cleanInput)

    .map(checkLengthSsn)

    .subscribe(

    ssn => ssn.isRight ? console.log('Valid') : console.log('Invalid'));
```

Subscribes to the change event

Extracts the value in the event

Applies functions to trim and clean the SSN (from previous chapters)

Checks whether the output of the validation is an Either.Right or Either.Left, to determine if it's valid

This code reuses the same functions from previous chapters, so the value passed in to `subscribe` is wrapped in an `Either` containing `Right(SSN)` on a valid input or `Left(null)` otherwise. RxJS excels at chaining linear asynchronous data flows to handle events, but that's not all. It also incorporates promises into its powerful APIs, so you can use one programming model for all things asynchronous. Let's look at that next.

8.4.3 *RxJS and promises*

RxJS can convert any Promises/A+–compliant object into an observable sequence. This means you can wrap the long-running `getJSON` function so that, on resolution, its value will be converted into a stream. Consider the example of showing a sorted list of students who reside in the United States:

```
Rx.Observable.fromPromise(getJSON('/students'))
    .map(R.sortBy(R.compose(R.toLower, R.prop('firstname'))))    ◁
    .flatMapLatest(student => Rx.Observable.from(student))    ◁
    .filter(R.pathEq(['address', 'country'], 'US'))    ◁
    .subscribe(
        student => console.log(student.fullname),    ◁
        err => console.log(err)
    );
// -> Alonzo Church
      Haskell Curry
```

Case-insensitive sort of all student objects by firstname

Converts the single array of student objects into an observable sequence of students

Filters students not living in the US

Prints the results

You can see that this code retains a lot of what you learned about promises, with a few differences. Notice the centralized error-handling logic in `subscribe`. If the promise can't be fulfilled because the web service you're accessing is down, it propagates the error through and invokes the error-callback printing (this is proper for a monad):

```
Error: IO Error
```

Otherwise, the list of student objects is sorted (in this case, by first name) and passed in to `flatMapLatest`, which converts the response object into an observable array of students. Finally, you filter out students not residing in the United States from the stream and print the results. The RxJS toolkit offers many more features, and you've only just scratched the surface of what it can do. For more in-depth information, visit https://xgrommx.github.io/rx-book.

In this book, we tackled all different types of challenging JavaScript problems using functional programming; these included processing collections, working with AJAX requests, database calls, handling user events, and others. Now that you've explored the theory in detail as well as programs that demonstrate real-world usage of these functional techniques, you grok the essence of thinking functionally and will soon be intuitively applying it.

8.5   Summary

- Promises provide a functional solution to callback-driven design, which has plagued JavaScript programs for a long time.
- Promises gives you the ability to chain as well as compose functions "in the future," abstracting out the low-level intricacies of temporally dependent code.
- Generators take another approach to asynchronous code by providing programming artifacts, backed by lazy iterators, that allow you to yield for data to be available.
- Functional reactive programming raises the level of abstraction of your programs so that you can focus on treating events as logically independent units. This lets you focus on your task at hand instead of coping with complex implementation details.

appendix
JavaScript libraries used in this book

Functional JavaScript libraries

Because JavaScript isn't a pure functional language, you have to rely on the help of third-party libraries that you can load into your project to emulate features, such as currying, composition, memoization, lazy evaluation, immutability, and so on, that are core in purer functional languages like Haskell. The libraries eliminate the need for you to implement the features yourself, so that you can focus on writing your business logic functions and delegate the orchestration of this code to these libraries. This section lists the functional libraries used throughout this book. These libraries are designed to do the following:

- Fill in any gaps of standard JavaScript environments by providing additional language constructs and high-level utility functions that encourage you to write code using simple functions
- When using JavaScript on the client, ensure that the functionality is consistent across browser vendors
- Abstract out the internals of functional programming techniques like currying, composition, partial evaluation, lazy evaluation, and others in a consistent manner

For each library, I'll include installation instructions for both browser and server (Node.js) environments.

Lodash

This utility library is a fork of Underscore.js (http://underscorejs.org/), which has been widely adopted by functional JavaScript programmers in the past, and it's a dependency in important JavaScript frameworks like Backbone.js. Lodash continues to track the Underscore APIs closely, but it's been completely rewritten under the hood to include additional performance enhancements. This book uses Lodash mainly to construct modular function chains.

- Version: 3.10.1
- Home page: https://lodash.com/
- Installation:
  - Browser: `<script src="lodash.js"></script`
  - Node: `$npm i --save lodash`

Ramda

This utility library is designed specifically for functional programming, which facilitates the creation of function pipelines. All of Ramda's functions are immutable and side effect–free. In addition, all the functions have automatic currying, and its parameters are arranged to be convenient for currying and composition. Ramda also contains property lenses, which are used in this book to read/write the properties of objects in an immutable manner.

- Version: 0.18.0
- Home page: http://ramdajs.com/
- Installation:
  - Browser: `<script src="ramda.js"></script>`
  - Node: `$npm install ramda`

RxJS

The Reactive Extensions for JavaScript implement a paradigm known as *reactive programming*, which combines the best ideas of the observer pattern, iterator pattern, and functional programming to yield a library that facilitates writing asynchronous and event-based programs.

- Version: 4.0.7
- Parent project home page: http://reactivex.io/
- Home page: https://github.com/Reactive-Extensions/RxJS
- Installation:
  - Browser: Download the needed packages from any JavaScript repository such as www.jsdelivr.com/?query=rxjs. These are the necessary packages for this book: `rx-async`, `rx-dom`, and `rx-binding`.
  - Node: `$npm install rx-node`

Other libraries used

This book also uses nonfunctional libraries to take care of some additional aspects of software development like logging, testing, and static code analysis.

Log4js

Log4JavaScript is a client-side logging framework that follows the same "Log4X" design of packages as other languages, such as Log4j (Java), log4php (PHP), and others. This library is commonly used for enterprise-level logging, which is much more powerful than the typical console.log.

- Version: 1.0.0
- Home page: http://stritti.github.io/log4js/
- Installation:
  - Browser: `<script src="log4.js"></script>`
  - Node: `$npm install log4js`

QUnit

QUnit is a powerful, slim, easy-to-use JavaScript unit testing framework. It's used by popular projects such as jQuery and is capable of testing any generic JavaScript code.

- Version: 1.20.0
- Home page: https://qunitjs.com/
- Installation:
  - Browser: `<script src="qunit-1.20.0.js"></script>`
  - Node: `$npm install --save-dev qunitjs`

Sinon

Sinon.JS is a stub and mocking framework for JavaScript. In this book, it's used in conjunction with QUnit to augment the testing environment with a mocking context and API.

- Version: 1.17.2
- Home page: http://sinonjs.org/
- Installation:
  - Browser: `<script src="sinon-1.17.2.js"></script>`
    `<script src="sinon-qunit-1.0.0.js"></script>`
  - Node: `$npm install sinon`
    `$npm install sinon-qunit`

Blanket

Blanket.js is a code-coverage tool for JavaScript. It's designed to complement your existing JavaScript unit tests (QUnit tests) with additional code-coverage statistics.

Code coverage measures the percentage of lines that execute through your code in a single pass of a unit test. It works in three phases:

1 Loads your source files
2 Instruments the code by adding tracking lines
3 Connects the hooks in the test runner to output coverage details

- Version: 1.1.5
- Home page: http://blanketjs.org/
- Installation:
  - Browser: `<script src="blanket.js"></script>`
  - Node: `$npm install blanket`

JSCheck

JSCheck is a specification-driven (property-based) testing library for JavaScript written by Douglas Crockford and inspired by Haskell's QuickCheck project. From the description of the properties of a function, it generates random test cases that attempt to prove those properties.

- Home page: www.jscheck.org/
- Installation:
  - Browser: `<script src="jscheck.js"></script>`
  - Node: `$npm install jscheck`

index

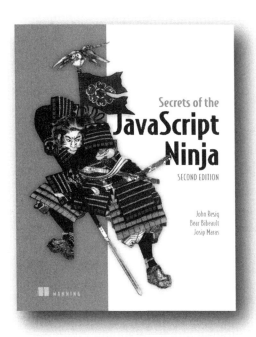

Secrets of the JavaScript Ninja,
Second Edition

by John Resig, Bear Bibeault,
   and Josip Maras

   ISBN: 9781617292859
   375 pages
   $44.99
   June 2016

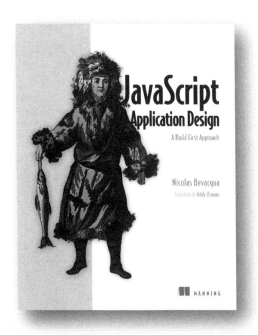

JavaScript Application Design
A Build First approach
by Nicolas G. Bevacqua

   ISBN: 9781617291951
   344 pages
   $39.99
   January 2015

For ordering information go to www.manning.com

MORE TITLES FROM MANNING

Node.js in Action, Second Edition
by Mike Cantelon, Alex Young, Marc Harter,
    T.J. Holowaychuk, and Nathan Rajlich

  ISBN: 9781617292576
  500 pages
  $49.99
  January 2017

Node.js in Practice
by Alex Young and Marc Harter

  ISBN: 9781617290930
  424 pages
  $49.99
  December 2014

For ordering information go to www.manning.com

Grokking Algorithms
An illustrated guide for programmers and
other curious people
by Aditya Y. Bhargava

ISBN: 9781617292231
256 pages
$44.99
May 2016

Functional Programming in Scala
by Paul Chiusano and Rúnar Bjarnason

ISBN: 9781617290657
320 pages
$44.99
September 2014

For ordering information go to www.manning.com

MORE TITLES FROM MANNING

Reactive Web Applications
With Scala, Play, Akka, and Reactive Streams
by Manuel Bernhardt

ISBN: 9781633430099
325 pages
$44.99
June 2016

Building the Web of Things
by Dominique D. Guinard and Vlad M. Trifa

ISBN: 9781617292682
375 pages
$34.99
June 2016

For ordering information go to www.manning.com